INDUSTRY, BUSINESS AND SOCIETY
IN SCOTLAND SINCE 1700

Edward Ryan
4 December 2001

Professor John Butt

INDUSTRY, BUSINESS AND SOCIETY IN SCOTLAND SINCE 1700

ESSAYS PRESENTED TO PROFESSOR JOHN BUTT

edited by
A. J. G. Cummings and T. M. Devine

JOHN DONALD PUBLISHERS LTD

EDINBURGH

ISBN 0 85976 401 X

British Library Cataloguing in Publication Data
A catalogue record for this book is available from the
British Library.

Typeset by ROM-Data Corporation Ltd, Falmouth, Cornwall
Printed and bound by
Hartnolls Limited, Bodmin, Cornwall

Preface

The publication of collections of essays in honour of distinguished academics is not uncommon. This particular volume is, however, unusual. Each chapter has been written by former undergraduate or postgraduate students of a single department, the Department of History in the University of Strathclyde. All were influenced by the teaching, research supervision and scholarly example of Professor John Butt, in whose honour these essays are published.

As the profile which follows makes clear John Butt has had a most distinguished academic career which has encompassed historical research, writing, teaching, university management and administration and public service. However, his first love has always been undergraduate teaching and the supervision of postgraduates and it is therefore appropriate that this *festschrift* has been edited and composed by some of those who have benefited from his instruction over the years. The wide range of themes studied reflect Professor Butt's own diversity of interests. Much of his most important work was concerned with industrial history, industrial archaeology and business history within a Scottish context. Several of the chapters in this collection therefore examine banking, coal, iron, granite and electricity as case-studies of the Scottish industrial experience over three centuries. But John Butt had also a deep interest in urban social history and this is also represented in the book in some of the remaining essays.

We hope Professor Butt enjoys reading this public tribute from his former students and approves of the standards of scholarship in the contributions which he himself has done so much to encourage.

A. J. G. Cummings
T. M. Devine
Glasgow, 1994

Contributors

Peter Clapham Research Assistant, Department of Architecture and Building Science, University of Strathclyde.

Robert D. Corrins Course Leader, Department of Law, Health and Social Administration, Bell College of Technology.

Graham Cummings Lecturer in Economic History, University of Strathclyde

T. M. Devine Professor of Scottish History and Dean of the Faculty of Arts and Social Studies, University of Strathclyde

Ian Donnachie Senior Lecturer and Staff Tutor in History, The Open University in Scotland.

Tom Donnelly Chair of Division of Strategy and Human Resource Management Coventry University Business School.

Jean Fraser Formerly Department of History and Vice Principal's Secretary, University of Strathclyde.

John C. Logan Lecturer in Economic History, Glasgow Caledonian University.

Charles W. Munn Chief Executive, The Chartered Institute of Bankers in Scotland.

Norman Murray Head Teacher, Calderhead High School, Lanarkshire.

Stana Nenadic Senior Lecturer in Economic and Social History, University of Edinburgh.

William Sloan Assistant Rector, St Andrew's High School, Kirkcaldy.

Christopher A. Whatley Senior Lecturer in Scottish History, University of Dundee.

Contents

Professor John Butt: An Appreciation

For over thirty years John Butt has had a distinguished career in university teaching, research and administration. Appointed in 1959 as a Lecturer in History at the Royal College of Science and Technology, Glasgow, he became a lecturer in economic history in the department created under Professor S. G. E. Lythe when the Royal College became the new University of Strathclyde in 1964. John has been an inspiring teacher and research supervisor, and even when his later career took him increasingly into the realms of administration he never faltered from his prime commitment to teaching. He was promoted to senior lecturer in 1968, to reader in 1975, and following Edgar Lythe's retirement, Professor of Economic History in 1976. Between 1978 and 1984 he was Dean of the Faculty of Arts and Social Studies. He became in turn Deputy Principal in 1986, Vice-Principal Designate and then Vice-Principal in 1990, playing a significant part in the merger of the university and Jordanhill College of Education.

Throughout his busy career he made a notable contribution to university life, while maintaining a succession of external appointments in the spheres of historical scholarship and education. Even those of us who know him well are astounded at the breadth of his contribution to local and national bodies and societies, ranging in a list too long to cite in detail from the David Livingstone Memorial Trust to the Royal Commission on the Ancient and Historical Monuments of Scotland and from Chairman of Governors of Craigie College of Education to membership of the General Teaching Council for Scotland. On the UK stage he served as a member of Council of the Economic History Society and as President of the Association for Industrial Archaeology. His multi-faceted contribution to education, historical studies, industrial archaeology and the historical conservation movement generally has been recognised by his election as a Fellow of the Royal Society of Arts and a Fellow of the Royal Society of Edinburgh. Of all his achievements, however, it is his contribution to historical study that is most outstanding.

One of John's first major research ventures, combining biography and industrial history, was his doctoral research on James 'Paraffin' Young, founder of the Scottish shale-oil industry. John knew of the extensive archive of Young's papers which had found its way into the Andersonian Library, and in a typically astute move realised the potential for a research project on a major Victorian scientist turned entrepreneur, which not only suited the mood of the time but also fitted well the developing ethos of the department. In this he was much encouraged by Edgar Lythe and his supervisor, the late Professor Sydney Checkland of the University of Glasgow—surely one of the few individuals John has ever held in awe. The resulting thesis was a model of scholarship, which strangely, though he often talked about it, was never published. But at least there were the spin-offs in a series of important articles telling the story of Young's inventions and business dealings—the basis of a successful Victorian novel had it ever been written. Incidentally his research on Young's transatlantic dealings developed further his interest in American history, which was to form an important component of his teaching in the future.

Meantime John had also become interested in a new branch of historical enquiry, called oddly, it seemed, industrial archaeology. Again its development came at an appropriate time, since the physical vestiges of the Industrial Revolution were fast disappearing in the face of redevelopment, particularly in Glasgow and the west of Scotland. Both Edgar Lythe and he saw that industrial archaeology could be a useful historical tool for the economic historian, and that apart from its research potential in helping to explain problems about industrialisation it could also be a remarkably useful teaching aid. Soon a Scottish Committee for Industrial Archaeology was established with Edgar as Chairman and John as Secretary. From Strathclyde John vigorously disseminated the propaganda of this new interdisciplinary study among local and national historical societies and individuals—as well as beginning to explore its potential himself by linking it to more conventional archival research.

A first venture into the field saw John and the associates he had gathered around him, including John Hume and Ian Donnachie, exploring the history of a series of late eighteenth-century iron works, which had left substantial if decaying relics of their existence. If the field-work was pioneering so too was the archival research in legal records, which helped to throw light on the business activities of the iron masters. Many of the archives he used at the Scottish Record Office were less accessible than they are now, but John was always doggedly persistent in his detective work. He assiduously cultivated the messengers who fetched the often voluminous sederunt books, and was one of the few search-room users to entertain them regally at lunch-time in the famous bar of the Café Royal next door to Register House. Research outings with John were always sociable occasions.

There followed more detailed and important work on the early iron industry and on the textile industry which again involved conventional research married to industrial archaeology. Probably his most successful exercise in industrial archaeology, partly under the auspices of an extramural class, was at Gatehouse-of-Fleet, an almost perfectly preserved industrial village dating from the late eighteenth century. There an examination of the industrial heritage raised a lot of interesting questions which could only be partly answered by the surviving documentation. The resulting paper was a model of its kind.

As his views on the potential of industrial archaeology came to be more clearly defined he realised that what was needed if the subject was to move forward was an overview of the scene in Scotland, a concept that fitted well with the aspirations of the publisher David St John Thomas of David & Charles, who had begun to produce work in this field. *The Industrial Archaeology of Scotland*, published in 1967, set the context for the future development of the subject, though there were certainly those in Scotland and beyond who were prepared to debate its philosophical underpinnings.

By 1968 John had taken over from Kenneth Hudson as editor of the journal *Industrial Archaeology*, whose centre of gravity moved north from the then Bath University of Technology. He was to continue in this role for nearly a decade, building up from Strathclyde a wide-ranging network of contacts nationally and internationally. He obtained a critical overview of developments which was to prove invaluable when, with Ian Donnachie, he came to write *Industrial Archaeology in the British Isles*, published in 1979. He continued to play an important role in the Association for Industrial Archaeology and with John Hume encouraged further development at Strathclyde by helping to establish the Scottish Industrial Archaeology Unit, now part of the Royal Commission on the Ancient and Historical Monuments of Scotland.

John's interest in the textile industry led him naturally to New Lanark and to Robert Owen. With Owen's bicentenary in the offing John initiated and edited an important volume of essays by Strathclyde scholars reappraising the man and the movement he inspired. His own contribution examined Robert Owen's business attributes and showed how New Lanark was turned into one of the most profitable enterprises of its time, giving Owen the wherewithal to promulgate his New View of Society. The book, appropriately entitled *Robert Owen. Prince of Cotton Spinners*, was launched at a major Owen Bicentenary Conference hosted by Strathclyde in 1971. At the same time he wrote detailed introductions to a reprint of Owen's *Life* and to a new edition of the Everyman's edition of *A New View of Society and Other Writings*. He later played an important role in raising awareness about the significance of New Lanark as part of Scottish national heritage.

John subsequently struck an interesting balance between economic and social history. He found the time with Edgar Lythe to write *An Economic History of Scotland 1100–1939*, published in 1975, a work which skilfully synthesised the increasing volume of literature on the subject and which filled a notable gap both for students and teachers of the subject. On the social side he turned to the housing of the working class, a subject on which he produced a series of much-quoted papers. His interest in the history of co-operation also went back a long way, though it was certainly rekindled by his work on Owen. With James Kinloch, one of his many research students, he wrote the definitive history of the Scottish Co-operative Wholesale Society. He also continued to research and publish on the history of textiles, culminating in a collection of essays on *Scottish Textile History* (1987), which he edited with the late Ken Ponting, and produce further good work on business history, with special reference to the Standard Life Assurance Company.

Apart from his own scholarship John encouraged and assisted a long line of successful research students, more than two dozen in all, between 1969 and 1992. Their dissertations reflected many of John's interests, from the history of the Scottish whisky industry, submitted by Iseabel Ann Glen in 1969 to the Scottish Special Housing Association and housing policy in Scotland by Tom Begg, sustained in 1992. Between the two were theses submitted by men and women who have since gone on to make their own significant contributions to historical research in Scotland and beyond.

The portrait sketched here, apart from a passing innuendo or two, says little about John himself. Always larger than life, his apparent bluffness might well intimidate the faint-hearted. But belying appearances to the contrary even the timid find in 'JB' a kindly and sympathetic listener. Enthusiasm for his subject always shines through—an enthusiasm which can inform and motivate undergraduates, research students and colleagues alike. John is an extremely congenial individual and formed many lasting friendships in the department, around the university and in Scottish educational circles. One friendship he valued more than most was that of his colleague, Professor John Ward, with whom he worked closely on a number of projects and whose premature death in 1987 greatly touched him. John's work within the department, the university and elsewhere has also been assisted by a succession of dedicated secretaries, most recently Jean Fraser, who has compiled the bibliography of his published works for this volume, and he would be the first to acknowledge the enormous debt he owes them. While John has had a busy career he has always devoted much time to his family of which he is enormously proud.

The contributors to this volume are in turn proud of their association with John Butt. As graduates of the Department of History of the University of Strathclyde they have all been influenced to a greater or lesser extent by his teaching, supervision and scholarly example. They hope that he sees some of that impact on the essays which follow.

Bibliography of the Academic Writings of Professor John Butt

Compiled by Jean Fraser

'General Studies at Glasgow', *Technology* (February, 1961).

'David Livingstone and the Idea of African Evolution', *History Today*, (June, 1963).

'Legends of the Coal-Oil Industry 1847–1864, *Explorations in Entrepreneurial History*,' 2nd Series (1964), pp. 16–30.

'The Story of Sir Paraffin', *B. P. Scottish News*, 1, 1–2, (Jan.-Feb., 1965).

'The Industrial Archaeology of County Down: A Review Article', *Scottish Studies*, VIII (1965).

'The Scottish Oil Rush', *B. P. Scottish News*, 1, 3, (March, 1965).

(with I. Donnachie), 'Three Eighteenth Century Scottish Ironworks', *Journal of Industrial Archaeology*, 1, 4 (1965), pp.

'Technical Change and the Growth of the British Shale Oil Industry', *Economic History Review*, 2nd Series, XVII, 3 (1965), pp. 511–21.

'The Scottish Oil Mania of 1864–6', *Scottish Journal of Political Economy*, XII (1965),' pp. 195–209.

'The Scottish Iron Industry before the Hot-Blast', *Journal of the West of Scotland Iron and Steel Institute*, 73 (1965–66), pp. 193–200.

'The Industrial Archaeology of Gatehouse-of-Fleet'. *Industrial Archaeology*, 3, 2 (1966), pp. 127–37.

'Glasgow at a Glance', *Industrial Archaeology*, 3, 3 (1966), pp. 215–16.

'Muirkirk, 1786–1802, the Creation of a Scottish Industrial Community', *Scottish Historical Review*, XLV, 2 (1966), pp. 160–83.

The Industrial Archaeology of Scotland, (Newton Abbot, 1967).

'The Wilsons of Wilsontown Ironworks (1779–1813): A Study in Entrepreneurial Failure', *Explorations in Entrepreneurial History*, 2nd Series (1967), pp. 150–68.

'Industrial Archaeology and Business History', *Business Archives Council of Scotland Newsletter*, 2 (1967).

'Glenbuck Ironworks', *Ayrshire Archaeological and Natural History Collections*, 2nd Series, 8 (1967–9), pp. 68–75.

'James Taylor of Cumnock and the Early History of Steam Navigation', *Ayrshire Archaeological and Natural History Collections*, 2nd Series, 8 (1967–9), pp. 76–92.

'The Role of Scottish Business History', *Journal of Economic Studies*, 3, 1 (1968), pp. 73–84.

(with I. Donnachie and J. R. Hume), *Industrial History in Pictures: Scotland* (Newton Abbot, 1968).

(ed. with Introduction), D. Bremner, *The Industries of Scotland, their Rise and Progress (1869)*, (Newton Abbot, 1969).

(ed.) 'Extracts from a Catalogue of Machine Tools prepared for Craig & Donald, Engineers of Johnstone *c.* 1900', *Industrial Archaeology Supplement*, (Newton Abbot, 1969).

'Wilsontown', *Field Excursions in West Scotland* (Rivingtons Press, London, 1970), pp. 68–72.

(with J. T. Ward), 'The Promotion of the Caledonian Railway Company', *Transport History*, 3, 2–3 (1970), pp. 164–92, 225–57.

(with K. Hudson and I. Donnachie), 'Annual Review of Literature on Industrial Archaeology and Industrial History', *Industrial Archaeology*, 7, 4 (1970), pp. 443–51.

'Robert Owen at New Lanark: a Note on the Relationship Between Robert Owen's Industrial Relations and his Social Theories', *Bulletin of the Robert Owen Bi-Centenary Association*, 1 (May, 1970), pp. 8–10.

'Robert Owen at New Lanark', *Co-partnership* (1971), pp. 14–17.

(ed.)., *Robert Owen, Prince of Cotton Spinners* (Newton Abbot, 1971).

'Robert Owen as a Businessman' in J. Butt (ed.)., *Robert Owen, Prince of Cotton Spinners*, (Newton Abbot, 1971).

'Robert Owen in His Own Time', in Robert *Owen and his Relevance to our Times*, Co-operative College Papers No.14 (1971).

'Robert Owen and Trade Unionism' in *Robert Owen, Industrialist, Reformer, Visionary, 1771–1858*, (London, 1971).

xiv

(ed. with Introduction), *Life of Robert Owen by Himself* (London, 1971).

(with I. Donnachie and J. R. Hume)), 'Robert Owen and New Lanark', *Industrial Archaeology*, 8, 2 (1971), pp. 186–93.

'Working Class Housing in Glasgow 1851–1914' in S. D. Chapman (ed.), *The History of Working Class Housing* (Newton Abbot, 1971), pp. 55–92.

(with K. Hudson and I. Donnachie), 'Annual Review of Literature on Industrial Archaeology and Industrial History', *Industrial Archaeology*, 8, 4 (1971), pp. 399–408.

(with K. Hudson and I. Donnachie), 'Annual Review of Literature on Industrial Archaeology and Industrial History', *Industrial Archaeology*, 9, 4, (1972), pp. 421–27.

(ed. with I. F. Clarke), *The Victorians and Social Protest*, (Newton Abbot, 1973).

'Robert Owen of New Lanark: His Critique of British Society' in J. Butt and I. F. Clarke (eds.), *The Victorians and Social Protest* (Newton Abbot, 1973), pp. 13–32.

(ed. with Introduction), *A New View of Society by Robert Owen*, (Everyman Library, London, 1973).

(with S. G. E. Lythe), *An Economic History of Scotland 1100–1939*, (Glasgow and London, 1975).

(ed. with J. T. Ward), *Scottish Themes: Essays in Honour of Professor S. G. E. Lythe* (Edinburgh, 1976).

'The American War of Independence and the Scottish Economy', in O. Dudley Edwards and G. Shepperson (eds.), *Scotland, Europe and the American Revolution* (Edinburgh, 1976), pp. 116–28.

'The Scottish Cotton Industry During the Industrial Revolution' in L. M. Cullen and T. C. Smout (eds.), *Comparative Aspects of Scottish and Irish Social and Economic History, 1600–1900* (Edinburgh, 1977), pp. 116–28.

'Capital and Enterprise in the Scottish Iron Industry 1780–1840', in J. Butt and J. T. Ward (eds.), *Scottish Themes* (Edinburgh, 1976), pp. 67–69.

'Working Class Housing in Glasgow, 1900–1939' in I. MacDougall (ed.), *Essays in Scottish Labour History: A Tribute to W. H. Marwick* (Edinburgh, 1978), pp. 143–69.

(with I. Donnachie), *Industrial Archaeology in the British Isles* (London, 1979).

(with J. A. Kinloch), *History of the Scottish Co-operative Wholesale Society* (Glasgow, 1981).

'Achievement and Prospect: Transport History in the 1970s and 1980s', *The Journal of Transport History*, 3rd Series, 2, 1 (1981), pp. 1–24.

James 'Paraffin' Young 1811–1863, (Edinburgh, 1983).

'Working Class Housing in the Scottish Cities' in G. Gordon and B. Dicks (eds.), *Scottish Urban History* (Aberdeen, 1983), pp. 253–67.

'Belfast and Glasgow: Connections and Comparison 1790–1850' in T. M. Devine and D. Dickson (eds.), *Ireland and Scotland 1600–1850, Parallels and Contrasts in Economic and Social Development* (Edinburgh, 1983), pp. 193–203.

'Life Assurance in War and Depression: The Standard Life Assurance Company and its Environment 1914–1939' in O. M. Westall (ed.), *The Historian and the Business of Insurance* (Manchester, 1984), pp. 155–72.

'The Changing Character of Urban Employment 1901–1981', in G. Gordon (ed.), *Perspectives of the Scottish City* (Aberdeen, 1984), pp. 212–35.

(ed. with G. Gordon), *Strathclyde: Changing Horizons* (Edinburgh, 1985).

'The Quality of Life' in J. Butt and G. Gordon (eds.), *Strathclyde: Changing Horizons* (Edinburgh,. 1985), pp. 124–33.

(ed. with K. Ponting), *Scottish Textile History*, (Aberdeen, 1987).

(with S. Chapman), 'The Cotton Industry 1775–1856', in C. Feinstein and S. Pollard (eds.), *Studies in Capital Formation in the United Kingdom 1750–1920* (Oxford, 1988).

The Good of Mankind and the Improvement of Science, Commemorative Brochure for the Silver Jubilee of the University of Strathclyde, 1989.

(with John Twidell), 'The Power of Scotland' in *The Nature of Scotland, Landscape, Wildlife and People*, edited by Magnus Magnusson and Graham White, (Edinburgh, 1991).

Part I

Industry and Business

1

New Light on Nef's Numbers: Coal Mining and the First Phase of Scottish Industrialisation, c.1700–1830

CHRISTOPHER A. WHATLEY

Economic historians have frequently emphasised the rapidity of the transformation of the Scottish economy from *c.*1760. Marked expansion in the urban sector had begun before this, but was undoubtedly furthered as manufacturing accelerated: most of the fastest growing towns in Scotland in the late eighteenth and early nineteenth centuries were centres of industrial production.[1] That coal played a part in this linked process of industrialisation and urbanisation is beyond doubt. However, close reading of the work of those historians who have written about the place of coal in the first phase of Scottish industrialisation reveals a measure of disagreement about the significance of the industry's contribution, as well as a range of different perceptions about its performance, particularly in the second half of the eighteenth century. Explanations for its alleged failings are far from uniform. This essay is concerned to examine what is a far from satisfactory historiographical situation, and provide, where possible, a clearer account of the progress and performance of the coal industry in the eighteenth and early nineteenth centuries.

On one thing there is a consensus: from the end of the seventeenth century until around 1760 the industry experienced only modest growth, while there was little technical or organisational change of any significance.[2] Of the few exceptions, the most notable was the colliery complex near Saltcoats in Ayrshire, where output rose dramatically in the 1720s and five Newcomen steam engines were erected between 1719 and 1747, their purchasers having been attracted by the prospects of coal sales in the lucrative Irish market.[3]

It is over the later decades of the eighteenth century and the first 30 years of the nineteenth that views diverge. According to the late Professor Henry Hamilton, the coal industry began to expand markedly in the last quarter of the eighteenth century, in response to rising industrial and domestic demand.[4]

A 'reckless increase in production and . . . unbridled competition', he declared, had followed the opening of the Monkland Canal in 1793, which had provided an economical route into the rapidly rising Glasgow market, and thereby stimulated the exploitation of the vast mineral reserves of Lanarkshire. Indeed such was the imbalance between supply and demand that two price and output-fixing cartels were established in Glasgow, in 1790 and 1813 respectively, to deal collectively with the twin problems of over-production and low sale prices.

Although recognising that the industry grew, most other historians have been inclined to lay greater stress on supply-side problems. Professor R. H. Campbell for instance has argued that 'even before the rapid industrial expansion which began in the 1780s, the coal industry found difficulty in meeting an increasing demand from domestic and industrial consumers', and that almost until the end of the century, 'the industry's problems arose less from a rapid increase in demand than from the exceptional problems of increasing supply'.[5] These, he was convinced, were poor drainage, and 'the problem, unique to Scotland, of improving the supply of labour'. Campbell's argument that the institution of serfdom had a deleterious effect on the industry, by deterring new recruits from entering it, has found considerable favour elsewhere.[6] It was only after these constraints were removed, from the end of the eighteenth century in the former case, somewhat later in the latter, Campbell argues, that coal was able to play its vital integral role in the expansion of Scotland's industrial base.[7]

In similar vein, in his major study of the Scottish coal industry, Professor B. F. Duckham referred eloquently to a 'loss of equipoise' after 1760, and pointed to a number of factors which restrained its growth. These were insufficient transport improvements, poor management and high wages, which in Midlothian were combined with 'idleness' of labour.[8] Both Duckham and Professor B. P. Lenman were convinced that east coast coalmasters suffered until 1793 from the 'burden' of a tax payable on coal shipped north of the Tay, thereby exposing the Scots to unfair competition from Tyneside. Duckham however was struck by the industry's progress over the course of the period with which he was concerned, 1700–1815, and acknowledged that it had 'made possible an industrial revolution without itself fully experiencing those changes we associate with the term'. He was reasonably certain that there was a four-fold increase in coal output between 1700 and 1800, with much of this coming after 1760, from the coalfields of Lanarkshire and Ayrshire, whose achievement, he described as 'most impressive'.[9] Less impressed however was Lenman, who, while conceding that coal mining was 'an essential adjunct to the general expansion of the Scottish economy in the late eighteenth and early nineteenth century', claimed that 'it did not adequately reflect the general rate of expansion, let alone provide an independent stimulus for growth'.[10]

Judged within the context of the British coal industry, the more cautious assessments of Scottish output performance appear to be fully justified. Although Scotland's more than four-fold increase in coal output over the course of the eighteenth century looks reasonable enough, output for the British industry reveals a five-fold increase over the same period.[11] The comparison is even less flattering if Professor Pollard's estimates are used: these produce a 3.2 increase for Scotland over the same time-span.[12] Nor is the picture improved if the period is extended to 1830: on the contrary, the British coal industry expanded its output 10-fold between 1700 and 1830, compared to a Scottish rate of 6.6. Some of the English regions did much better, with the South Wales coalfield registering a 21-fold increase, while the Cumberland collieries managed to increase output by a factor of 20. It may be objected that these regions started from a lower base. Production at the turn of the eighteenth century in the West Midlands however was greater than in Scotland, and a faster rate of growth was achieved thereafter. The only comfort that can be derived is from comparison with the other two early large-scale producers, Yorkshire and the North-East, both of which grew slightly more slowly than Scotland. Like them, Scotland's share of British output fell, from 15.1 per cent in 1700, to 13.3 in 1800 and 9.9 in 1830.

The benchmark for all of these calculations is Professor J. U. Nef's 60-year old estimate of output for 1681–90. Nef however was acutely aware of the grave limitations of his Scottish data. Unfortunately, too few of his successors have heeded his warning that it was impossible 'to do more than hazard a guess concerning the output in Scotland'[13], and Nef's 'guesstimated' production figure for the late seventeenth century, 475,000 tons, has subsequently been used with varying degrees of confidence as the foundation stone upon which calculations about the industry's growth rate in the following century have rested. Indeed, some historians have been tempted to round it upwards, to 500,000 tons.[14]

What has been entirely overlooked however, is that Nef calculated lower as well as upper estimates. Although he finally opted for a high figure, the sum of his lower estimates of coal output for the three main coalfields, the Firth of Forth district, Lanarkshire, and Ayrshire, was 395,000 tons, that is over 100,000 tons, or 21 per cent, less than the figure quoted above, or almost 25 per cent below his own highest estimate of 525,000 tons. If the lower estimate is used (and assuming that a figure of c.two million tons for 1800 is accurate), Scottish output rose five-fold in the eighteenth century. Yet it is possible to reduce Nef's 475,000 tons by more persuasive means. Close scrutiny of the assumptions he made when compiling his estimates reveals that these are far from soundly based, and in some cases his figures are demonstrably wrong.

Perhaps the best example of an unfounded assumption concerns Nef's global output figure for the Forth mining district. This, he concluded, was between 300,000 and 400,000 tons. The basis for his calculation however was the output figures from two collieries, Tulliallan and Torry, which together put out 25,000 tons. To obtain his total, Nef took these as 'fair samples' of the 'more important' producers, of which he guessed there were around 50. Recent research however has confirmed what has long been suspected, that while there was in Scotland a handful of mining enterprises which ranked amongst the biggest in Britain, there were insufficient numbers of collieries of the size Nef needed to achieve his most optimistic output figure of 400,000 tons, that is 50 producing an average 8,000 tons per annum each.[15] At least in the case of the Forth district Nef's figures did have an arithmetical core. The output figure for Lanarkshire, of between 70,000 and 100,000 tons, is conjured out of an impressionistic survey of the district's collieries, for which not a single production figure is given.[16] Doubts also surround the manner in which the Ayrshire figure of 25,000 tons was compiled, and this can reasonably be reduced by half.[17]

Rightly, it has been observed that it is easy to criticise Nef's figures and 'notoriously hard to do better'.[18] In two specific areas however he has been bettered, and there are grounds for believing that Dr John Hatcher's recently-published total is nearer the mark than Nef's, although as will be seen later, even this may not be low enough.

Some 30 years ago, Professor T. C. Smout made a persuasive case for slashing Nef's estimates of Scottish coal exports by half, to between 25,000 tons and 30,000 tons for the 1660s and 1680s respectively.[19] There is nothing to suggest that there was any improvement in the 1690s – indeed all the indications are that the position worsened. Tariffs and competition from Tyneside and Liege, and better fuel husbandry in the Netherlands, reduced opportunities for sales abroad; intensive working of the most accessible shore-side seams on the Forth (the main exporting region), allied to heavy rain in the mid-1690s and at the turn of the eighteenth century, led one informed contemporary to observe that the 'whole Coals' on both sides of the Forth were in an 'ill condition'.[20] Export levels failed to recover for over a century and were still below the 70,000-ton peak of the early 1660s as late as the 1790s.[21]

The major industrial users of coal at the end of the seventeenth century were the sea salt manufacturers. Their pans burnt some 150,000 tons of coal each year according to Nef, who was convinced that the Scottish industry was bigger than its counterpart on Tyneside and the north-east of England.[22] There seems no doubt however that Nef grossly exaggerated the productive capacity of the Scottish industry, which may have been producing as little as a third of the salt being made by its southern equivalent. The Scottish saltworks can have been using no more than 50,000 tons at the end of the seventeenth century, and possibly as much as 10,000 tons less.[23] Other industrial users, lime-burners, brewers, potters, smiths and the like, can hardly have accounted for more than a few thousand additional tons.

If the re-worked figures are correct, something in the region of 130,000 tons of coal can justifiably be shaved from Nef's preferred total, 475,000 tons. The remaining outlet was the domestic market, consumption of coal by which has recently been estimated at 200,000 tons.[24] This is based on the quite proper assumption that most coal was consumed in the cities and towns of central Scotland, the bulk of which were either situated on the major Scottish coalfields, or, as in the cases of Dundee and Perth, were within reach of coastal shipment. Coal was also shipped further north, to Arbroath, Montrose and Aberdeen. Coal usage much beyond these points is likely to have been slight, with peat being the main source of heat for the great majority of rural dwellers until much later in the eighteenth century, when coal began to replace it on a wide scale.[25] It is suggested here that the figure of 200,000 tons may be too high.

There was a substantial rise in the proportion of the population living in towns with over 10,000 inhabitants in the second half of the seventeenth century, with most of the increase being accounted for by Edinburgh and Leith, which were major coal consumers. The fortunes of medium and smaller towns were more varied, with some declining, and others, Stirling, Linlithgow and Dunfermline for example, rising, with the overall result probably being a small net increase in the size of the urban population of Scotland between 1639 and 1691. Nevertheless only some 11.9 per cent of the Scottish population lived in towns of more than 2,000 people in 1691.[26] It should be noted however that this does not include the unknown – but overall rather small – numbers of the inhabitants of the many newly-created burghs of barony whose populations were lower than 2,000.

If indeed the towns did consume 200,000 tons, and allowing an urban population of 148,149 (i.e. 12 per cent of 1,234,575) in 1691, per capita consumption per annum must have been around 1.3 tons. This however seems highly unlikely, given that the average for London was only 0.75 tons in the 1610s, and only reached one ton during the final quarter of the century during the most prosperous years.[27] Scottish living standards were considerably lower (and seem to have fallen from mid-century)[28], and the supply of coal to the domestic market was far from steady. It became less so during the 1690s, for reasons which have already been outlined. Even making the generous assumption that urban dwellers in Scotland managed to consume an annual average of one ton per head, total domestic consumption cannot have been greater than 150,000 tons per annum. Although this would be less if the much more realistic per capita consumption figure of 0.75 tons (or less) was applied, the adoption of a higher multiplier at least has the virtue of allowing for landsales and the unknown output of marginal inland pits which supplied consumers in their immediate vicinity.

With any revised Scottish total there is bound to be a wide margin of error. The methodology used has been crude, has necessarily failed to distinguish sales from output, and makes no allowance for coal consumption at the collieries, mainly in the form of worker's concessionary coal, theft, and coals used by smiths in mining-related work. The precise size of the Scottish population is far from certain and 'urban' figures often confuse burgh with parish (i.e. landward) dwellers, who are likely to have used more peat and turf fuel.

Even so, Nef's preferred total can be reduced substantially, to 250,000–300,000 tons per annum (which is Hatcher's range) if it is assumed that domestic consumption was 200,000 tons, and even further if this is revised downwards to 150,000 tons or less. It is proposed here that total Scottish coal output in the early 1690s was no more than 225,000 tons, and that this was almost certainly lower at the turn of the eighteenth century. The consequences of this for the growth trajectory of the Scottish coal industry in the eighteenth century are profound. Rather than rising four-fold, Scottish output appears to have risen eight- or 10-fold between *c.*1700 and 1800, almost double the rate for Britain as a whole, which makes Scotland one of the faster growing coal producing regions. Depending on whether a base figure of 300,000 tons or 225,000 tons is used, there was a 10- or 13-fold increase in output between 1700 and 1830. Furthermore, on the basis of these figures, rather than shrinking, Scotlands's share of British coal output clearly increased between the 1690s and the end of the eighteenth century, from some 8.1 per cent (or at most 10.5 per cent) to 13.3 per cent.

The impressively-rapid rate of growth of coal output which the figures compiled here point to cannot easily be squared with the catalogue of reasons which have been advanced to explain the industry's alleged supply-side weaknesses and laggard performance in the later eighteenth century, and failure to meet the burgeoning demands of domestic and industrial users. Indeed there must have been somewhat more activity during the first half of the century than has been supposed hitherto, with output in 1750 rising to anything between 700,000 tons[29] and (far less likely) 900,000 tons.[30] Given the continued growth of the urban population – the proportion of Scots inhabiting towns of 10,000-plus almost doubled between 1700 and 1750 – and the emergence on a bigger scale of coal-using industries such as brewing and bleaching, this makes much sense, although it must be assumed that expansion was more rapid after around 1740, when population had recovered from the crises of the 1690s and sustained economic growth got under way on a broader front.[31] Rigorous examination of the more significant of the restraints referred to above reveals that they have either been misunderstood or overemphasised. Much more stress, it will be argued in what follows, should be placed on the manner in which they were overcome.

Of the factors which allegedly constrained the coal industry's growth in the eighteenth century, the easiest to dismiss is the so-called 'burden' of the coastwise duty on coal. This, it has been demonstrated elsewhere, was nothing of the sort.[32] From the time of the Union of 1707 coal shipped from Forth-side collieries which was sold within the designated estuarial limits of the Forth had in fact been *relieved* from the payment of duty, which, it was readily conceded by the Forthside coal proprietors who had benefited from this arrangement, had given them a monopoly of that market, by protecting them from cheaper Newcastle coal.[33] Far from being opposed to the tax, a number of them waged a brief, vehement, but ultimately unsuccessful campaign to maintain it. Nevertheless, while the coal duty did not have the effect which some historians have claimed, by shielding the East coast coalmasters from the cold winds of competition, it may well have induced in some a sense of complacency.

Labour supply is more problematic. Periodic crises did occur, as for example at Stevenston colliery in Ayrshire in the early 1720s, of which it was remarked by one observer that, there were 'Several pits laid dry . . . Which may be carried down to two Several valuable Coals', but for a 'want of Coaliers' to exploit them.[34] In the first half of the eighteenth century however, shortages were local and short-lived. Coal miners and female bearers (who could be as hard to find as hewers)[35] could be attracted both from other pits with offers of bounties and higher wages, and simply by the prospect of work, when, as frequently happened, production at the pit where such individuals had previously been employed ceased.[36] This could occur for a variety of reasons, as when the accessible coal was worked out, because of problems with water or geological difficulties, or owing to slack demand which was insufficient to 'Defray the Charge of keeping the Coall going'.[37] Consequently it is not unusual to find registers of coal workers which reveal a high level of labour mobility. One such list, from Strathore colliery on the Rothes estate in Fife in 1739, shows that eleven of the hewers then working had come from other collieries, while several men who had been bound at Strathore had gone to work in other pits. A similar source, from Grange colliery in Stirlingshire in August 1774, reveals that of 45 'bound' colliers, 41 were 'absent'.[38]

Overall however, there is nothing to suggest a serious imbalance between the supply and demand for labour before 1760. There were local labour shortages, but these could usually be overcome by a modest level of poaching and by agreements between colliery proprietors to lend each other currently unwanted workers.[39] Although, as has been seen, a shortage was reported at Stevenston in 1723, the colliery's proprietors had managed to double the labour force prior to that date, and achieve a marked expansion in output; the problems which emerged there towards the end of the 1720s had little to do with the availability of labour. It was during the later decades of the eighteenth century that what has been described as a bottleneck in the supply of labour for the Scottish coal industry appeared. Support for this hypothesis is to be found in the increased incidence of poaching by coalmasters and subsequent court battles over colliery employees, complaints from some collieries of labour combination and high wages, and above all, in the campaign which was waged by a body of coal proprietors in the early 1770s to abolish serfdom and thereby remove from the colliers the 'stigma' attached to those working in the industry, which many masters considered to be a principal cause of their difficulties. As has been seen, several historians have been inclined to agree with them.

Yet there are grounds for exercising caution when considering both the severity of the problem and in particular its uniqueness to the Scottish coal industry, and indeed the extent to which this was a consequence of serfdom. Particular complaints about recruitment difficulties do not always signify a national problem. James Dewar of Vogrie, for example, who was, significantly, a leading light in the campaign which led to the so-called 'Emancipation Act' of 1775, had acquired a colliery in 1764, from which he hoped to sell coal in the large lucrative Edinburgh market. Expansion however depended upon his ability to attract more colliers.[40] Nevertheless, almost at the same time as Dewar was searching for colliers in Midlothian, where they clearly were in short supply, an agent of the Cadells at Grange colliery, in Stirlingshire, was confident that he would be able to get men from Fife, where 'coaliers are plenty and wages very low', as well perhaps, from the West of Scotland.[41] In 1774, during the downturn in trade which followed the boom of 1770–72, it was reported that colliers were relatively easy to find, and that perhaps more than half of the industry's workforce was either un- or under-employed.[42]

It must be conceded that 1774 was a particularly bad year, and in more buoyant conditions there were indeed complaints about labour shortages and high wages. Colliery proprietors were not alone in facing this problem though: skill was at a premium virtually everywhere throughout Scottish industry where attempts were made to achieve rapid and substantial output increases.[43] Wage levels too were rising across the board in Scotland between 1760 and 1793.[44] Much more pertinent however is the fact that labour shortages in coal mining were not peculiar to Scotland. These were also commonly experienced in similar circumstances at collieries in England, where recourse was also had to recruitment practices like poaching, accompanied by offers of generous sums of 'binding money', the offer of higher rates of pay, and other inducements such as the promise of easier working conditions. Strictly-enforced period labour contracts were also used to retain workers, who, on occasion, could, like their Scottish counterparts, find themselves chased and incarcerated if they deserted.[45]

The renowned Bond system, increasingly used at collieries in the north of England from the 1760s, had its origins in the desire of coalowners to stabilise their labour force at a time when it was in short supply.[46] So too did the much more extreme option of life-binding in Scotland, the legal basis of which was established in 1606, during a series of booms in coal mining activity which had commenced some three decades earlier.[47] Both of these systems were inadequate however, and north and south of the border, coalmasters were to be found, before the end of the eighteenth century, making use – on a small-scale – of immigrant Irish workers.[48] Evidence of a modest cross-border traffic in colliery labour – in both directions, both during the era of 'serfdom' and afterwards – is an indication that at some collieries at least, conditions of employment in the two countries' coal industries may not have been as great as is sometimes supposed, although it should be noted that prior to the Carron era, most Englishmen coming north were hired to perform specific tasks and were rarely simply hewers.[49] The pattern altered thereafter however and indeed in 1777 striking Bond-bound pitmen from Hartley colliery on Tyneside fled to Scotland.[50] In locations where there was either no mining tradition or it was very weak, enterprising coalmasters in Scotland recruited skilled men from the south, although deep-seated antipathy towards the English meant that this was not always a successful strategy.[51]

Thus compelling grounds exist for qualifying the notion that Scottish coalmasters were alone in having insufficient numbers of coal workers. Undoubtedly the intensity of demand in Scotland, where the existing pool of colliery labour was small, did create severe short-term difficulties for ambitious coalowners and lessees, but this was a matter of degree rather than a difference in kind. Thus on the fast-growing Cumberland coalfield, colliery proprietors during the eighteenth century had to resort to what was in that district the unprecedented step of employing female labour to carry out a range of underground tasks – unlike slower-growing Tyneside, where it was unusual to find females below ground.[52]

The extent to which the problem of labour recruitment was a consequence of serfdom may also have been exaggerated. Not all coal hewers in Scotland were bound for life. Unfortunately however the proportion of men (and women, who were invariably bearers) who were 'free' cannot be ascertained, and estimates range from 'negligible'[53], to what must be assumed to have been fairly substantial numbers in the West of Scotland, where independent colliers are thought to have been 'more common'.[54] There must however have been a significant number in the East as well, particularly outside Midlothian, as one of the principal aims of the River Forth Coal Proprietors Association (established c.1773) was to reduce their colliers' bounty payments, that is the sums paid annually in order to encourage them to enter in the first place, or to stay at a particular colliery. In the East too there are instances where colliers were hired on the understanding that they would be free to leave after a certain time, or to renegotiate their contracts.[55] In short, forms of labour contract other than life binding were adopted, not only in the West, but wherever coal mining was carried on in Scotland. This was so long before the first legislative steps were taken to abolish life-binding;

one-year bonds like those of the north-east of England, and other schemes, did not simply replace serfdom[56], but developed alongside it.

There was, however, little uniformity, and custom and practice could vary from estate to estate.[57] Thus at the Rothes pits in central Fife one year contracts were 'common' in the 1740s, but at nearby Lochgelly the colliers were life-bound.[58] Nor was it always clear to contemporaries whether or not a particular group of colliery employees was bound for life.[59] Neither did the courts take a uniform view as to what constituted serfdom. If the outlines of a pattern can be discerned, it is that life-binding was more likely be found at long-established collieries where competition from outside was relatively weak. Nowhere was this more so than in Midlothian, where a handful of aristocratic proprietors had a virtual monopoly of the Edinburgh market for coal until the first pricks of competition were felt with the abolition of the tax advantage they had over Newcastle in 1793, and the opening of the Union Canal in 1822.[60]

A central plank in the argument that the 'stigma' of serfdom discouraged new recruits from entering the industry is that coal workers were members of a despised 'caste', who 'lived apart from the rest of the population'.[61] And indeed, at its worst, collier serfdom could be a barbaric institution. Instances of life-bound colliers and bearers being subjected to the most humiliating treatment can readily be found, especially when they tried to leave for any reason without their master's permission.[62] Again however, it is worth noting that although far less common, instances where deserting hewers were hunted down and imprisoned can be found in England too.[63]

Yet the suggestion that coal workers were particularly brutal or brutalised, culturally distinct from the rest of the labouring poor in Lowland Scotland, has of late been subjected to critical scrutiny.[64] Colliery workers shared with others of their class many of the same values and interests, and were not alone in displaying a high level of occupational endogamy.[65] A similar historiographical shift has taken place in England, where coal workers had also been perceived by observers from the higher ranks as well as historians as a 'race apart'.[66] A much more convincing concept is that of colliers forming communities within a wider community.

This is not to discount altogether the possibility that the 'stigma' of serfdom had an adverse impact on recruitment, although the argument that it did is largely based on the testimony of those masters who wished to change the existing arrangements in 1774 and 1775. There were colliers who evidently detested the system and petitioned for its abolition.[67] Equally however there were those who perceived the benefits of their situation: in terms of earnings colliers were relatively well-rewarded from the 1770s, almost certainly for shorter hours of work than most other comparable groups of workers. Significantly, it was the coalmasters who campaigned most energetically for the abolition of serfdom, a system which had outgrown its usefulness, and was seen to be interfering with the market mechanism and understood to be keeping wages high.[68]

As is widely recognised, despite the ending of life-binding for new recruits in 1775, labour did not flood into the Scottish mining industry and wages remained high. A lingering fear of serfdom may partly account for this, as well as the colliers' practice of of restricting the entry to pits of unwelcome 'strangers'.[69] The adoption of a wider perspective however provides a more convincing explanation. Many of the ills associated with colliery work in Scotland had little or nothing to do with serfdom and much more to do with the nature of coal mining, which was arduous, dirty and dangerous work, into which labour could only be recruited – and retained – with the greatest difficulty everywhere.[70] This was true not only of hewing but also of the back-breaking job of bearing: in 1803, in order to encourage female bearers at Pencaitland colliery to enter and stay for a year, they were given half a guinea entry money and only permitted to engage with those colliers who agreed to give them 'proper work and wages'.[71] North as well as south of the border the best underground workers were judged to be those who had been raised in the industry and who would therefore have the necessary skills and experience to do underground work. Cutting coal under the widespread stoop and room (or 'pillar and stall') system required years of observation and practice if lives were not to be lost and the pit endangered. Adult recruits from outside the industry were therefore rarely employed. Accordingly, by and large, unless productivity could be improved, increases in the size of the coal mining labour force were dependent on the rate at which the colliery population could reproduce itself, and the success coalmasters had in dissuading workers and their offspring from leaving the industry. That the industry did achieve quite remarkable output gains during the eighteenth and early nineteenth centuries suggests that they did succeed, although towards the end of the 1700s this was increasingly due to the use of a new form of bondage, 'debt slavery'.[72]

More effective labour management also made a difference. Most complaints concerning colliers were made not about their numbers but about their performance. They had a strong 'disposition to mutiny' and were a 'far from passive inarticulate group', as the Clerks of Penicuik discovered as they spent the best part of a century in a largely forlorn attempt to create a disciplined regiment of coal workers.[73] The mushrooming of the industry in the eighteenth century involved the sinking of larger, deeper pits which could no longer be run on the informal lines of their typically smaller seventeenth century predecessors. The pool of underground supervisors, 'oversmen', upon which proprietors could draw was necessarily small, and accordingly, underground management was often insufficient or weak, with competent and reliable men, who were almost always former colliers, being extremely difficult to obtain.[74] Consequently, colliers were able to exercise considerable collective power both below and above ground, and until the defeat of the Associated Colliers of Scotland in 1826, revelled in the status of the 'independent collier'. 1826 however was the result of determined and concerted action on the part of the leading coal and ironmasters who were increasingly likely to dismiss troublesome workers.[75] Yet decades earlier, individually and occasionally collectively, colliery employers had begun to take steps to seize the managerial initiative, and slowly chip away at the colliers customary freedoms.[76] Part and parcel of this attack was the introduction, from the 1760s, of longwall working, one of the advantages of which was that it facilitated a greater division of labour and stripped from the hewer a layer of his bargaining power.[77] As with labour shortages however, workplace organisation and control (and labour combination) was not a distinctly Scottish problem, although it may well be that it was more acute in the buoyant conditions which prevailed north of the border.

There were however very real barriers to expansion in Scotland. One was that there were insufficient senior mine managers and mining engineers – that is men above the rank of oversman whose guidance was necessary for the strategic development of collieries.[78] Inland transportation was poor (although not absent) in the first half of the eighteenth century.[79] Turnpike development lagged behind that of England and Wales, and although much-discussed, few canal schemes actually came to fruition, and then late in the century.[80] Export and coastal trading was hampered by the existence of too many small and often exposed piers and harbours, which restricted the size and numbers of vessels which could load coal from them.[81] The significance of shipping accommodation can be well illustrated by examples from Ayrshire, where the major ports experienced very different fortunes, despite the fact that they were all within easy reach of the buoyant Irish market. Thus Ayr, described in 1723 as having an old pier 'out of Repair', and unable to handle any shipping during the winter months, accounted for less than three per cent of the county's Irish coal shipments in 1744. By contrast, the main coal shipping port, Saltcoats, was 'capable of holding 30 Sail of Ships, has $10\frac{1}{2}$ or 11 foot water at a spring tide' and was 'well secur'd'.[82] Even Saltcoats however was disadvantaged in its competitive struggle with Cumberland, not least because the average burden of the vessels belonging to the Scottish port was only two-thirds that of its custom-built, shallow-draughted Workington rivals.[83] A further difficulty for the owners and lessees of coastal collieries (in the East as well as Ayrshire) was that as they had little direct financial interest in shipping, they were at the mercy of the ship's masters, who had considerable freedom about which port to take coal from, and how much they were prepared to pay.[84]

Much of the coal which could be mined was of a poor quality, or unsuitable for its intended market. Even during Ayrshire's early eighteenth century heyday for example, coal had commanded a lower price than that from

Whitehaven, principally because it was not the 'caking' coal sought by Irish distillers and other industrial users.[85] This and the fact that urban demand for coal in Ireland was relatively weak [86] provides part of the explanation for Ayrshire's failure to increase coal shipments between c.1730 and c. 1780. Similar constraints were experienced on the East coast. Scottish coal, it was reckoned, was less 'oeconomical' than that of Newcastle or Sunderland, and for this and other cost reasons, little of it was consumed in London.[87] Although geological conditions varied across the Scottish coalfields, on the whole, Scotland was less well placed than many English mining districts.[88]

It has rightly been argued that the development of coal mining in Scotland required the industry's leaders to tackle and overcome the problem of underground drainage. As has been seen, during the the 1690s and early 1700s there was serious flooding at the pits which had been sunk along the banks of the Firth of Forth. Water posed particular difficulties in Ayrshire, where the most productive pits for much of the century were located along the low-lying raised beach which skirted the county: 'wet and slavish' is how one former manager of the pits at Auchenharvie described them in 1723, and indeed around the same time the Lowther collieries in Cumberland referred gleefully to the 'distress' the Scots were having in coping with inrushes of water and sand.[89] It was a supply-side constraint with which successive owners and lessees of the colliery had to struggle.

Over the course of the eighteenth century, and especially after c.1760, sometimes as a direct result of pressure from within the coal industry itself, or its potential customers, all of these constraints were tackled. The shortage of Scottish-bred mining engineers for instance was overcome by importing men from England, when they were required.[90] Some, William Dixon from Newcastle for instance, stayed, and became 'Scotland's mightiest coal master in the west'.[91] English coal and iron companies too came north from time to time, and in several cases, Carron for example, introduced a new dynamism, along with technical and managerial innovation, into the Scottish mining districts.[92] They were joined in the Glasgow region by members of the city's thrusting mercantile elite, who purchased coal-bearing estates. It was one of their number, Archibald Smellie of Easterhill, who was partly responsible for anti-combination clauses in the 1775 'Emancipation' Act.[93]

Inland transportation was substantially improved too, largely through the efforts of individual landowners and turnpike trusts, some 350 of which were enacted between 1750 and 1844.[94] Much of the increased and improved mileage which resulted enabled coal to be carried many miles from the pits. Carrying coal by road continued to be relatively expensive however, and even by the 1790s there were still many parts of the country – even in the Lowlands – which were ill-served[95]. Waggonways and, above all, water carriage, were preferable options. Although only one waggonway was constructed in Scotland before 1750, over the next 75 years, at least 30 more were added, mainly for the carriage of coal. Over half of the total mileage was laid down in Fife and Clackmannan, its builders being intent on tapping the coal-hungry Edinburgh market.

As waggonways resulted in undoubted advantages for the proprietors of inland pits by producing major savings in transport costs, and were also relatively inexpensive to lay[96], that more were not constructed is surely an indication that by and large, the potential market for coal, which prior to 1830 was almost wholly confined to Scotland and Ireland, was being satisfied. A further benefit of transport improvement was that varieties of coal which had previously been effectively cut off from the market, or restricted by shortcomings in transport facilities, became saleable, as in the case of the colliery belonging to the fourth Duke of Portland, who wished to increase his sales of coal – and in particular the more expensive 'blind' coal – in the Irish market. To facilitate this he constructed a new harbour at Troon in 1808 which was linked to his pits at inland Kilmarnock by a $9\frac{1}{2}$-mile long waggonway. By 1839 it was carrying over 130,000 tons of coal. Other locally important waggonways were constructed at Ayr.[97]

Arguably, it was the provision of steam pumping engines in Scotland after mid-century which reveals most vividly the energy – and capital commitment – with which the fortunes of the Scottish coal industry were transformed. After the flurry of steam engine construction in Ayrshire between 1719 and 1734, and their occasional appearance elsewhere, Newcomen engine building in Scotland came to a virtual halt. Thereafter however, the Scots record is singularly impressive, and between 1760 and 1769 as many as 20 were added. Of all the British coal mining regions, between 1734 and 1775, only in the North-east of England were more built than in Scotland and the West Midlands, which shared second place. For the century as a whole, Scottish collieries accounted for 17 per cent of all steam pumping engines erected in Britain (including the improved and more efficient Boulton and Watt engines) – at a time when Scotland accounted for only 13.3 per cent of British coal production.[98] Steam-powered winding engines too were introduced in the early 1790s.

Just how influential these and other factors can be seen not only in the revised growth rate for the Scottish coal industry generally, but also at the regional and local level. Close inspection reveals that historians' doubts about the ability of the industry to match demand have little foundation.

In Glasgow during the second half of the eighteenth century there were undoubtedly times when coal was in short supply. These *periodic* short-term crises however appear to have been overcome by 1790, if not beforehand. The Edinburgh-Glasgow road was turnpiked in the 1780s and the city was served by a carting system which was noted for its efficiency. Glasgow's coal prices were significantly lower than they were in Edinburgh.[99] The opening of the Monkland canal enabled even greater quantities of coal to be brought into the city. The establishment of the Glasgow Coal Combine at virtually the same time, and evidence of colliery company failures in the depression of 1797, indicate that supply of and demand for coal was in closer harmony than is sometimes supposed.[100] Indeed such was the level of output around Glasgow by the early 1800s (leading, presumably, to fears that prices would fall even further) that coal was being 'dumped' on the Irish market.[101] Efforts too were made to cart coal from the eastern end of the Forth & Clyde canal into Edinburgh. That coal prices in Glasgow were substantially higher than pithead prices had much to do with the monopoly which the Monkland Canal had, until the opening of the Monkland & Kirkintilloch railway in 1826, which allowed the Forth & Clyde canal to halve coal prices within two years.[102] Others quickly followed in its wake: the Ballochney (1828) and the Garnkirk & Glasgow (1831).

Over-production appears to have posed temporary difficulties for the Forth-side coalmasters in the 1770s, as from 1773 until 1776, and perhaps for longer, several of them met as River Forth Coal Proprietors, and made arrangements to dispose of 'any surplus quantities [of coal] that may in future be raised', and increase the selling price of coal within the Forth estuary.[103] It is true that two decades later, complaints about shortages and high prices on the East coast, mainly in Edinburgh and north of Fife, led to the removal in 1793 of the coastal coal tax. It should not be assumed however that Forth-side colliery proprietors were lacking in enterprise or enthusiasm: more steam engines were erected on coal mines in Fife and the Lothians than in Ayrshire and Lanarkshire between 1750 and 1800 for instance, while the coal port of Alloa generated one of the fastest increases in coastal shipments in Scotland between 1760 and 1784.[104] 1793 was an exceptionally bad year economically, while demand in the years immediately preceding it appears to have been unusually intense, the result of unprecedented prosperity and the establishment of coal-consuming manufactures in towns such as Perth and Dundee.[105] By the mid-1830s the coalmasters were once again combining in an attempt to raise the price of their product.

None the less, initially, the tax change was a severe blow for some of the formerly protected collieries of the Forth estuary, who watched in alarm as English imports flooded into ports – including Leith – which they had previously monopolised.[106] Yet coastal shipments continued to grow, if modestly, and did so much more strongly after the nadir of 1812. Coal ports on the Forth were improved and coalmasters displayed a new-found competitive spirit: Alloa for example increased its shipments of coal to the emergent industrial town of Dundee from 10 in 1820 to 395 in 1830; impressive increases in shipments also came from the collieries of Fordel, Halbeath and Elgin. Whereas in 1820 only 38 per cent of coal cargoes into Dundee were from Scotland, by 1830 the proportion had grown to 64 per cent.[107] The exception in the East was Midlothian, whose aristocratic coalowners managed to retain a powerful grip on the Edinburgh market, despite the challenges from Fife and Newcastle. It is here that allegations of conservatism, poor management and inefficiency stand up best to inspection.[108] Only after 1822 and the opening of the Union canal was there a marked change, as coal prices and wages began to fall – as coal proprietors from Lanarkshire made determined efforts to break into the newly-opened market, and landowners through whose estates the canal ran, began to exploit the opportunities it created.[109]

In Ayrshire, coal proprietors overcame the difficulties which had caused the county's share of the Irish coal trade to plummet from 16 per cent in 1720 to 11 per cent in 1740. Capital investment, in collieries and waggonways (and minor canals) and improved harbours, and entrepreneurial enthusiasm and ability (and good luck) were principal factors in the process of recovery which saw Irish coal shipments rise to 153,000 tons in 1825 (compared to 25,000 in 1729, and 39,800 in 1790) and capture something like 20 per cent of the market.[110] A leading figure in the later eighteenth century was Robert Reid Cunninghame of Auchenharvie, who sunk new pits, constructed a short canal and built a waggonway in order to move his Stevenston coal more efficiently and cheaply to the harbour which he had reconstructed at Saltcoats. Unlike his predecessors, he exercised considerable skill and firmness in persuading shippers that they should take his coal, although he was undoubtedly assisted in this by the powerful position that most Scottish-Irish coal suppliers found themselves in at this time.[111] Elsewhere in the county complaints that the domestic market was being sacrified in the interests of the better returns which could be had from selling to the shore were rarely heard after the early 1790s[112]; all the indications are that wherever demand was sufficient to justify commercial coal mining, efforts were made to satisfy it. After the end of the Napoleonic Wars in 1815 the evidence of a more or less sustained fall in coal prices suggests that this market too was being well-served.[113]

In this essay it has been argued that the performance of the Scottish coal industry throughout the eighteenth and early nineteenth centuries was much more impressive than has sometimes been assumed. While there were supply-side constraints, it is suggested here that these were overcome with remarkable speed: certainly most of them had been broken through by the early 1800s. The role of the coal tax has clearly been misunderstood. The adoption of a comparative perspective leads to the conclusion that the labour supply bottleneck is unlikely to have been much tighter in Scotland than was the case in other fast-growing mining regions. In tackling the problem of water, faced by all deep-mining enterprises, judged by the application of steam pumping technology, the Scottish record is impressive.

The consequences of this for our understanding of the process of industrialisation in Scotland are of considerable importance. Recently, much greater emphasis has been placed on the contribution of coal to the Industrial Revolution.[114] The argument is no less potent as far as Scotland is concerned. Far from checking growth, as some historians have been inclined to believe, it eased and encouraged it. Without the increases in output which were achieved, prices would have risen to prohibitive levels and the swelling urban population – which grew by a remarkable 132 per cent between 1750 and 1800 – could not have been sustained; towns thereafter could hardly have fulfilled their function as 'dynamic centres of economic change'.[115] Rural-urban migration would have been less attractive.

Coal fuelled not only domestic hearths and urban manufacturers' furnaces, but also rural limekilns, the lime from which was used not only to raise agricultural productivity, but also in the construction of houses, mills and workshops. Although water provided much of the power for industry before 1830[116] coal usage was growing. There is no evidence however to suggest that any of the coal-using industries suffered in the long-run from fuel shortages; on the contrary, it has been argued that cheap coal was a crucial factor in the emergence of a competitive coarse linen bleaching industry in Scotland prior to the introduction of chlorine in 1788.[117] Although there is debate about how critical natural endowments such as coal were for industrialisation in Ireland and elsewhere in Europe[118], few would dispute its significance for the Scottish economy as it actually developed, by encouraging the establishment of coke-using ironworks for example. Yet coal was not only a facilitating factor; it stimulated economic change and development in its own right – in agriculture, for instance, where the rapid expansion of a colliery in a locality created demand for foodstuffs and animal feed. Its most notable effect however was in the field of transport, although unlike England, where the needs of coal transporation encouraged canal construction, in Scotland its impact was felt most powerfully by the waggonways, built mainly to take coal to water; and later, the first railways.[119] Pessimistic assessments of the response of the Scottish coal industry to the demands placed on it in the first crucial phase of Scottish industrialisation should be discarded.

REFERENCES

1. T. M. Devine, 'Urbanisation', in T. M. Devine and R. Mitchison, eds., *People and Society in Scotland, Vol 1, 1760–1830* (Edinburgh, 1988), p. 35.
2. B. F. Duckham, *A History of the Scottish Coal Industry* (Newton Abbot, 1970), p. 14; S. G. E. Lythe and J. Butt, *An Economic History of Scotland, 1100–1939* (Glasgow, 1975), p. 162; B. Lenman, *An Economic History of Modern Scotland, 1660–1976* (London 1977), p. 63.
3. C. A. Whatley, 'The Process of Industrialisation in Ayrshire, *c.*1707–1871' (unpublished Ph.D. thesis, University of Strathclyde, 1975), pp. 103–9; 'The

Introduction of the Newcomen Engine to Ayrshire', *Industrial Archaeology Review*, II (1977), pp. 69–77. It was Professor John Butt who first aroused the author's interest in Scottish coal mining, in the former's stimulating Economic History Honours class at the University of Strathclyde on Scottish Business during the Industrial Revolution. He began to work on it seriously in 1975, during research for his doctoral thesis, supervised by Professor Butt (and John R. Hume). He is deeply indebted to Profesor Butt for his encouragement at that stage in his career.

4. H. Hamilton, *The Industrial Revolution in Scotland* (London, 1966), p. 170.
5. R. H. Campbell, *Scotland Since 1707: The Rise of an Industrial Society* (Oxford, 1965), p. 128.
6. J. Butt, *The Industrial Archaeology of Scotland* (Newton Abbot, 1967), p. 86; A. Slaven, *The Development of the West of Scotland, 1750–1960* (London, 1975), p. 113; Lenman, *Economic History*, p. 132.
7. R. H. Campbell, *The Rise and Fall of Scottish Industry, 1707–1939* (Edinburgh, 1980), p. 15.
8. Duckham, *Scottish Coal*, pp. 32–8.
9. Duckham, *Scottish Coal*, p. 30.
10. Lenman, *Economic History*, p. 134.
11. M. W. Flinn, *The History of the British Coal Industry, Volume 2, 1700–1830* (Oxford, 1984), p. 26.
12. S. Pollard, 'A New Estimate of British Coal Production, 1750–1850', *Economic History Review*, XXXIII (1980), p. 216.
13. J. U. Nef, *The Rise of the British Coal Industry* (2 Vols., London, 1932), i, p. 42.
14. Slaven, *West of Scotland*, p. 113; Lythe and Butt, *Economic History*, p. 163.
15. J. Hatcher, *The History of the British Coal Industry, Volume 1, Before 1700* (Oxford, 1993), p. 109; Hatcher however may be guilty of overestimating the size even of the larger collieries. Although he suggests that four (Clackmannan, Methil, Tulliallan and Wemyss) may each have been capable of putting out 20,000 tons or more per annum, in no case does he provide any actual output data; where this has been calculated by the present author, at Tulliallan in 1679–80 for example, the actual figure is 15,000 tons. See C. A. Whatley, 'Salt, Coal and the Union of 1707: a revision article', *Scottish Historical Review*, LXVI (1987), p. 34.
16. Nef, *Coal Industry*, i, pp. 48–9.
17. C. A. Whatley, 'The Finest Place For a Lasting Colliery: Coal Mining Enterprise in Ayrshire c.1600–1840', *Ayrshire Arch. and Nat. Hist. Soc.*, 14 (1983), p. 54.
18. Duckham, *Scottish Coal*, p. 20.
19. T. C. Smout, *Scottish Trade on the Eve of the Union 1660–1707* (Edinburgh, 1963), pp. 226–7.
20. Whatley, 'Salt, Coal', pp. 62–3.
21. Duckham, *Scottish Coal*, p. 230.
22. Nef, *Coal Industry*, i, pp. 207–8.
23. C. A. Whatley, *The Scottish Salt Industry: An Economic and Social History, c.1570–1850* (Aberdeen, 1987), pp. 146–7, n. 22.
24. Hatcher, *British Coal*, pp. 107–8.
25. Duckham, *Scottish Coal*, p. 28.

26. I. D. Whyte, 'Urbanisation in Early-Modern Scotland: A Preliminary Analysis', *Scottish Economc & Social History*, 9 (1989), pp. 23–9.

27. Hatcher, *British Coal*, pp. 40–2.

28. L. Cullen, T. C. Smout and A. Gibson, 'Wages and Comparative Development in Ireland and Scotland, 1565–1780', in R. Mitchison and P. Roebuck, eds., *Economy and Society in Scotland and Ireland 1500–1939* (Edinburgh, 1988), pp. 109–11.

29. Duckham, *Scottish Coal*, p. 20.

30. Pollard, 'Coal Production', p. 230; Pollard fails to explain why he favours an estimated per capita consumption figure of 15 cwt. (for the population as a whole) over Duckham's more realistic 11 cwt.

31. A. Durie, *The Scottish Linen Industry in the Eighteenth Century* (Edinburgh, 1979), pp. 55–9; Devine, 'Urbanisation', p. 28; M. W. Flinn, et. al., *Scottish Population History from the seventeenth century to the 1930s* (Cambridge, 1977), p. 246; T. C. Smout, 'Where had the Scottish economy got to by the third quarter of the eighteenth century?', in I. Hont and M. Ignatieff, eds., *Wealth and Virtue: The Shaping of Political Economy in the Scottish Enlightenment* (Cambridge, 1983), pp. 45–72.

32. Whatley, 'Salt, Coal', pp. 40–1.

33. Scottish Record Office (hereafter S.R.O.), GD 172/496/32, Henderson of Fordel MSS, Observations on the Proposed Repeal of the Coal and salt Tax, n.d., GD 172/496/24, Sir John Henderson to James Chalmers, 28 January 1792.

34. Whatley, 'Industrialisation', p. 82.

35. National Library of Scotland (hereafter N.L.S.), MS 5723, Wemyss MSS, Tutors Sederunt Book, 1719–33, 6 April 1733; S.R.O., RH15/119/16/11, Hamilton of Pencaitland MSS, Memoranudum concerning Pencaitland Colliery, 15 September 1803.

36. Whatley, 'Finest Place', p. 83.

37. G. P. Bennet, *The Past at Work: Around the Lomonds* (Markinch, n.d.), p. 14.

38. C. A. Whatley, 'A Caste Apart? Scottish Colliers, Work, Community and Culture in the Era of Serfdom, *c*.1606–1799', *Journal of the Scottish Labour History Society*, 26 (1991), p. 4; N.L.S., Acc. 5381, Box 15/2, Cadell MSS, Note, 'Bound Colliers at Grange', 29 August 1774.

39. Bennet, *The Past*, p. 26; S.R.O., GD224/388/6/1, Buccleuch MSS, Memorandum concerning the Sheriffhall Coalliers belonging to his Grace the Duke of Hamilton, n.d., *c*.1756; Signet Library, Court of Session cases, CS 166:6, Appendix, Sir James Clerk and John Clerk of Penicuik v. their colliers, 1773.

40. C. A. Whatley, ' "The Fettering bonds of brotherhood": combination and labour relations in the Scottish coal-mining industry, *c*.1690–1775', *Social History*, 12 (1987), p. 146.

41. N. L. S., Acc. 5381, Box 28 (1), Cadell MSS, James Frish to (?), 6 June 1768.

42. Whatley, 'Fettering bonds', p. 147.

43. This much-neglected topic is referred to briefly in C. A. Whatley, 'The Experience of Work', in Devine and Mitchison, *People and Society*, p. 225, and 'Women and the Economic Transformation of Scotland, *c*.1740–1830', *Scottish Economic & Social History* (forthcoming, 1994).

44. J. H. Treble, 'The Standard of Living of the Working Class', in Devine and

Mitchison eds. *People and Society*, pp. 194–200.
45. Flinn, *British Coal*, p. 350.
46. R. Colls, *The pitmen of the northern coalfield: work, culture and protest, 1790–1850* (Manchester, 1987), pp. 45, 68.
47. I. Guy, 'The Scottish Export Trade, 1460–1599', in T. C. Smout, ed., *Scotland and Europe, 1200–1850* (Edinburgh, 1986), p. 66.
48. Flinn, *British Coal*, p. 386.
49. B. F. Duckham, 'English Influences in the Scottish Coal Industry 1700–1815', in J. Butt and J. T. Ward, eds., *Scottish Themes: Essays in Honour of S. G. E. Lythe* (Edinburgh, 1976), p. 40.
50. Colls, *Pitmen*, p. 69.
51. Whatley, 'Finest Place', p. 88; Duckham, 'English Influences', p. 41; J. Strawhorn, *The History of Ayr* (Edinburgh, 1989), p. 98.
52. Hatcher, *British Coal*, p. 384; Flinn, *British Coal*, p. 334.
53. Duckham, *Scottish Coal*, p. 249.
54. T. C. Smout, *A History of the Scottish People, 1560–1830* (1969), p. 405; Slaven, *West of Scotland*, p. 113.
55. Glenrothes Development Corporation Archives (hereafter G.D.C.A.), 40/82/11, Rothes MSS, Contract between the Earl of Rothes and Christen Gray, 3 March 1753; 40/87/4, Agreement between the Earl of Rothes and George Blair, 27 October 1752; N.L.S., Acc. 5381, Box 15/2, Cadell MSS, John Grieve to William Cadell jnr., 16 and 22 January 1774.
56. Flinn, *British Coal*, p. 361.
57. Duckham, *Scottish Coal*, p. 244.
58. Bennet, *The Past*, p. 25; N.L.S., MS 13252, f.147, Minto SS, William Black to Andrew Chalmer, 12 November 1744.
59. See, for example, Strathclyde Regional Archives, RU2/1/15/68, Petition to the Provost of Rutherglen of the Tacksmen of Rutherglen Coalwork, 17 February 1750, and RU2/1/15/71, Answers for Robert Bryson and others.
60. J. A. Hassan, 'The Supply of Coal to Edinburgh, 1790–1850', *Transport History*, 5 (1972), pp. 132–3; see too 'The landed estate, paternalism and the coal industry in Midlothian, 1800–1880', *Scottish Historical Review*, LIX (1990), pp. 73–91.
61. Smout, *Scottish People*, pp. 168–70; I. H. Adams, *The Making of Urban Scotland* (1978), p. 53.
62. See, for example, S.R.O., CS96/2146, Dryden Coal Book, 1725–8.
63. Flinn, *British Coal*, p. 350.
64. Whatley, 'A Caste Apart?'.
65. R. Houston, 'Marriage Formation and Domestic Industry: Occupational Endogamy in Kilmarnock, Ayrshire, 1697–1764', *Journal of Family History* (Fall, 1983), pp. 220–6.
66. Hatcher, *British Coal*, p. 377; J. Benson, *British Coalminers in the Nineteenth Century: A Social History* (1980), pp. 1–5; even contemporary Scots observers were prepared to admit that there were 'remarkable exceptions' to the generally perceived rule that coal miners were 'more rude in their manners and more ignorant . . . than the generality of other work men', S.R.O., GD 345/742/2, Grant of Monymusk MSS, 'An Attempt towards the laying down of a proper

method of Enquiring into and writing upon Coal', n.d. It should be noted that even though critical, this account points to a difference of degree rather than of kind.

67. Smout, *Scottish People*, pp. 407–8; A. Campbell, *The Lanarkshire Miners: A Social History of their Trade Unions, 1775–1874* (Edinburgh, 1979), p. 12.
68. Whatley, 'Fettering bonds', p. 148.
69. Whatley, 'Finest Place', p. 145; 'A Caste Apart?', p. 7.
70. Flinn, *British Coal*, p. 339; this was recognised by the astute contemporary coal 'viewer' Robert Bald, who remarked in 1808, that after 'Emancipation', 'even the allurement of double wages . . . induced . . . very few . . . to forego the busy haunts of men, and cheerful light of the sun, for the damp, gloomy and dangerous regions of a coal-pit'.
71. S.R.O., Hamilton of Pencaitland MSS, Memorandum concerning Pencaitland Colliery, 15 September 1803.
72. Campbell, *Lanarkshire Miners*, p. 13.
73. R. Houston, 'Coal, class and culture: labour relations in a Scottish mining community, 1650–1750', *Social History*, 8 (1983), pp. 1–18; Whatley, 'Fettering bonds', p. 144.
74. Duckham, *Scottish Coal*, pp. 119–26; Whatley, 'Industrialisation', pp. 120, 126;
75. A. Campbell, 'The Scots Colliers' Strikes of 1824–1826: The Years of Freedom and Independence', in J. Rule, ed., *British Trade Unionism: 1750–1850: The Formative Years* (1988), p. 143–9; Whatley, 'Fettering bonds', p. 153; N.L.S. MS 17249, f.28, Saltoun MSS, Henry Davidson to Robert Farmer, 31 December 1825.
76. Duckham, 'English Influences', p. 41; Whatley, 'Work', pp. 236–9; G.D.C.A., MS 40/87/1, Rothes MSS, Mr Robertson's Directions as to the Coal, June 1752; N.L.S., MS 13257, f. 48 Minto MSS, Robert Beatson to Sir Gilbert Elliot, 27 January 1767.
77. Duckham, 'English Influences', p. 141.
78. Duckham, *Scottish Coal*, p. 130; 'The Emergence of the Professional Manager in the Scottish Coal Industry, 1760–1815', *Business History Review*, XLIII (1969), pp. 21–38.
79. Duckham, *Scottish Coal*, p. 205.
80. A. Gordon, *To Move With the Times: The Story of Transport and Travel in Scotland* (Aberdeen, 1988), p. 5; C. J. A. Robertson, *The Origins of the Scottish Railway System, 1722–1844* (Edinburgh, 1983), pp. 3–5.
81. B. Lenman, *From Esk To Tweed* (Glasgow, 1975), pp. 16–54.
82. Whatley, 'Finest Place', p. 92; L. E. Cochran, *Scottish Trade with Ireland in the Eighteenth Century* (Edinburgh, 1985), pp. 30–1.
83. Whatley, 'Finest Place', p. 94.
84. Whatley, 'Industrialisation', pp. 50a–51; 'Finest Place', p. 93; N.L.S., Acc. 5381, Vol. 2, Cadell MSS, Minutes of meetings of the Proprietors of Grange and Pitfirrane Collieries, 6 August 1772.
85. Whatley, 'Industrialisation', p. 50.
86. Cochran, *Scottish Trade*, pp. 37–8.
87. Whatley, 'Salt, Coal', p. 33.
88. Flinn, *British Coal*, p. 6.

89. Whatley, 'Industrialisation', pp. 122–3.
90. Duckham, 'English Influences', pp. 41–3.
91. Duckham, *Scottish Coal*, p. 184.
92. Duckham, 'English Influences', pp. 35–9.
93. Duckham, *Scottish Coal*, 179–81; T. M. Devine, *The Tobacco Lords* (Edinburgh, 1975), pp. 40–3.
94. Gordon, *To Move*, p. 36.
95. Duckham, *Scottish Coal*, p. 206.
96. Robertson, *Railway System*, pp. 5–6; 25–30.
97. Whatley, 'Industrialisation', p. 44; Robertson, *Railway System*, pp. 21–5; H. Broad, 'Rails to Ayr', *Ayrshire Arch. Nat. Hist. Soc.*, 13 (1981), pp. 104–10.
98. Flinn, *British Coal*, pp. 122, 127.
99. Robertson, *Railway System*, p. 26.
100. Hamilton, *Industrial Revolution*, pp. 193–6.
101. Cochran, *Scottish Trade*, p. 32.
102. Robertson, *Railway System*, p. 307.
103. N.L.S., Acc. 5381, Box 12/1, Cadell MSS, Minutes of River Forth Coal Proprietors, 10 January 1776.
104. Duckham, *Scottish Coal*, pp. 363–5; G. Jackson, 'Scottish Shipping, 1775–1805', in P. L. Cottrell and D. H. Aldcroft, eds., *Shipping, Trade and Commerce: Essays in Memory of Ralph Davis* (Leicester, 1981), p. 123.
105. Perth and Kinross District Archives, PE 1/1/4, Perth Town Council Minutes, 1786–1794, Petition to Parliament as to the Duty on English Coal, p. 398.
106. Duckham, *Scottish Coal*, p. 233.
107. G. Jackson and K. Kinnear, *The Trade and Shipping of Dundee 1780–1850* (Dundee, 1991), pp. 26–7.
108. Hassan, 'Supply of Coal', pp. 131–2; 'The landed estate', pp. 73–9.
109. Hassan, 'Supply of Coal', pp. 134–5.
110. Whatley, 'Industrialisation', p. 43.
111. L. M. Cullen, *Anglo-Irish Trade, 1660–1800* (Manchester, 1968), p. 126; Whatley, 'Industrialisation', pp. 116–92.
112. Whatley, 'Industrialisation', p. 57; Strawhorn, *History of Ayr*, p. 98.
113. Whatley, 'Industrialisation', p. 47.
114. Pollard, 'Coal Production', p. 232; Flinn, *British Coal*, pp. 442–57.
115. Devine, 'Urbanisation', p. 31.
116. J. Shaw, *Water Power in Scotland 1550–1870* (Edinburgh, 1984), p. 102.
117. A. Durie, 'Textile Bleaching: A Note on the Scottish Experience', *Business History Review*, XLIX (1975), pp. 141–2.
118. For discussion of this in the Irish context see Mokyr, *Why Ireland Starved: A Quantitative and Analytical History of the Irish Economy, 1800–1850* (1985 ed.), pp. 152–8.
119. Robertson, *Railway System*, pp. 306–9.

2

Industry and Investment in the Eighteenth Century Highlands: The York Buildings Company of London

A. J. G. CUMMINGS

In recent years the economic effects of the Union of 1707 have been subject to a considerable degree of scrutiny by, among others, R. H. Campbell, T. M. Devine and C. A. Whatley.[1] Generally, historians are agreed that the first two or three decades after 1707 were ones of economic stagnation,[2] although Devine has stressed that this cannot be seen as caused by the union.[3] By the 1730s it has been claimed that manufacturing was on the road to recovery based on evidence derived from the linen, wool and salt industries.[4] Much attention has been given to these industries, to the cattle trade and to the potential markets opened up to Scots as a consequence of the union, but the role of Scotland as a recipient of English direct investment in the early post union decades has virtually been ignored. The object of this essay is to examine attempts by English capitalists to exploit the natural resources of the Highland region of Scotland, particularly minerals and timber, in the 1720s and 1730s.[5] Contemporaries had been made aware of the long-term prospects of both of these, in parts of the north of Scotland, by the writings of Daniel Defoe.[6] Much of this spurt of investment centred around the activities of the York Buildings Company and the reasons for this outburst of activity, and its comparative lack of success will be discussed. The role of the York Buildings Company will form the main basis of the study, although the scope and nature of other ventures will also be considered.

The York Buildings Company was a London waterworks which had been acquired by a group of city speculators during the boom which preceded the South Sea 'Bubble' in 1720. The aim of the new owners, led by Case Billingsley a noted speculator, was to exploit a loophole in the company's charter which gave it unlimited landholding powers by acquiring estates forfeited after the Jacobite Rebellion of 1715 and using their revenues to fund a life annuity scheme.[7] In this they were actively encouraged by the government which was having difficulty disposing of the estates, and accordingly passed the necessary measures to make the purchase possible.[8] The company was relaunched in 1719 with an authorised capital of £1,200,000 and proceeded to buy estates in England and Scotland to a total value of £264,191.[9] After a spectacular rise, the company was caught up in the panic surrounding the collapse of the 'Bubble' and left in fairly dire straits.[10] However, the company was confident of solving its problems. These hopes were ill-founded. A series of lotteries designed to issue annuities and raise cash were unsuccessful in raising ready money, but left the company with an annuity debt, placing it deeper in the mire.[11] The company also tried to exploit its estates. That of the Earl of Winton at Tranent in East Lothian was noted for its coal works, and these the company proceeded to develop.

As well as being an age of speculation, the period was also one of considerable intellectual curiosity. This was the age of Newtonianism and this manifested itself not only in things theoretical but in things mechanical. Public lecturers on scientific matters such as physics were extremely popular, and a more practical interest in science is indicated by the fact that it was also an age when patent registrations abounded.[12] The York Buildings Company took full advantage of the new technology this made available. It installed the first steam engine in the South of England built by Thomas Savery at its waterworks around 1713–14, and acquired a more advanced Newcomen machine in 1725. In 1722, the company built the first railway in Scotland to link the coalworks at Tranent with the harbour at Cockenzie and installed one of the first steam engine in Scotland to drain the mines.[13] None of this capital expenditure, however, met with the success its foresight deserved. The venture also provided the first indications that the company's industrial investment in Scotland was going to provide no worthwhile returns.

The link between advanced technology and water supply revived the interest of James Brydges, 1st Duke of Chandos, in the affairs of the York Buildings Company. Chandos had been involved in the company when it had been relaunched during the promotions boom of 1719. However between 1721 and 1724 he had attempted to revive the fortunes of the ailing Royal African Company.[14] Realising that slaves and ivory were losing propositions for the company, he was keen to develop its trade in gold, potash, cotton and medicines.[15] Potash was of interest to him as he was attempting to establish glass and soap production on some of his estates.[16] This brought him into contact with a fellow director, Samuel Horsey,[17] who was to become his principal agent within the York Buildings Company. Chandos revived interest in that company came about because of the need to supply water to his property in the Marylebone area of London.[18] His speculative instincts were soon aroused by the prospects of developing the company's coal works in Tranent, not only to provide fuel for the waterworks engine, but for general sale in London and in France and Holland.[19] These dreams were never realised as higher costs meant that the coal could not compete with that of Tyneside but this was the first of a series of ventures in Scotland that would arise from the fertile minds of Chandos and his associates.

Chandos's first step was to place his own men in the company. He contrived to have his friend Samuel Horsey elected as a director in 1724, and made governor in 1726.[20] During the same period, one of his stockbrokers, James Marye, was causing serious trouble within the company, but Chandos denied that he had anything to do with these manoeuvres.[21] Whatever the truth of the matter, the resultant destabilisation of the York Buildings Company made it easier for Horsey to take charge. Around this time, Chandos and Horsey thought first of exploiting the woods on the company's estates in the North-east of Scotland to provide potash, an interest dating from their African Company days.[22] Horsey and Chandos then cast their eyes even further afield to possibilities existing in other parts of northern Scotland.

Part of the reason for looking further afield was economic, and part was political. In economic terms, the Scottish estates had not proved the bonanza for the company which had been hoped. Partly this was due to the difficulties of collecting rents, which could still be paid partly in kind. Also the company's agents were notorious for milking their employers. Furthermore there was the difficulty of remitting funds to London, again the company seeming to be the loser. Finally, it was still the case that there was a great degree of underlying sympathy for the forfeited families, a fact which had led to difficulties in disposing of the estates in the first place. Such sympathy could extend even to the highest places, and this convinced Chandos and Horsey that perhaps the way to reviving the company's fortunes was to sell the estates back to the dispossessed families at a suitable price.[23] The scheme made no headway as opposition from London proved too strong. The situation was complicated by the fact that the company's annuitants saw the estates as security for their debts and in 1727 their trustees gained control of the revenues.[24] Thus it was no longer possible for the company to exploit its estates for its own profit.

To solve its problems, the company was forced to look to new ventures and Chandos and Horsey became attracted to the Highlands as a possible source of investment. The link, once again, was potash. In 1726, Aaron Hill, a noted speculator, dramatist and theatrical entrepreneur had visited Abernethy on Speyside and with the assistance of equipment sent to him from London by John Essington, a former director of the York Buildings Company and close associate of Case Billingsley, had attempted to produce potash.[25] This was unsuccessful, but he saw possibilities in the woods themselves. He convinced Horsey and Chandos that they were capable of producing timber for masts large enough for first rate ships. This was very attractive as to obtain such naval stores at home was not only strategically desirable but would reduce the need to import them from potentially hostile areas. From the company's point of view, the fact that it had to pay charges amounting to around 3 per cent to transfer its money from Scotland to London made it an attractive proposition to convert part of these funds into timber and sending it instead.[26]

The woods had been worked to some extent as there were already sawmills on the site.[27] However Hill's record as a businessman did not bode well for the operation. Two of his enterprises, the Beech Oil project of 1714 and the Golden Islands scheme of 1720 had been well publicised, abject failures.[28] So great was Hill's notoriety, that when the company adopted the scheme it was attributed to its agents Thomas Fordyce and William Adam, concealing Hill's involvement from the stockholders and the public.[29]

Despite the range of its previous activities, however, the company was clearly acting outwith its charter and so it was obliged to seek additional powers to carry on what was, in effect, trade and manufacturing. The Attorney-General Philip Yorke was slightly wary of the application but with some reservations approved an extension to the company's charter.[30] Indeed the range of powers enjoyed by the York Buildings Company was unusual. Most companies, even the largest such as the Bank of England and the East India Company, were set up with fairly narrow functions in mind. The York Buildings Company, however, with its broad range of activities and interests was more akin to a twentieth century conglomerate seeking profits wherever they may be found. In that sense at least it was perhaps too advanced for its time.

On 7 December 1727, Horsey and the banker John Ewer entered into a bargain with Sir James Grant of Grant to purchase 60,000 trees at a price of £7,000 Sterling. On 5 January 1728, the company affixed its seal to the contract,[31] one week before the Attorney-General approved their power to do so, and over eight months before the final draft of the required letters patent extending the range of the company's activities was approved by the Privy Council.[32] On the date this was finally granted, the company petitioned the Treasury to introduce a measure creating a bounty for the home production of naval timber and this was finally set at £1 per ton on specified timber.[33]

As with the potash scheme, the timber scheme was doomed to failure. A report showing that the trees were not of a sufficient size to produce masts for large ships was not presented in full to the directors.[34] The terrain was not suitable for a cost effective operation. The base of the operations was at Culnakyle, some twenty-five miles from the rivermouth. Timber had to be floated downstream to the Moray Firth. Horsey had painted a favourable picture of the scheme's prospects.[35] In reality, the river was unsuitable for such traffic. It was shallow and liable to flash flooding during heavy rain making passage dangerous and the river likely to change its course. Timber could be carried out to sea causing a danger to shipping.[36] Also the river had to be cleared at one point to ensure free passage.[37] Costs were extremely high, making Scandinavian timber cheaper. Chandos felt that the scheme would never cover its cost let alone make a profit.[38] Some voyages did result in bounties, one cargo also receiving sufficient to cover the freight costs despite a glutted market.[39] Chandos became a little more cheerful about the prospects, stressing the need to finish the sawmills and load the timber at Garmouth instead of Findhorn, the original point of despatch.[40]

Investment was considerable. By 1735 there were at least twenty sawmills on the site and a boring mill for producing pipes, noted in 1771, has also been attributed to the Company.[41] Neil Munro has even claimed that ships were built at the rivermouth, but this has never been substantiated.[42] Despite such expenditure, Chandos' original forebodings proved to be correct. In all, the company felled some 20,000 trees but lost around £26,000 on this operation between 1728 and 1732, the only period for which we have any meaningful figures.[43] Bad management is one possible explanation for this failure. However the principal manager at Abernethy was one William Stephens, a bankrupt former MP., who was said to have been given the job to get him out of London to avoid his creditors. On leaving his position in 1734, Stephens went to South Carolina to look after Samuel Horsey's interests there, and ended up as an administrator in Georgia.[44] It is not outwith the bounds of possibility that the basis of his recovery was laid in the North of Scotland.

Despite the problems of the Speyside operation, the York Buildings Company attempted to extend its operations in the timber industry. In 1730, the company entered into an agreement with Roderick Chisolm to develop woodlands on his estate in Strathglass, Invernesshire.[45] As on Speyside the stated aim was to produce naval timber, deals and planks, floating them down to the Beauly Firth. Again this was unsuccessful and 2,400 trees felled were left to rot.[46] The company also leased woods from Lord Lovat in the Beauly area, but like Strathglass, the scheme appears to have failed.[47]

Timber also provided a basic ingredient for iron production, the second venture on Speyside. The idea of producing iron in the North of Scotland was not new. The most important bloomery in medieval Scotland had been situated near Elgin.[48] On Speyside, Sir John Grant of Grant had toyed with the idea in 1630s, but nothing had come of it.[49] The basis for the optimism for new investment in the iron industry in the Highlands seemed sound. Between 1710 and 1720, difficulties in importing Swedish iron due to warfare led to the building of new plant in England.[50] In the 1720s, product prices had risen and charcoal prices were falling. With nine charcoal blast furnaces being built in the country and only one closed during the decade, the potential for profit seemed to be present.[51] In terms of location, the fragility of charcoal meant that it was not feasible to move it any great distance. Thus rather than force prices up in an area due to increased competition for fuel, it was often seen as more practical to set up in a new location and move ore to the charcoal.[52]

Four new iron ventures were established in the Highlands in this period. In addition to Speyside there were works at Achray near Loch Katrine, Glenkinglass near Loch Etive in Argyll, and Invergarry in Invernesshire.[53] The latter was operated by the Rawlinsons of Furness using local charcoal to smelt imported ore.[54] The York Buildings Company established that ore was obtainable between Tomintoul and Strathdown, around twenty miles from Abernethy.[55] As waterpower for bellows and other equipment was available at the timber works, Chandos and Horsey became keen to exploit this to the benefit of the company. Chandos saw excellent prospects for the production of pig iron, claiming that forges in Gloucestershire and Herefordshire producing bar iron were idle because of a lack of pigs, a statement given some credence by the fact that much of the produce of the Invergarry works was shipped through Bristol to Chepstow merchants, Nehemiah Champion and John Beckett.[56]

Once again the company invested heavily in the venture. A furnace was shipped from Bristol to Scotland, and there were also forges and other equipment on the site.[57] Transporting the ore required one hundred and twenty horses and scores of men.[58] In April 1730, Chandos was informed that the company had agreed to take thirty-six square miles of woods for charcoal in order to stop any other organisation entering the iron trade in the area. Francis Place and Benjamin Lund, the company's technical experts, planned five new furnaces to be built near the woods, which along with three on the original site meant the plan was for a total of eight furnaces. It was reckoned that output would be upwards of 6,500 tons per annum, which at a profit of £6 per ton would yield £39,000. Production was due to commence in May.[59] This seemed a gross overestimation, not only of the company's capabilities, but of the country's needs. In 1717, it has been estimated that the total production of pig iron in Britain was only 20,000 tons and that output did not grow significantly until after 1750.[60]

By July, there appeared to be a change in the company's plans. Lund had stopped work on the furnace at Culnakyle and had commenced work on another in 'Inverness', by which was probably meant the Invergarry works. Chandos felt this was strange and asking why, if it was now more convenient to have a furnace elsewhere, had money been wasted at Culnakyle. The lack of production was fuelling rumours and Chandos felt a good load of iron was necessary to show the public and the markets that the venture was sound.[61] Chandos was also worried that if the furnace at Culnakyle was abandoned but the forges kept, transferring pig iron from Invergarry to be made into bar iron would prove a costly business unless water transport was available. However, the tenor of his correspondence would seem to suggest that those in Scotland were trying to convince him that pig iron should be made at Invergarry and bar iron at Culnakyle.[62] In January 1731, Chandos requested Brodie of Brodie to ascertain whether or not any furnaces or forges had actually been constructed at Culnakyle.[63] What is certain is that between June and September 1730, Lund purchased one hundred tons of pig iron from Invergarry for which the latter had trouble obtaining payment from the York Buildings Company.[64]

Some of the forges and furnaces were completed and bar and pig produced.[65] However by 1734, the company was in serious trouble. John Grant of Burnside, Sir James Grant of Grant's factor, seized fifty two tons of locally produced iron and a further two and a half tons imported from Invergarry, for sums owed to his employer.[66] Iron had also been given to employees in lieu of wages.[67] As early as 1732, accumulated losses were over £6,000 Sterling.[68]

The York Buildings Company's activities proved of mixed benefits to Speyside. Successive cash flow crises led to the company issuing notes for goods and services which became almost worthless when the company crashed, following the disclosure of grave irregularities by a parliamentary committee in 1733.[69] The company had tried to keep the locals quiet by organising large scale celebrations with bonfires and hogsheads of brandy which horrified the local minister by killing five people in a single night! In the longer term the company built proper sawmills, created roads through the woods and developed a system of floating timber down the Spey on rafts, all of which were used after the company left the area.[70] After the company's failure in 1733 the timber operation and possibly the iron works were carried on by the company's agents in the short term, ultimately falling into the hands of the company's governor, Thomas Pembroke in 1742.[71] Just how much iron was produced is uncertain. Operations were bedevilled by creditors trying to obtain payment and seizing property and goods to do so.[72] Even the company's landlord, Sir James Grant of Grant and his heirs, were forced into almost interminable legislation to try to obtain some redress.[73] Thus considerable capital investment brought no long term returns to the company and only marginal benefit to the locality.

The Highland iron industry as a whole was in serious trouble in the early 1730s. The Invergarry works effectively ceased production in February 1734. It cannot be determined when production ceased in Glenkinglass, but it was certainly before 1738, and possibly earlier.[74] One reason for this was that the market situation in Britain had changed. The price of Swedish iron, always desirable because of its quality, fell.[75] Average annual imports of bar and pig iron which had stood at 19,650 tons and 328 tons respectively in the 1720s rose to 23,727 tons and 2,544 tons on average in the five year period 1730–1734.[76] Thus the York Buildings Company and other Highland operators were exposed to stronger competition. The Abernethy works, as we have seen, had been conceived on a large scale to produce pig and bar iron. Even scaled down, they still failed to show a profit, despite Chandos' optimism. Costs and location were a further problem. The York Buildings Company's operations, as we have already seen, were a considerable distance from the sea, requiring shipment through either Garmouth or Findhorn. Iron from Invergarry was transported by land and water to Corpach on Loch Linnie, and from there to markets in the south.[77] In both cases this added to costs and rendered them vulnerable when the cost of more desirable imports fell. Invergarry iron was also subject to competition from the iron industry on the west side of England, and here too, costs were a significant factor.[78]

The potential markets for Glenkinglass iron are even more difficult to determine, but they did in fact supply the York Buildings lead works at Strontian with a new type of hearthplate.[79] Alfred Fell has gone so far as to state that the Glenkinglass works were controlled by the York Buildings Company in 1727.[80] Lindsay makes no mention of this but shows that the works were controlled by a mainly Irish partnership, but which by 1733, included Daniel Campbell of Shawfield.[81] Shawfield had become the tenant of the York Buildings Company's estate at Kilsyth in 1727 with Horsey's connivance.[82] In the ensuing years the two men developed a stronger financial relationship and Campbell claimed to be owed over £10,000 by the company, including payments on behalf of the Strontian operation.[83] Thus a potential connection between the two iron concerns cannot be totally ruled out. As we have seen, the York Buildings Company purchased a fair amount of iron from Invergarry and closer links between the two were at least envisaged. It is also not outwith the bounds of possibility that the lease of Chisolm's woods in nearby Strathglass might have been taken with the possibility of charcoal in mind. The intriguing possibility therefore occurs that at some stage, the York Buildings Company controlled, or at least had a strong influence over all three ironworks operating in the Highlands in the late 1720s and early 1730s. Market forces certainly played a significant part in their decline, but one must also consider the fact that none really survived the crash of the York Buildings Company in 1733.

As the iron and timber works were being developed, Chandos and Horsey were spreading the net of the York Buildings Company's Scottish interests still further. This time the objective was lead mining and Horsey now conceived a great plan which, according to David Murray, was no less than an attempt to monopolise the lead industry of Scotland.[84] This is in fact an exaggeration but there is no doubt that there were considerable moves afoot in the lead industry in Scotland. In 1729, Horsey had been in Scotland visiting the company's estates and its works on Speyside. During his stay, he negotiated a lease of the lead mines in West Lothian owned by the Earl of Hopetoun.[85] In the same year, a group of expatriate Scots including Sir Archibald Grant of Monymusk and Thomas Watts obtained a charter for the

Scotch Mines Company which was to operate out of the Sun Fire Office, controlled since 1720 by Watts, yet another close associate of Chandos,[86] who himself subscribed for shares.[87] The Scotch Mines Company was to become significant in the exploitation of Leadhills in Lanarkshire, and Sir Archibald Grant also had a personal interest in lead mines in Morvern in the Western Highlands.[88]

Grant, together with several others including General George Wade, also held a lease on the lead mines owned by Sir Alexander Murray of Stanhope at Strontian Ardnamurchan, just across Loch Sunart from Morvern.[89] Murray, a lowlander who had acquired this estate in 1714, had, like many other improvers of the age, an optimistic view for the future. He felt that the whole of the Argyllshire coast had 'advantageous Prospects of great Improvement by Husbandry, Planting, Iron-works, Mining and Fishery'.[90] This keeness of outsiders to develop Highland assets was a sign of the change in the region implying more commercial landowning as noted by Devine.[91] Horsey soon became keen to add the Strontian mines to the York Buildings Company's industrial ventures. In March 1730, the company's mining expert, Francis Place was sent to view the mines, and his report, sent to Horsey in April was generally favourable. On 2 May, Horsey wrote to Place telling him that he had entered into negotiations to lease the mines. Place advised caution as he felt there was a heavy burden of royalties payable on the mines.[92] Chandos was also sceptical about the worth of the mines feeling too much was being asked for them.[93] However, the York Buildings Company was led to believe the Company of Mine Adventurers, another speculative concern, was also interested in Strontian, and thus the company entered into an agreement to sub-lease the mines for an annual payment of £3,600 Sterling, a rent Place regarded as excessive and far in excess of what they were really worth.[94]

The Strontian mines were relatively undeveloped when the York Buildings Company took them over. At first the ore was recovered on an open cast system, or at least from very near the surface.[95] As with the venture on Speyside, the York Buildings Company invested a large sum on their new acquisition. Francis Place found that the works were not in a good state of repair.[96] Thus, considerable works were carried out in the area. Shafts were sunk at the lead veins, although some of them were in the wrong place.[97] At Strontian itself, they built a quay, a smelting mill, furnaces, hearts, a cooperage and housing for their workers as well as a large house for their senior officials and for offices. At New York, nearer to the lead workings, they created a settlement that included a brewhouse, kilns, workshops and coal and timber yards. They also built a road between Strontian and New York.[98] The malthouse and brewhouse were not properly authorised and never finished. Francis Place later reckoned that buildings alone had cost around £5,000.[99] Thus the company added considerably to the infrastructure of an isolated and remote area, an achievement compared by Lieutenant Alexander Bruce of the Engineers to General Wade's roadbuilding programme in the Highlands.

It is hard to estimate exactly how much was actually invested in the works. The company later claimed to have spent 'upwards of £40,000 more than the produce of the mines.'[100] However there were problems. Local hostility as well as logistical problems meant food had to be imported and coal for the works was also required, some of the latter coming from Sir James Lowther's mines in Cumberland. Some of the timber needed came from Speyside, but an additional quantity had to be imported from Norway and hearthplates were ordered from Glenkinglass.[101] Such was the bad feeling in the area that Place was relieved when arms were sent for protecting the miners from the locals.[102] Even in the early days, if a ship did not arrive in time the position could be bad. In February 1731 there was an outbreak of sickness due to people drinking water owing to a lack of malt.[103] As the company's financial position worsened, supplies became more difficult to obtain and the plight of the workers, many of them skilled men imported from England, Wales and the Low Countries because of the lack of experienced local labour, grew ever more dire. By 1734 some were even forced to resort to begging to seek funds to return home.[104] The precise amount expended on these works cannot be determined, but by the end of 1732, losses incurred amounted to over £25,000,[105] thus estimates of capital expenditure in excess of £30,000 cannot be discounted.

The whole issue, however, is complicated by the fact that the Company had become involved, whether inadvertently or otherwise, in what was to be one of the greatest financial scandals of the eighteenth century, namely the Charitable Corporation affair. Put at its simplest, Sir Archibald Grant, William Burroughs and William Squire, who controlled the Charitable Corporation, together with John Thompson its warehousekeeper and George Robinson its banker, had been speculating in the shares of that organisation with money they had embezzled from it. George Robinson swindled his partners by taking all their shares for himself. To try to retrieve the situation and avoid discovery, they had been forced to trust Robinson again, and embezzle more money. This they planned to invest in York Buildings Company stock in which the conspirators already held an interest, force up the price and then sell to recover their losses. It was for this reason that Grant was so keen to rent the Strontian mines to the company.[106]

It was realised that Chandos was a big player in York Buildings stock as he had asked Grant for his opinion on the state of the mines. The latter told Chandos he felt their success could double the company's value. Burroughs also reported to Chandos on the great potential of the mines. Acting on such advice, Chandos ordered Robinson, who was also a stockbroker to buy £20,000 of York buildings stock for him. Chandos as usual let his enthusiasm run away with him. He had initially been very sceptical about the mines, but fuelled by further reports from Grant, he felt that an estimated annual output of 5,000 tons of lead would not show a profit and thus the company should think of sending out 10,000 tons per year as well as 2,000 tons of iron.[107] This was a wildly overoptimistic estimation as in 1733 Place reckoned 1,500 tons per annum was a more realistic figure.[108] To add to the speculative fever, a series of reports appeared in the press, eulogising the prospects of the company both on Speyside and in Ardnamurchan, culminating in a report that six ships laden with ore were on the way from Scotland.[109] This had the desired effect of raising the price of York Buildings stock. The price of £100 of stock which had stood at £19 on 1 August had risen to £38 on 2 October.[110] However the myth created by the conspirators could not be sustained. Partly the rise was due to the optimistic climate they created, but it was also caused by their own excessive purchases. When one takes into account that Chandos was playing the market to a greater extent than he had done since 1720, it is obvious that another bubble had been created.

The company certainly proved incapable of turning optimism into profits. In August 1731, Francis Place was dismissed by the York Buildings Company and his place taken by Horsey's son Jerome. This would appear to have been a mistake as the works were building up to a production figure of 50 tons of lead per week.[111] During Francis Place's year at Strontian, 750 tons of lead were shipped. Between then and April 1733, only another 537 tons were shipped and recorded, a further 170 tons shipped and not recorded and 82 tons left at Strontian.[112] This was a far cry from the potential of around 1,500 tons a year and the amount of capital expended. In all the company' loss on the venture by Christmas 1732 was estimated at £25,856.[113]

The difficulties were exacerbated by the fact that the frauds of the directors of the Charitable Corporation were exposed when Robinson and Thompson fled in October 1731. Although the real commercial contacts between the two companies were slight, the City of London believed them to be greater than they were and the rumours that the Charitable corporation might have lost £400,000 affected the York Buildings Company.[114] The full extent of the scandal became apparent in 1732 when Parliament investigated the corporation and Grant was expelled from the House of Commons on 5 May 1732.[115] Thompson returned to Britain in February 1733 and later gave evidence to a further Commons investigation of the scandal.[116] Meanwhile the shareholders of the York Buildings Company, fearful of their own mounting losses had already voted to petition parliament for an investigation into the company's affairs.[117] All of this had a devastating effect on the price of York Buildings stock. On 1 October 1731, before Robinson and Thompson's disappearance, it had been quoted at £23. 10s. per cent. By the end of the year it had sunk to £14. However, by the end of 1732, damaging revelations of its own affairs and those of the

Charitable Corporation meant that at £2. 15s per cent, the stock was practically worthless.[118]

Despite the upheavals in London caused by the parliamentary investigations, work at Strontian continued. Francis Place was sent by the stockholders to examine the mines and found that their condition had declined. Sir Alexander Murray, fearful for his interest had ordered the company to rectify their neglect.[119] Place continued to oversee the mines on behalf of the company but as finance from London was not forthcoming, the managers had to pledge their own credit to get supplies. They had also made use of stores left by the company.[120] As the company's interest waned, Place came more to look after the interests of Sir Archibald Grant who held a one-third share in Sir Alexander Murray's interest in the mines.[121] Problems such as cash flow, a shortage of provisions and the poor state of repair continued to haunt the works. In 1734, Francis Place found difficulty in obtaining a cargo of coal, and his brother Abraham was claiming that timber was needed to make underground workings safer. Any attempt to re-equip and work the mines would be expensive. To get out of such difficulties, the company tried to return the mines to the original lessors, but this plan fell through. The company continued to neglect the works and Place was continually harassed by irate unpaid workmen.[122]

A last attempt to achieve something concrete with regard to the mines led Sir Archibald Grant to agree to his brother Francis taking a sub-lease of the mines in his own interest.[123] Francis Grant was no more successful than his predecessors. In just over two years he managed to produce around 1,000 tons of lead. He abandoned his lease on 25 March 1740, but operated the mines on behalf of the company until 29 September 1741.[124] Accusations of poor working were continually levelled at Grant, and John Richardson, judicially appointed factor on Murray's sequestrated estates, had forcibly entered the mines on 20 January 1741.[125] Despite the efforts of Richardson to seize lead and ore, Grant continued to sell some of the output of the works. After his departure at the end of 1741, Francis Grant tried to control the operation from a distance but failed.[126] On 18 August 1742, the mines were let to the then governor of the York Buildings Company, Thomas Pembroke, in a private capacity.[127] Thus, as with the Speyside operation, control passed from the company to Pembroke, but it is impossible to tell whether he profited from either deal.

The question that now arises is, was the huge investment in industry in the Scottish Highlands merely cover in a giant stock jobbing scam, or was it a genuine attempt to create assets which would produce longer term returns? Evidence certainly exists to sustain the former explanation. The parliamentary committee investigating the York Buildings Company discovered that Horsey was dealing quite extensively in stock. Chandos' share dealings were also enormous at this time. In both 1730/31 and 1731/2, R.S. Neale has estimated Chandos share dealings to have been over £1.3m, only fractionally below the peak year of 1720.[128] However Chandos role was kept away from public scrutiny so in that sense, the investigation never uncovered the complete truth.

Chandos's own correspondence gives us far more insight into both his and Horsey's activities. To both of them, speculation and technical development were inextricably interwoven. This was true of their activities in developing sources of potash and soap and glass manufacture in the earliest days of their association, hence their links with the Royal Africa Company. Chandos was also heavily committed to developments on his estates near the town of Bridgewater in Somerset, where again scientific and financial development went hand-in-hand. The nature of the correspondence between Chandos and Horsey, Grant and others show how absorbed he was in costs, potential profitability and other aspects of the plans which indicated he clearly saw them as long term commercial prospects, not just the hype that was appearing in the press. Likewise Horsey was far too involved to be merely a part of a scam. Like Chandos he had a track record of experimentation and an interest in matters scientific and even after the debacle of the York Buildings Company affair was actively pursuing his aim of being made Governor of South Carolina. To men such as Chandos, speculation was as much part of the new society as technical advances. They wished to use their ideas to make money and were only too eager to do so when the stock market seemed to give them the opportunity. Even Sir Archibald Grant, for all his involvement in the Charitable Corporation scandal, was not merely out to make a quick killing. His continued involvement with the Speyside and Strontian ventures after the frauds were uncovered showed he still believed in the possibility of their longer term profitability.

Unfortunately for all of those involved in the development of the Highlands in the 1720s and 1730s, their ideas and inventions had outrun the capacity of the local economy to absorb them. The infrastructure needed to sustain such ventures was simply not there, and everything, including skilled labour had to be imported, thus adding to costs. Nor were there any significant local markets, apart from the York Buildings Company itself. The way forward in industry in the ensuing years, in the main, was not going to be in large scale corporate enterprise such as the York Buildings Company, but in the smaller businesses conducted by sole traders and partnership with steady, soundly based, longer term growth rather than an overnight fortune created by a stock market 'bubble'.

As far as the development of the Highlands is concerned, on the surface at least, a golden opportunity was missed. Lt. Bruce of the Engineers drawing up his plan of the Strontian area for General Wade saw the development as part of the wider improvement and civilising influence that must come from the road and bridgebuilding programme in which his commander was engaged.[129] However he was over optimistic. The ventures were over-capitalised. This added significantly to their costs and meant that any serious competition would make them unviable. In each instance, a more modest operation would perhaps have stood more chance of success. The involvement of the York Buildings Company in the Charitable Corporation scandal did not help matters. Both organisations were serious losers in the affair but there is no concrete evidence of widespread collusion between the two concerns. The actions of both Horsey and Chandos can be explained in terms of a reaction to market opportunities rather than conspiracy. Horsey was guilty of malpractice and bad management, but no more so than many another manager of his day who had not been bred to business since his youth. Ironically in 1734, shortly after his dismissal from the York Buildings Company, Horsey wrote to Chandos trying to interest him in another venture, Chandos replied somewhat testily that he was having no more to do with such affairs.[130] Defoe's vision that exploitation of the mineral resources of the North would 'fill their harbours full of ships, their towns full of people'[131] was not to be realised. The York Buildings Company, and indeed the Rawlinsons and others had clearly tried to take advantage of the new, more commercial spirit prevailing among some Highland landowners, but their ideas had outstripped economic reality. Not for the last time Scotland was to see the construction of large-scale industry built on hope and false promise, but with little long-term hope for commercial success.

REFERENCES

1. R. H. Campbell, 'The Anglo-Scottish Union of 1707, II, The Economic Consequences', *Economic History Review*, Vol. XVI (1964), pp. 455–477; T. M. Devine, 'The Union of 1707 and Scottish Development', *Scottish Economic and Social History*, Vol. 5, (1985), pp. 23–40; C. A. Whatley, 'Economic Causes and Consequences of the Union of 1707: A Survey' *Scottish Historical Review*, Vol. 68, (1989), pp. 150–181.
2. Ibid., pp. 168–169.
3. Devine, 'The Union of 1707', p. 29.
4. Whatley, 'Economic Causes and Consequences', p. 174.
5. Aspects of this have been dealt with in A. J. G. Cummings, 'The York Buildings Company: A Case Study in Eighteenth Century Corporation Mismanagement', Ph.D. Thesis, University of Strathclyde, 1981, Ch. 4; J. M. Lindsay, 'Some aspects of Timber Supply in the Highlands, 1770–1850', *Scottish Studies*, Vol. 19, (1975) pp. 39–53; J. M. Lindsay, 'The Iron Industry in the Highlands: Charcoal Blast Furnaces', *Scottish Historical Review*, Vol. 56, (1977) pp. 49–63.
6. Daniel Defoe, *A Tour through the Whole Island of Great Britain*, (Penguin English Library ed., Harmondsworth, 1971), p. 633.
7. Aspects of Billingsley's career are dealt with in A. J. G. Cummings and Larry Stewart,

'The Case of the Eighteenth Century Projector: Entrepreneurs, Engineers, and Legitimacy at the Hanoverian Court in Britain', in Bruce Moran (ed.), *Patronage and Institutions: Science, Technology and Medicine at the European Court, 1500–1750*, (Woodbridge, 1991), pp. 235–261.

8. Cummings, 'York Buildings Company', p. 33.
9. *Reports of Committees of the House of Commons*, [Henceforth RHC], (1803), Vol. 1, p. 595, Report on York Buildings Company, 1733.
10. Cummings, 'York Buildings', Ch. 2.
11. Ibid., pp. 110–149.
12. See in particular, Larry Stewart, *The Rise of Public Science: Rhetoric, Technology, and Natural Philosophy in Newtonian Britain, 1660–1750*, (Cambridge, 1992); Christine Macleod, *Inventing the Industrial Revolution: The English Patent System 1660–1800*, (Cambridge, 1988).
13. Cummings, 'York Buildings Company', p. 310; H. W. Dickinson, *The Water Supply of Greater London*, (Leamington Spa, 1954), p. 59; Stewart, *Rise of Public Science*, pp. 340–354.
14. Huntington Library, San Marino, California, [Henceforth, Hunt. Lib.], Stowe MSS 57 Vol. XXV, f. 61, Letter Chandos to Mr. Zollicoffre, 19 December, 1724; K. G. Davies, *The Royal African Company*, (London, 1957), pp. 344–345.
15. Stewart, *Rise of Public Science*, p. 321.
16. Ibid., pp. 355.
17. Hunt. Lib., Stowe MSS, 57, XXIII, f. 33, Letter Chandos to Mr. Desaguliers, 24 October, 1723; *ibid.*, f. 36, Letter, Chandos to Horsey, 27 Oct., 1723.
18. Joan Johnson, *Princely Chandos: James Brydges 1674–1744*, (Gloucester, 1984), p. 71.
19. Bodleian Library, Oxford, Gough MSS, Somerset 7, ff. 335–339, Papers relating to the York Buildings Company; Hunt. Lib., Stowe MSS, 57, XXVI, f. 42, Letter Chandos to Mr. Arbuthnot, 17 May, 1724; *ibid.*, f. 86, Letter Chandos to Horsey, 8 June, 1725.
20. Cummings, 'York Buildings', pp. 516–518; Stewart, *Rise of Public Science*, p. 371.
21. Marye was dealing in York Buildings stock for Chandos from late 1724. Hunt. Lib., Stowe MSS, 57, Vol. XXV, f. 32, Letter Chandos to Marye, 22 November, 1724; *ibid.*, Vol. XXVI, ff. 159–160, Letter Chandos to Horsey, 7 July, 1725.
22. Stewart, *Rise of Public Science*, p. 216.
23. National Library of Scotland, Fletcher of Saltoun MSS, 16534, Letter S. Horsey to Lord Milton, 5 July 1726.
24. Signet Library, Edinburgh, Court of Session Papers, [Henceforth SL CSP] F29 24, Delavalle & ors. v. York Buildings Co. 1788, Case of the Appellants; Scottish Record Office, [Henceforth SRO], GD345/576/11, Grant of Monymusk MSS, Queries for Norfolk & ors.
25. British Library, [Henceforth BL] 8223. d. 44 (7), *A Letter from a Gentleman at Edinburgh to his Friend at London*, (1727).
26. PRO PC4/66/6, Sworn statement of John Ewer, 19 December, 1727.
27. *House of Commons Journal* [Henceforth HCJ], Vol. 22, p. 180.
28. W. R. Scott, *The Constitution and Finance of English Scottish and Irish Joint-Stock Companies to 1720*, (repr. New York 1968), Vol. 3, pp. 115–117, 458; David

Murray, *The York Buildings Company: A Chapter in Scotch History*, (repr. Edinburgh, 1973), pp. 55–57.

29. *HCJ*, Vol. 22, p. 181.
30. PRO PC1/4/66, Opinion of P. Yorke, 12 January, 1728.
31. PRO C11/1833/23, Grant & ors. v. York Buildings Co. 1736, Answer of Company.
32. PRO PC2/90/358, Minute of the Privy Council, 2 August 1728.
33. PRO T1/269/50, Memorandum of York Buildings Company to Treasury, 21 October, 1728; SRO CS232/Y13/3, York Buildings Company v. Grant, State of 28,000 Fir Trees.
34. *HCJ*, Vol. 22, p. 181.
35. *Daily Post*, 21 November, 1727; BL 8223. d. 44 (1), *Short Abstract of the Hon. Col. Samuel Horsey Governor of the York Buildings Company, His Speeches at their General Courts*.
36. BL ADD MSS, 36, 149, ff. 186v.–187, Part of a Plan of the River Spey 1726.
37. H. M. Steven, *The Native Pinewoods of Scotland*, (Edinburgh, 1959), p. 116.
38. Hunt. Lib., Stowe MSS 57 Vol. XXXIII, f. 198, Letter Chandos to Horsey, 10 July, 1729; *ibid.*, 268, Letter Chandos to Horsey, 28 July, 1729.
39. Ibid., Vol. XXXIV, f. 4, Letter Chandos to Thomas Watts, 26 November 1729; *ibid.*, 4–5, Letter Chandos to Horsey, 26 Nov., 1729.
40. Ibid., Vol. XXXIV, f. 94, Letter Chandos to Mr Corbett, 27 December, 1729.
41. A. Forsyth, 'Notes on the York Buildings Company in Abernethy, 1728', *Transactions of the Inverness Scientific Society and Field Club*, p. 192; Stevens and Carlisle, *Native Pinewoods of Scotland*, p. 116.
42. Neil Munro, *The History of the Bank of Scotland 1727–1927*, (1928), p. 106.
43. *HCJ*, Vol. 22, pp. 180, 189–190.
44. Romney Sedgewick, (ed.), *The History of Parliament: The House of Commons 1715–1754*, (London, 1970), Vol. 2. p. 445; Phinizy Spalding, *Oglethorpe in America*, (Chicago, 1977), pp. 37–38.
45. M. L. Anderson, *A History of Scottish Forestry*, (London, 1967), Vol. 1, p. 443.
46. SRO GD345/854/17, Grant of Monymusk MSS, Proposal to York Buildings Company for managing their fir wood in Strathglass.
47. Anderson, *History of Scottish Forestry*, Vol. 1, p. 443.
48. J. R. Harris, *The British Iron Industry 1700–1850*, (London, 1988), p. 13.
49. Lindsay, 'Iron Industry in the Highlands', p. 54.
50. Sven-Erik Astrom, 'Swedish Iron and the English Iron Industry about 1700', *Scandinavian Economic History Review*, Vol. XXX, 1982, p. 140.
51. C. K. Hyde, *Technological Change and the British Iron Industry 1700–1870*, (Princeton, 1977), pp. 45, 218.
52. Harris, *British Iron Industry*, p. 24.
53. Ibid., pp. 56–59.
54. Alfred Fell, *The Early Iron Industry of Furness and District*, (repr. London 1968), pp. 343–389; A. Raistrick, *Quakers in Science and Industry*, (Newton Abbott, 1968), p. 102.
55. Forsyth, 'Notes on York Building Company', p. 189.
56. Hunt. Lib., Stowe MSS 57, Vol. XXXII, f. 224, Letter Chandos to Horsey, 10 August, 1729; Henry Hamilton, *An Economic History of Scotland in the Eighteenth Century*, (1963), p. 190; Lindsay, 'Iron Industry in the Highlands', 58.

57. Ibid., Vol. XXXIII, f. 277, Letter Chandos to Horsey, 10 October, 1729; Forsyth, 'Notes on the York Buildings Company', p. 193.

58. W. Forsyth, *In the Shadow of Cairngorm*, (1900), p. 199.

59. Hunt. Lib., Stowe MSS 57, Vol. XXXIV, f. 303–304, Letter Chandos to Thomas Watts, 27 April, 1730.

60. Eric Pawson, *The Early Industrial Revolution: Britain in the Eighteenth Century*, (London, 1979), p. 113.

61. Hunt. Lib., Stowe MSS 57, Vol. XXXV, f. 133, Letter Chandos to Horsey, 5 July, 1730.

62. Ibid., Vol. XXXV, f. 161, Letter Chandos to Horsey, 16 July, 1730; *ibid.*, f. 183, Letter Chandos to Horsey, 25 July, 1730.

63. Ibid., ff. 345–346, Letter Chandos to Mr. Brodie, 9 January, 1731.

64. Fell, *Early Iron Industry*, pp. 380–381; Lindsay, 'Early Iron Industry in the Highlands', p. 59.

65. SRO GD248/135/1, Seafield MSS, York Buildings Company Bundle, Inventory taken on 28 August 1734.

66. Forsyth, 'Notes on York Buildings Company', p. 190.

67. SRO CS232/Y/13/3, York Buildings Co. v. Grant, Letter William Stephens to York Buildings Company, 2 March 1734.

68. *HCJ*, Vol. 22, pp. 189–190.

69. Cummings, 'York Buildings Company', p. 221.

70. Murray, *York Buildings Company*, pp. 61–62.

71. SRO CS232/Y13/3, Account between the York Buildings Company and Thomas Pembroke, 1742.

72. Murray, *York Buildings Company*, pp. 64–65.

73. SL CSP F34;13 Grove and ors. v. Grant. This shows the matter was still being pursued in 1785.

74. Lindsay, 'The Iron Industry in the Highlands', pp. 57–58.

75. J. C. T. Rogers, *A History of Agricultural Prices in England*, (1902), Vol. VII, pt. i, p. 387.

76. Hyde, *Technological Change*, pp. 45–46.

77. Lindsay, 'Iron Industry in the Highlands', p. 58–59.

78. Hamilton, *Economic History of Scotland*, p. 191.

79. *HCJ*, Vol. 22, p. 196.

80. Fell, *Early Iron Industry*, pp. 379–380.

81. Lindsay, 'Iron Industry in the Highlands', p. 56–57.

82. Cummings, 'York Buildings Company', pp. 378–380.

83. Guildhall Library, London, Folio Pamphlet 631, Information for Daniel Campbell, 1765.

84. Murray, *York Buildings Company*, p. 67.

85. SL CSP, F34;7, Grove & ors. v. Hopetoun 1785, Hopetoun's Case.

86. P. G. M. Dickson, *The Sun Insurance Office 1710–1960*, (London, 1960), p. 272.

87. Hunt. Lib. Stowe MSS 57, Vol. XXXIII, f. 334, Letter, Chandos to Mr. Drummond, 18 November, 1729.

88. *Estates of the Directors of the Charitable Corporation: Inventory of Sir Archibald Grant*, [Henceforth *Grant's Estate*] (1733), p. 8; T. C. Smout, 'Lead mining in

Scotland, 1650–1850' in P. L. Payne, (ed.), *Studies in Scottish Business History*, (London, 1967), p. 108.

89. Edinburgh University, Laing MSS II 693, Defences for Norfolk etc. against John Pringle, 1739; *Grant's Estate*, p. 8.

90. BL. 522 m. 4, Sir Alexander Murray, *The True Interest of Great Britain*, (1740), p. 7.

91. T. M. Devine, *From Clanship to Crofters War*, (forthcoming 1994), ch. 2.

92. *HCJ*, Vol. 22, pp. 190–192.

93. Stowe MSS 57, Vol. XXXIV, f. 343, Letter Chandos to Sir A. Grant, 11 May, 1730.

94. *HCJ*, Vol. 22, pp. 186, 193–194.

95. Hunt. Lib., Stowe MSS 57, Vol. XXXVI, ff. 76–78, Letter Chandos to Capt. Robinson, 15 October, 1730; Smout, 'Lead Mining in Scotland', p. 108.

96. *HCJ*, Vol. 22, p. 195.

97. SRO GD 345/576/13, Grant of Monymusk MSS, Queries and Answers anent the present state of the mines.

98. BL 522. m. 4, Murray, *True Interest of Great Britain*, Map VII, A Plan of Loch Sunart, (1733).

99. *HCJ*, Vol. 22, pp. 186–187.

100. Edinburgh University, Laing MSS, Add. 11, Petition of York Buildings Company, 24 February 1743, p. 9.

101. SRO GD 345/895, Grant of Monymusk MSS, Account of York Buildings Company with the Morvern Company; *RHC*, Vol. 1, p. 592; *HCJ*, Vol. 22, p. 196.

102. Ibid., pp. 196–197.

103. SRO GD 345/830, Grant of Monymusk MSS, Letter T. Blackball to Sir A. Grant, 27 February 1731.

104. SRO GD 345/576/13, Grant of Monymusk MSS, Queries and answers; Smout, 'Lead Mining in Scotland', pp. 120–121.

105. *HCJ*, Vol. 22, p. 189.

106. A. J. G. Cummings, 'The Business Affairs of an Eighteenth Century Lowland Laird: Sir Archibald Grant of Monymusk, 1696–1778' in T. M. Devine, (ed.), *Scottish Elites*, (Edinburgh, forthcoming 1994).

107. Hunt. Lib., Stowe MSS 57, Vol. XXXIV, f. 343, Letter Chandos to Sir A. Grant, 11 May 1730; *ibid.*, Vol. 35, f. 214, Letter Chandos to George Robinson, 20 August 1730; *ibid.*, f. 224, Letter Chandos to William Burroughs, 27 August 1730; *ibid.*, ff. 247–248, Letter Chandos to Sir A. Grant, 8 September 1730.

108. *HCJ*, Vol. 22, p. 186.

109. *Daily Courant*, 2 October 1730.

110. *Daily Journal*, 1 August 1730; *Daily Courant*, 2 October, 1730.

111. Hunt. Lib., Stowe MSS 57, Vol. XXXVIII, ff. 10–11, Letter Chandos to Watts, 15 July 1731.

112. *HCJ*, Vol. 22, p. 186.

113. Ibid., p. 189.

114. Hunt. Lib., Stowe MSS 57, Vol. XXXVIII, f. 241, Letter Chandos to Mr. Arnold, 24 October, 1731; *ibid.*, f. 301, Letter Chandos to Dr. Stuart, 13 November 1731.

115. Sedgewick, *History of Parliament*, Vol. 2, pp. 77–78.
116. *Daily Journal*, 26 February 1733.
117. Ibid., 13 January 1733.
118. *Daily Courant*, 1 October 1731; *ibid.*, 31 December 1731; *ibid.*, 30 December 1732.
119. SRO GD345/830 Grant of Monymusk MSS, Notice given by Sir A. Murray to York Buildings Co., 5 January 1733; *HCJ*, Vol. 22, p. 186.
120. SRO GD345/830, Grant of Monymusk MSS, Proposal to York Buildings Company by Mr. Halley, 20 July, 1742; SRO CS271/19878, York Buildings Co. v. Richard Graham 1739; SRO CS271/52438, York Buildings Co. v. Telphord, 1734.
121. *Grant's Estate*, p. 5.
122. SRO GD345/576/13 Grant of Monymusk MSS, Queries and Answers; *ibid.* GD345/725, Timberman's declaration, 28 September 1734; SRO GD345/830, Letter Abraham Place Sir A. Grant 4 January, 1735; *ibid.*, Letter A. Ouchterlony to Sir A. Grant, 28 January, 1735; *ibid.*, Letter F. Place to Sir A. Grant, 17 February 1735.
123. SL CSP F32;12, Norfolk v. York Buildings Company., 1742, Case of Sir A. Murray.
124. SRO CS228/G2/27, F. Grant v. York Buildings Co. 1744.
125. EU Laing MSS Add. 11, Petition of York Buildings Company, 24 February 1743.
126. SL CSP 14;1, Crawfurd v. Campbell 1753, Petn. Of Crawfurd 12 November 1753.
127. SRO CS232/Y13/3, York Buildings Co. v. Grant, Account between Co. & T. Pembroke 1742.
128. *HCJ*, Vol. 22, p. 181; R. S. Neale, *Bath 1680–1850: A Social History* (1981), p. 122.
129. Murray, *True Interest of Great Britain*, Map VII, Plan of Loch Sunart (1733).
130. Hunt. Lib., Stowe MSS 57 Vol. XLII, f. 39, Letter Chandos to Grant, 18 June, 1733.
131. Defoe, *A Tour through the Whole Island*, p. 633.

3

A Tour of the Works: Early Scottish Industry Observed 1790–1825

IAN DONNACHIE

> We cam na here to view your works
> In hopes to be mair wise
> But only, lest we gang to hell,
> It mae be nae surprise.
>
> But when we tirled at your door,
> Your porter dought na bear us,
> So may (should we to hell-yetts come)
> Your billy Satan sair us.

John Butt has always displayed an enormous enthusiasm for contemporary descriptions, illustrations and surviving artifacts of the process that has long fascinated him and been a major subject of his research, the era and main components of early industrialization in Scotland. He was among the first to marry documentary research with physical evidence on the ground, what is now called industrial archaeology, retracing the steps of those who, two hundred years before, had visited the mines, mills and factories which had so captured his own imagination. So the economic historian turned industrial archaeologist was able to deploy a whole new tool kit of and approaches and techniques to help him see his way into the minds of those who created or witnessed the burgeoning of industry. In the years of research that followed Butt and his acolytes not only pioneered industrial archaeology in Scotland but also carried investigations into previously unexplored archives, such as legal records, which helped to through fresh light on industrial and business history. This chapter provides a modest celebration of these enthusiasms, by looking through contemporary eyes at the impact of industry on the Scottish scene. Of course, industry was an established if unobtrusive part of the Scottish landscape long before its rapid advance during the closing decades of the eighteenth century, but it was not much remarked upon by contemporaries. Once under way, however, industrialization proceeded rapidly and had a dramatic and immediate impact on the Scottish environment, particularly in some parts of the Lowlands. There both residents and foreign visitors alike were impressed by the speed with which huge textile mills, iron works, and chemical plant were established, collieries sunk to ever greater depths, with road, bridge, harbour and canal building also proceeding at rapid pace to provide the necessary infrastructure for commerce. Moreover there were the new communities which grew up to house the emerging industrial workforce – modelled to some extent on the planned villages which by that time peppered the landscape of agricultural improvement almost everywhere south and east of the Highland Line. Appropriately on our own tour we will visit many of the places which have figured in John Butt's own researches into Scottish economic and industrial history over the past thirty years.

For its period the first Statistical Account is clearly the major and most comprehensive source of what contemporaries of the 1790s saw of Scottish industrialization on the ground and impressions about its impact on their communities. The local accounts, as others have observed, varied greatly in quality and usefulness with regard to industrial matters and related economic and social concerns. While the great bulk of the entries were written by the clergy, who might not have been expected to be au fait with industrial matters, almost everywhere that the march of industry had occurred, it was sketched in varying degrees of detail by the contributors. Some parish ministers in compiling their accounts, sought out the advice of local industrialists and landowners, and occasionally their managers or foremen, so their accounts are generally better informed and invariably more detailed than those who relied on their own observations. It's worth noting, however, that since patronage was still very much a live issue and that in many localities major industrial developments were inspired by landowners, as for example, at the planned village of Gatehouse-of-Fleet in Galloway or in the parish of Muirkirk in Ayrshire, whose histories Butt was to research nearly two centuries later, the ministers had to be circumspect in their views, since unfavourable comment might upset their patron and prejudice their living.

What did such observers make of the changes taking place in their localities? The majority were amazed at how rapidly industrialization had impacted, a phenomenon now recognised by historians (and thanks partly to Butt's work) as a significant feature of the process in Scotland. In many contexts, particularly those affected by the technological revolution in textiles, writers could trace the changes back to the previous decade, while in other places, where mining or salt manufacture had been the prime economic activities, the lead-in time was longer. Most commented favourably on the benefits industry brought in its wake particularly cheaper fuel and better transport.

However, many were suspicious of the social changes, notably the rapid increase in population and its concentration in villages and towns and the adverse consequences on living conditions, the potentially increased burden on poor relief, and above all the danger of adverse social behaviour. If the bulk of accounts are taken at face value Scottish workers were a quiescent lot, yet there are numerous comments on crime, immorality and drunkenness – allegedly brought about by the new mills, bleach works, mines and other industrial enterprises. Such social concerns Butt was to address in his studies of communities built to house textile and iron workers.

A few observations from selected parishes are sufficient to indicate that the dynamism of the industrialization process, the rapidity of its impact on localities, the value of land, prices, wages, and food supplies was both readily appreciated and well enough understood by contributors to the Statistical Account. For example, in the north Lanarkshire parish of Old or West Monkland, with its rapidly expanding coal pits, ironworks, pottery and bleach fields, the economic benefits of industry were there for all to see, as the Rev. John Bower observed, 'wherever manufactures and commerce seat themselves, their influence on landed property is felt in an inconceivable degree; and how much is it the interest of landholders to cherish and protect them! Consequently the rise of the value of the land in this parish is astonishing'. The impact of improvement on the landscape bounding the still rural eastern environs of Glasgow was spectacular. The district still had 'the appearance of an immense garden' for agriculture was an enormously important activity thanks to enterprising farmers and successful merchants who had bought into the area and adorned it with elegant gentlemen's seats. Monkland already had a well-developed transport infrastructure, with the Glasgow to Edinburgh turnpike running through the parish and toll revenue worth a vast sum annually. The Monkland Canal connecting the pits to Glasgow was virtually complete and the coal carried was able to undercut that from other collieries in the environs of the city by a substantial margin.[1]

Likewise at Inverkeithing, formerly a moribund Forth port, the level of economic activity had been much enhanced and the population greatly increased 'owing to the flourishing state of the coal trade brought from Halbeath and shipped here; to a considerable distillery and brewery in the neighbourhood of the town, and a branch of the iron foundery [sic] business lately introduced'. The minister there, the Rev. Andrew Robertson, not only noted a few of the traditional saltpans but also a significant new feature on the landscape, now also of considerable interest to the industrial archaeologist, 'a proper waggon road laid with timber for the distance of five miles, and kept in good repair at great expense'.[2]

To the south west, at Muirkirk, an apparently 'desert place', where agricultural modernization had made little progress on poor, marginal land, industrial development had an immediate and dramatic impact. There, as in other superficially unpromising and relatively remote situations, the wealth lay underground awaiting exploitation by entrepreneurial incomers willing to risk capital and harness up even very basic technology in new contexts. Despite the obvious drawbacks, Muirkirk, according to the minister:

> . . . . boasts, of late, *other* advantages, still greater in one respect, because they enhance its natural ones, give them value, and call them forth into effect, I mean the manufactures lately established. The success of these is an object truly desirable. Every friend of his country and of the public must, upon all occasions, wish well to laudable and useful enterprise. We respect, nay we *praise*, that man who can improve or enrich the surface of the earth, can mow down rich crops from fields formerly barren, or even double the grains of corn, upon those that bore before. But surely an equal share of praise is justly due to that man, who in countries that are ungrateful to the labours of cultivation, and either discourage or forbid its ungainful toil, can drag from the sluggish bosom of the earth, in which they lie concealed, inactive and useless, those minerals, which under the forming hand of art gradually assume every figure and every shape, and serve to accommodate, or adorn life.[3]

Hence the development locally of two 'very considerable manufactures', coal-tar and iron. The latter has been explored in considerable detail by Butt (and his erstwhile colleague, John Hume) as part of a wide ranging investigation into the history and archaeology of the nascent Scottish iron industry, which we will see again at first hand later in our tour.[4]

Finally, in the remote fastness of the western Highlands, lacking the critical resources, few Lowland style industries flourished but one which established a fitful existence there was a direct predecessor of developments at Monklands and Muirkirk, the charcoal iron industry. It was more than the ancient woodlands that attracted the English iron masters, because, as Butt has shown, labour costs were lower, water power was readily available and high grade bog ore was found where bloomeries had earlier been established. Moreover demand for iron in the Highlands for peaceful uses was greater than we might imagine and additional inducement was the favourable terms offered by landlords. The Craleckan furnace (*c.*1775), south of Inveraray was typical, in that its owners Jonathon Kendall & Company, were able to secure from Archibald, Duke of Argyll, 'a tack of cuttings of his woods in this and some other parishes, upon very reasonable terms'. 'The Company', continued the statisist, 'import ore and ironstone in vessels of their own, from the west of England, which they return loaded with pig iron of very superior quality, timber, oak-bark, etc. The establishment of this Company was particularly advantageous to this country, in raising the price of woods, and serviceable, in giving employment and bread, to a considerable number of hands, both male and female, in cutting and peeling the woods and making charcoal'.[5] The environmental damage over much of this part of Argyll was considerable, but the furnace and its more dramatic counterpart further north at Bonawe now stand as silent monuments to this incursion of early industry into the Highlands. It was partly due to the enthusiasm of Butt and Hume that Craleckan survives and Bonawe came into the care of the then Ministry of Public Buildings and Works, now Historic Scotland, as a prelude to becoming an outstanding relic of the era of charcoal iron smelting.[6]

The highly informative General Views of Agriculture in counties or wider localities where less detailed coverage was deemed appropriate were also largely inspired by the ubiquitous and energetic Sinclair. While at first glance these volumes seem an unlikely source for contemporary comment on the march of manufactures they dealt not only with the progress of agricultural modernization but also the major industrial developments occurring in their respective areas.[7] This was highly appropriate (as Butt himself was one of the first modern scholars to observe) given the abiding and close relationship between Scottish proto-industrialization and agriculture during the eighteenth century, particularly the vitally important primary processing industries like textiles, tanning, milling, brewing and distilling, on which the earliest stage of the Scottish Industrial Revolution was built.[8] Some writers for the series were also aware of this relationship and commented at length on the part agricultural improvement had played in diversifying the local economy.

Industry for its part reciprocated by generating demand for primary products including manufacturing raw materials like wool and flax as well as the grain, meat and dairy products needed to feed a growing and increasingly urbanised population. This important two-way relationship was summed up neatly by Sinclair himself, writing in his own contribution to the series, *A General View of the Agriculture of the Northern Counties*, that:

> There cannot be a doubt that the kindly influences of trade and manufactures direct their effects as immediately to agriculture as to any other object or art capable of improvement, for they must of course go to quicken and increase the demand for the husbandman's produce and stock. This is a self-evident truth, wherever commerce and manufactures have found footing.[9]

From direct observation he was able to cite the case of Cromarty which:

> on account of its safe anchorage, and also its very convenient pier, the extensive hempen manufacture of sacking and biscuit bagging, established about twenty years ago, its capital well constructed brewery, erected at the same period, and a manufacture of nails; these together with some dealers in provisions and victualling stores, and the retail trade carried on by the different shopkeepers, are the branches which as yet distinguish this commodious, well adapted, and finely situated town, and occasion a circulation of money, that has certainly been so far serviceable to agriculture in its neighbourhood.[10]

Time has treated most of what Sinclair observed kindly for in this architectural gem of a community the industrial heritage still embraces the former hemp and rope works, the old brewery (originally built to discourage spirit drinking) – both restored and put to other uses – and the fine harbour which were all later to be described in the pages of Butt's pioneering volume on the *Industrial Archaeology of Scotland*.[11]

The juxtaposition of agriculture and industry and of old and new was nowhere better illustrated than in the Rev. David Ure's description of Dumbarton, a diverse and scattered agricultural county much affected in parts by the early impact of industry, for in his words 'the manufactures at present carried on in this district are very far from being inconsiderable; and their influence on agriculture is very discernable'. The most significant activity there was cloth bleaching and printing, initially an adjunct to the linen industry but by Ure's time also embracing the new cotton industry. It dated back to 1768 when John Todd, a Glasgow merchant, had established the first plant in the Vale of Leven, the Levenside works. The industry grew to such an extent that by the early 1790s it accounted for more than two-thirds of the total cloth printing business in Scotland, paid £44,000 duty on printed linens and muslins, and was estimated to be worth £400,000 per annum besides capital of £70,000 sunk in buildings and machinery. It employed nearly 4,000 and the print fields at Leven, Milton and Dalmuir alone occupied 364 acres. The textile industry had itself become quite significant locally with a woollen mill, three cotton mills and a paper mill. Other industries in and around Dumbarton included several distilleries and breweries which had – as at Alloa – generated enhanced demand for local barley and spawned the construction of the glass and bottle works. The by-product of the drink trades was returned to agriculture in the form of draff which went to feed 60 cattle owned by the inhabitants of Dumbarton which even then still grazed the town common. Moreover a tanworks had greatly expanded production to meet the demand for leather products both from industry and the population at large. All of this, as Ure observed, had a big impact on agriculture and other older established proto-industries. The old Dalnotter forge and smithy, which had lost some of its export market to the North American colonies found that business had rallied with a keen demand for edge tools, nails, and other iron goods; while local slate and stone quarries were greatly enlarged to meet the demand for building materials in town and countryside alike.[12]

One of the most perceptive and best-informed observers of his generation was undoubtedly Robert Heron, who worked for Sinclair as a leading member of the team that assembled and edited the entries for the Statistical Account project and consequently was very familiar with much of the country and the changes occurring in different places. One area he certainly knew like the back of his hand was his native south-west and the account of his travels through the western counties provide considerable insight into the impact of industry in the area, particularly at Gatehouse-of-Fleet, a place that subsequently held a particular fascination for John Butt and was his first major exercise in the then new field of industrial archaeology. There, on the margins of early Scottish industrialization, the local landowner, James Murray of Broughton and Cally, joined forces with Yorkshire and Ulster merchants to establish cotton spinning mills and a range of related enterprises.

When Heron visited Gatehouse-of-Fleet in 1792 he was greatly impressed both by Murray's Palladian mansion in its parkland setting and the neat new village nearby. It soon attracted craftsmen, traders and industries, the most significant being cotton spinning for which:

> ... the Messrs Birtwhistle built a large fabric, at a great expense, at the western end of the village. Water to drive the machinery, by the apparatus of wheels and cranks, was to be brought from a lake, several miles distant, among the hills to the north-east, by an aqueduct ... the Fleet lying too low to leave it possible to obtain water from it which might be conveniently raised to such a height as to command the wheels. Every difficulty was overcome. The works were prepared; and the manufacture begun.

This was just the beginning because the Fleet was deepened and widened to take small ships, two additional cotton mills were built, and a machine building shop and a brass foundry opened to supply and service the new plant. Two breweries were soon doing good business to drown the thirsts of the drouthy cotton spinners. Local agriculture was booming, as was the sale of imported food commodities and fuel. Two tanneries and a soap works prospered. 'The village of Gatehouse', wrote Heron, 'has thus been greatly enlarged within this short time by the addition of new streets and the extension of those which had been before begun. Its inhabitants are multiplied to the number of 1,500'. Heron was perhaps less enthusiastic about the social impact of this rapid expansion for he did not think 'the morals of these good people have been improved with their circumstances'. He was certainly not to know that Gatehouse's flirtation with industry would be short-lived and that like many other Scottish mills of the water-power phase of cotton spinning would eventually fall victim to technological changes and competition from larger-scale producers.[13]

What struck Butt when he first visited it in the early 1960s was the fact that practically everything survived as Heron had described it, 'a rare and beautiful example of an arrested industrial village'. Butt was able to show through his study of Gatehouse's surviving buildings and other relics the value of industrial archaeology as a historical tool. The estate and community, which, thanks to the enterprise of the Murrays and their associates, had grown up around it, were certainly very well-documented, but in trying to put together a picture of change through time a lot of pieces were missing from the jig-saw. Only by abandoning books for boots was it possible to understand what actually happened on the ground and gain some appreciation of the enormous technical problems which had to be overcome in building the cotton mills and supplying them with adequate water power. In the longer-term, as at Bonawe, his enthusiasm and pioneering research brought Gatehouse's industrial relics to the attention of a wider audience and the reconstructed cotton mill buildings now form the focus of a fascinating museum to Gatehouse's industrial history.[14]

The travel diaries of men of science have a special value and significance because such savants could comment with understanding on what they saw during their factory visits. The individuals themselves are of considerable interest, invariably products of the Enlightenment, knowing each other and moving in the same scientific or philosophical circles. The earliest cited here, Charles Hatchett, was a distinguished geologist, who later became a Fellow of the Royal Society. His diary of a tour in 1796 'visiting mines and manufactories' is an invaluable commentary on Scottish industry at a critical stage in its development. Hatchett was specially interested in the progress of the mining and the chemical industries, devoting particular attention to everything he saw as he went about. Hatchett certainly knew Eric Svedenstierna, a Swedish metallurgist, who visited Britain in 1802–3 in search of scientific knowledge, mainly chemistry, which might assist the re-orientation of the troubled Swedish iron industry. Svedenstierna, by his own admission an industrial spy, left a fascinating diary of his tour in Scotland which took in Edinburgh, Glasgow and neighbouring industrial districts.

Continental visitors like Svedenstierna were rare but given John Butt's other great enthusiasm, American history, it is appropriate to review what travellers from the United States thought about Scottish industry. And, if the declarations of aliens registered in Edinburgh and signatories in the visitor's book at New Lanark for this period are anything to go by, there were plenty of them. Louis Simond, a merchant, was unusual, being French and a naturalised United States citizen. Another American, the Quaker, John Griscom, a chemist and ultimately a professor of chemistry at Columbia University in New York, was sufficiently knowledgable about technical and business matters to provide highly informed comment on what he saw of industrial premises during his tour of Scotland in 1819. Like many others with an interest in educational and social reform a visit to New Lanark was high on Griscom's agenda. But the most distinguished American by far was William Maclure, a successful merchant and scientist, a founder of the Academy of Natural Sciences in Philadelphia, a friend of Svedenstierna and later one of Robert Owen's associates at New Harmony, returned to his native country in 1824 and visited Glasgow, Edinburgh and New Lanark.

Given the danger of espionage and the threat of patent-busting some visitors to industrial premises, especially iron works, were not guaranteed a warm reception. As Burns found, and immortalised in the lines above, sightseers were regularly turned away from Carron for fear they might discover the deep secrets of cannon casting, boring and milling. Hatchett was luckier than Burns in gaining access to Carron and recording in his diary:

> . . . went to Carron to see Iron Works. They say they employ 1000 Men but I do not believe it. They have five blast furnaces 36 feet by 18 each make from $2\frac{1}{2}$ Tons to 3 Tons. Here they cast Cannon, Shells, Shot and all sorts of Iron Kettles etc. The Ore is Argillaceous (not rich) found in the neighbourhood. The coal also – the Limestone is brought from Fyfe. To each Blast Furnace they have 4 cylinders. They cast twice in 24 hours. **Not** equal to Mr Walkers Works [near Rotherham]. They do not allow the boring of the cannon to be seen. Make coke on the spot – only use the Ore of the country.[15]

Hatchett also visited the Clyde ironworks, which were later to be closely inspected by Svedenstierna.

Hatchett observed, evidently at first hand in the Monklands parishes, that 'very good pit coal is raised in many places about Glasgow, the strata of which all dip towards the Bed of the Clyde on each side and often appear at the Day in the neighbouring mountains'. Transporting the coal to Glasgow was made possible by the Monkland and Forth and Clyde Canals, on the latter as Hatchett noted being 'a celebrated Aqueduct [Maryhill] on which Vessels are seen sailing above whilst carriages are passing underneath', just the sort of novelty that often caught people's imagination.[16]

Iron was not the only strategically valuable mineral worked by Scottish industry, for the wars brought about a resurgence of lead mining, notably in the Lowther Hills around Leadhills and Wanlockhead, where the mineral had been worked for many centuries. 'The appearance of the place', Hatchett recorded of Leadhills, 'is dreary beyond description [and] uncommonly subject to Stormy Weather in all Seasons for Wind and Snow prevail in Winter and Wind and Rain in summer'. In this apparently hostile environment the mining company, whose principal partner was the landowner, the Earl of Hopetoun, had created a modest but successful enterprise. According to Hatchett 'the Vein (which consists of Galena principally) runs from North to South and dips to East at the rate of about $2\frac{1}{2}$ or 3 feet in a Fathom. The total depth of the mine is 167 fathoms each shaft is about 13 fathoms – there are not any footways and the miners descend and the ore is raised by Ropes and Wheels'. The ore was 80 per cent pure and smelted on the spot 'and as they have the advantage of much Peat they permit the fuel to be in contact with the ore without prejudice to the produce'. Output was said to be worth £36,000.[17] The relics that survive there were documented by Butt in the 1960s and together with those at neighbouring Wanlockhead now provide the focus for another innovative industrial heritage centre, the Scottish Lead Mining Museum.[18]

Foreigners were treated with even more suspicion than natives and Svedenstierna was remarkably lucky to see what he did on his tour of industrial and mining enterprises, particularly during his visit to several ironworks and chemical plant which both had considerable strategic significance in a time of war. Svedenstierna, being primarily interested in the progress of the iron industry and any lessons this might hold for Sweden, managed to look at no fewer than five ironworks at Cramond near Edinburgh, Leven in Fife, Wilsontown near Lanark, Clyde near Glasgow, and Muirkirk in Ayrshire. Next to Carron, which Hatchett managed to penetrate but Svedenstierna probably had no expectation of seeing, the Clyde plant then had the largest foundry in Scotland also specializing in cannon production. The Swede was undoubtedly most impressed by Wilsontown, where he could see 'the struggle between wild Nature and creative Scottish industry' in the large works established there by the Wilson brothers around 1780. In a remote inland location, not dissimilar to that of Muirkirk, two blast furnaces and associated buildings had been erected all connected to ironstone mines, coal and limestone pits by waggonways at a cost of £100,000 and at the time of Svedenstierna's visit further costly improvements were under way:

> A part of the old works was pulled down already and in its place the installation of puddling furnaces and rolling mills for an annual production of 1,500 tons of bar iron was begun.

> During this not yet completed building work, they had collected a supply of 1,400 tons of pig iron besides a quantity of castings, among which were flywheels and other pieces of 7 to 8 tons weight, for the requirements of this works. A tourist cannot expect straight answers to improper questions, so I could not ask to be told the cost of this alteration, but from the knowledge which I believe I have of the expenses of this kind of work, I would hazard the guess that before it is all in working order, the costs may run to £30,000 or more.[19]

Svedenstierna then sounded a note of caution saying that 'although there are plentiful supplies of coal and ore here, and the transport of these materials can be arranged more easily in time, it yet seems inconceivable how this works, which must take its iron more than two (Swedish) miles overland to the nearest port, can yield a return on the capital invested'.[20]

With its Boulton & Watt engines harnessed up to provide the blast Wilsontown was the most modern ironworks in Scotland and for a short while, despite Svedenstierna's pessimism, was also one of the most profitable. But Wilsontown and its patriotic owners were geared up to war-time demand and the works faced financial problems when conditions changed. It paid the price of overcapitalization when the bottom fell out of the iron market at the close of the Napoleonic War. So the Swede was proved right in the end – and the business books that survive in the Scottish Record Office, as Butt (and the present writer) discovered, tell a tale of family jealousy and intrigue that would have provided a ready made plot for an early nineteenth century novel.[21]

Understandably very few French visitors – apart from prisoners of war – saw much of Scotland during the period of the Revolutionary and Napoleonic Wars. One who did, was Louis Simond, who had emigrated to America and become a citizen of the United States, where he subsequently prospered as a ship owner. His visit to Glasgow in the summer of 1810 caused him to observe that 'we have seen carding and spinning mills, weaving mills, mills for everything', some being steam-powered. Mechanisation was everywhere, but 'the human hand and human intelligence are not separated, and mere physical force is drawn from air and water alone, by means of the steam-engine'. 'Manufactories, thus associated with science', wrote Simond, 'seem to produce with the facility and fecundity of nature'. He was greatly enthraled by the process of cotton manufacture, for:

It is impossible to see without astonishment these endless flakes of cotton, as light as snow, and as white, ever pouring from the carding-machine, then seized by the teeth of innumerable wheels and cylinders, and stretched into threads, flowing like a rapid stream, and lost in the *tourbillion* of spindles. The eye of a child or of a woman watches over the blind mechanism directing the motions of her whirling battalion, rallying disorder and broken threads, and repairing unforeseen accidents. The shuttle likewise, untouched, shoots to and fro by an invisible force; and the weaver, no longer cramped upon his uneasy seat, but merely overlooking his self moving looms, produces forty-eight yards of cloth in a day, instead of four or five yards.[22]

Large factories – mainly associated with the textile industry – were still unusual and hence attracted the attention of visitors and tourists. New Lanark, though located near the scenic and romantic Falls of Clyde, already high on the agenda of tourists, artists and poets, was by no means unique. But it did have an enormous number of visitors, during both the Dale and Owen eras and quickly became a tourist attraction in its own right. Griscom, the American Quaker, who visited New Lanark in 1819, left a perceptive description of the place which presented 'a very neat and interesting appearance, affording, in this respect, a remarkable contrast with old Lanark, about two miles distant'. 'It is beautifully situated', he continued, 'and has grown entirely out of the manufactory, which is exclusively that of spinning cotton. The houses are mostly uniform in their structure, built of stone, with a roof of slate, and kept to all appearance, in great decency, attention evidently being paid to cleanliness throughout the whole establishment'. 'The buildings of the factory', he observed, 'are very large, and the machinery is in excellent style. The whole of it is made on the premises, by workmen skilled in all the complicated operations of metal and wood, connected with the fabrication and erection of the extensive apparatus of such an establishment'. But Griscom's main concern was the school, where in the evening he saw the usual mutual instruction, singing and dancing. The following day he saw the infant school judiciously noting that 'this baby school is of great consequence to the establishment, for it enables mothers to shut up their houses in security to attend to their duties in the factory, without concern for their families'. While 'humanity to the laborers' was clearly an avowed principle at New Lanark, the whole community was subject to 'a strict discipline'.[23]

For his part William Maclure was impressed by Glasgow which he found to be 'a handsome town – the streets are wide and the foot pavements are more spacious than in any place I have been in'. Which was just as well for 'such a tussle and crowd as I have not been accustomed to for some time: everyone elbowing you in the streets, and all of them anxious pigs of business. Even the atmosphere is saturated with smoke and dust to such an extent that it would not agree with people with weak lungs and do no good to those with sound ones'. A major environmental pollutant was the smoke from Tennant's 'chemical manufactory of sulphuric acid' where the product was made 'by burning the suplhar and the nitre in an oven on the outside if the lead chamber, although it is not designed to save much of the nitre as the oven was close'. 'They sell it', observed Maclure, 'at 1 $1/2$d per liter. Blacking of lime and chlorine sells at 3d per liter, soda at 39 shillings per bushel, white soda at 68 shillings per liter and yellow soap at 58 shillings. It is one of the most extensive establishments I ever saw. It burns fifty tons of coal per day, and every process goes on with great regularity and economy'.[24]

Another plant that owed much to chemical technology and clearly fascinated him was Henry Monteith's bandanna and colour printing factory. There bandannas were printed using a hydraulic press with a pressure of 130 tons. According to Maclure, 'this method secures the red part of the dye from the chlorine (chloride) of lime which discharges the white spots and stripes through 14 plies by the means of lead plates, which are excavated opposite the part intended to be white, through which the chlorine of lime circulates under high pressure and discharges to the read dye, leaving all the rest of the cloth a permanent Turkey-red. Likewise the block printing employs the red tint exclusively. The power looms they have here are operated by one girl who attends two looms and weaves about 20 yards of cloth a day on each'.[25] Maclure later called on Monteith at the 'immense palace' he was building at Carstairs.

The highlight of Maclure's Scottish tour was a visit to New Lanark but the account of his sojourn there, like Griscom's, has been little quoted. Maclure found the workshops 'on the best construction' and was impressed by the 'order, happiness and comfort that pervades the whole of Mr Owen's establishment'. The school and the curriculum clearly fascinated him:

> The children are taught geography at a very early age in a simple, easy way by the use of a large map; all answering at a time . . . They are taught by representations (reproductions, models) in all the cases that can be obtained, the

transparencies being used only in part for the explanation of the elements of botany for the shape of the leaves, etc. The representation of the different ages of the world, as far as it is connected with history, etc, the birds quadrupeds, insects, and plants are drawn by the boys and girls in oil colors. They are done exceedingly well and are tolerably accurate.[26]

So impressed was Maclure by what he saw that he was encouraged, so he wrote, to undertake his own 'long projected plan of forming experimental schools in so superior a field as the United States, which can scarcely fail when such an extensively profound and beneficial system seems to flourish here in spite of all the opposition of despotism, both church and state'.

It is hardly surprising that Butt, like those distinguished visitors from the past, found himself fascinated by New Lanark, which when he came upon it was still a working mill village and not a fossil from the past like Gatehouse or Wilsontown. The community and mills survived much as they had been in 1824 when Robert Owen had abandoned it as he left in some haste for his new venture at Harmonie in Indiana. For Butt what started out as an exercise in industrial and business history soon broadened to become a critical reappraisal of Owen, his economic and social philosophy and the movement he inspired. His introductions to re-issues of *The Life of Robert Owen* and of *A New View of Society and other writings* were based on much original research and called into question many long-cherished notions about Owen. The collection of Owen Bi-Centennial Essays by Strathclyde scholars which he edited was undoubtedly one of his major achievements.[27] With John Hume and others Butt aided the campaign which saw New Lanark through its darkest days in the 1970s so he can legitimately claim to have played a role in rescuing what is perhaps the most important monument to early industry internationally.

Through his studies of Scottish industry and entrepreneurship John Butt has pieced together parts of the jig-saw which help to make up the picture of a dynamically changing industrial scene during the closing decades of the eighteenth century and the first two decades of the nineteenth. As he realised, contemporary sources, familiar and unfamiliar, like those quoted above, need to be treated with a degree of circumspection, which necessarily involves some reading between the lines. But they do bring a vitality to the story of industrialization in Scotland – a vitality that Butt has always successfully conveyed in his own work. The genuine wonder and enthusiasm of those who viewed at first hand the dramatic impact of industry in late eighteenth and early nineteenth century Scotland is captured both in Butt's publications and the work of the numerous acolytes he inspired to follow a similar course exploring further the economic and social history of Scotland during the era of the Industrial Revolution. So this tour of the works concludes at its cut-off point in 1825, but many of John Butt's publications dealing with later nineteenth and twentieth themes are cited elsewhere in this volume.[28]

REFERENCES

1. *Statistical Account of Scotland*, vol. VII, pp. 375–90.
2. *Ibid.*, vol. X, pp. 503–07. Despite his firm west of Scotland base, Butt's researches extend the length and breadth of Scotland, particularly in his studies of the metal and textile industries, in the history of transport and in industrial archaeology. One of his research students, Dr Walter Stephen, produced a detailed study of Fife industrial history and archaeology.
3. *Ibid.*, vol. VII, p. 614.
4. See in particular: J. R. Hume and J. Butt, 'Muirkirk 1786–1802. The Creation of a Scottish Industrial Community', *Scottish Historical Review*, vol. XLV, no. 2, 1966, pp. 160–183; and J. Butt, 'Glenbuck Ironworks', *Ayrshire Archaeological and Natural History Collections*, Second Series, vol. 8, 1967–69, pp. 68–75.
5. *Stat. Acc.*, vol. V, pp. 297–98.
6. J. Butt, 'The Scottish Iron and Steel Industry Before the Hot-Blast', *Journal of the West of Scotland Iron and Steel Institute*, vol. 73, no. 6, 1965–66, pp. 1–22.
7. For a handy, comprehensive list of volumes in the series see J. A. Symon, *Scottish Farming Past and Present*, Edinburgh, 1959, pp. 445–47.
8. See, for example, J. Butt, *The Industrial Archaeology of Scotland* (Newton Abbot, 1967), pp. 28–55.
9. Sir John Sinclair, *General View of the Agriculture of the Northern Counties and Islands of Scotland* (London, 1795), p. 62.
10. *Ibid.*, pp. 63–4.
11. Butt, *Industrial Archaeology of Scotland*, p. 302.
12. Rev David Ure, *General View of the County of Dumbarton*, (London, 1794), pp. 11, 59, 77, 87–90.
13. R. Heron, *Observations Made in a Journey through the Western Counties of Scotland; in the Autumn of 1792* (Perth, 1793), vol. II, pp. 211–35.
14. J. Butt, 'The Industrial Archaeology of Gatehouse-of-Fleet', *Industrial Archaeology*, vol. 3, no. 2, pp. 127–37.
15. A. Raistrick (ed.), *The Hatchett Diary. A Tour through the counties of England and Scotland in 1796 visiting their mines and manufactories* (Truro, 1967), p. 89.
16. *Ibid.*, p. 99.
17. *Ibid.*, pp. 101–03.
18. Butt, *Industrial Archaeology of Scotland*, pp. 91–2, 281.
19. Eric T. Svedenstierna, *Tour through a part of England and Scotland in the years 1802 and 1803 with particular reference to mining and metallurgical, technological and mineralogical matters* (Stockholm, 1804 Eng. ed.) with introduction by M. W. Flinn, Newton Abbot, 1973, pp. 145–6.
20. *Ibid.*, p. 146.
21. I. Donnachie and J. Butt, 'The Wilsons of Wilsontown Ironworks (1779–1813): A Study in Entrepreneurial Failure', *Explorations in Entrepreneurial History*, vol. 4 No. 2, 1967, pp. 150–168.

22. C. Hibbert (ed.), *An American in Regency England. The Journal of a Tour in 1810–1811* (London, 1968), p. 78.
23. J. Griscom, *A Year in Europe. Comprising a Journal of Observations in England, Scotland etc. in 1818 and 1819*, 2 vols. (New York, 1823), pp. 374–6, 385–6.
24. J. S. Doskey (ed.) *The European Journals of William Maclure*, (American Philosophical Society, Philadelphia), 1988, p. 714.
25. *Ibid.*, p. 716.
26. *Ibid.*, pp. 721–22.
27. J. Butt (ed.), *Robert Owen. Prince of Cotton Spinners*, Newton Abbott, 1971.
28. Further work on textiles includes:
J. Butt, 'The Scottish Cotton Industry during the Industrial Revolution, 1780–1840', in L. M. Cullen and T. C. Smout (eds.), *Comparative Aspects of Scottish and Irish Economic and Social History* (Edinburgh, 1977); and J. Butt and K. Ponting (eds.), *Scottish Textile History* (Aberdeen, 1987) in which there is useful article by Butt on 'Labour Relations in the Scottish Cotton Industry during the Industrial Revolution' in Butt and Ponting (eds.), pp. 139–160.

4

The Scottish Business Elite in the Nineteenth Century – The Case of William Baird & Company

ROBERT D. CORRINS

William Baird & Company, although officially formed in 1830, had its roots in a single small gin pit developed by William and his brother in 1816. Within a generation they, together with five other brothers, had built up one of the world's largest industrial enterprises and had become in the process stereo-typical Victorian self-made men. Down to the outbreak of the First World War the firm and those who controlled it played a prominent part not only in the economic life of Scotland but in many other aspects as well, most notably social, political, and religious, and did so in a way for which there is really no modern parallel. The Baird brothers and their successors are the subjects of this essay which explores the history of the firm in the nineteenth century in terms of the actions and motives of the men who led it.

The Victorian entrepreneur has been the subject of interest and debate at least since the time of Samuel Smiles. Contemporary historians have found him no less fascinating[1]. Yet the wide ranging debate seems if anything to be moving away from rather than towards a consensus on even the most basic issues. The study of origins, and its related dimensions of social class, religious persuasion and education has produced qualified agreement on the overwhelming predominance of the middle class[2], but continued dispute about the significance of Anglicanism vis-a-vis non-conformity, and equally about the contribution of the schools – especially the public schools – to the formation of businessmen[3]. Their motivation beyond the mere acquisition of wealth has proved equally disputatious. Their assumed enthusiasm to join landed society is assumed no longer[4], while their political impact – the bourgeois revolution – may, it seems, never have happened[5]. The most vigorous debate of all has concerned the part played by the entrepreneur in Britain's decline from a position of mid-Victorian hegemony. The earlier assumption that the heroic pioneers were succeeded by lesser men was powerfully criticised by the cliometricians only for their arguments in turn to come under attack[6]. In the present generation the focus of the debate has had a number of major themes each with its own sub-themes and specific issue. There has been a tension between the individual biography approach to entrepreneurial studies and the 'group characteristics' approach, with the recent development of prosopography[7] in the field representing something of a bridge.

The firm of William Baird & Company offers a case study particularly well-suited to illuminate many aspects of the discussion on the Victorian entrepreneur. Single firm studies have certain limitations but nevertheless they can contribute to testing general explanations. As the largest of the Scottish coal and iron combines of the nineteenth century William Baird & Company has often been cited but, in the absence of a comprehensive company history, such references have inevitably been based on brief and superficial secondary sources. This essay will, it is hoped add some breadth and depth to the picture at least so far as the entrepreneurial aspect is concerned. Its growth over the period 1830–1914 reflected, and indeed significantly contributed to, Britain's rise to industrial prominence. The partners/directors, of whom there were twenty-one, provide a sizeable and varied group for study. Moreover the firm and the men who led it came to occupy a particularly important position in Scotland as it in turn rose to industrial prominence within Britain.

William Baird & Company was formally established in 1830 when Alexander Baird made over to five of his eight sons the non-agricultural leases he held in the rapidly developing Monklands iron and coal field.[8] Descended from a long line of small tenant farmers he had been fortunate to be able to take over from a childless uncle the farm leases which were virtually hereditary to the Bairds. He worked hard to develop and extend these holdings and soon became a prominent member of the community, with close links to a number of local landowners. By 1815 he was the principal tenant of 250 acres and a mill at an annual rental of 250 pounds. In 1825 he made the vital breakthrough when he purchased the lands of Lochwood and became a modest member of the local gentry.

In 1794 he married Jean Moffat, daughter of a local farmer who over the next twenty-two years gave birth of eight sons and two daughters all of whom, surprisingly for the time, survived to adulthood. Alexander obviously appreciated that his sons could not all inherit the farm leases without reversing the gains achieved in his lifetime. Nor did they appear anxious to follow in his footsteps. The oldest, William, who had been sent to Tweedside to learn the most advanced agricultural techniques returned full of knowledge but with little enthusiasm. An alternative readily suggested itself. Coalmining, following the opening of the Monkland canal, had begun rapidly to transform the district. In 1816 Alexander leased the coalfield at

Rochsolloch in neighbouring New Monkland. He personally continued to concentrate on farming. Management of the pit was the responsibility of William aged 20, while Alexander junior then only 16 years old, was sent into the very demanding environment of the canal basin at Port Dundas to act as selling agent[9]. Such an approach was guaranteed to test whether the brothers had ability. This they demonstrated in abundance and in 1822 Alexander leased the much larger coalfield at Merryston bordering the farm of Newmains which had become his principal residence in 1819, and a third son, James, joined in the reopening and rapid extension of the pits. When the boom of 1825 tempted the landlord, Buchanan, to reclaim the colliery the outraged brothers acted immediately to secure their position in the coal trade. Before the six months notice to quit Merryston had expired they had a new pit in operation on the estate of Gartsherrie, so beginning an association which was to last for almost the next century and a half.

By 1828 deliveries by the Monkland canal alone were running at 1000 tons per month and the thoughts of the brothers were already turning to new ventures. In September 1828 J B Neilson, a friend of William,[10] patented the Hot-blast process which proved such a stimulus to the exploitation of the Lanarkshire blackband ironstone and the brothers began the erection of the first Gartsherrie furnace which commenced production on 4th May 1830.

Some writers[11] have described Alexander senior as the first of the 'industrialists' but this should on balance be rejected. He was certainly the foundation of the family's rise to prominence but he did this by very astute exploitation of the opportunities presented to agriculturalists by the Napoleonic wars. The original coal leases were in his name but from the beginning in 1816 he left their exploitation to his sons while he and his second son, John, continued to concentrate on agriculture. Far from reducing his activities, or at least limiting himself to the farms already held, he expanded his farming interests significantly by leasing Newmains farm in 1819, and after 1825 he was taken up with the improvement of his new estate at Lochwood. As head of the family, and given his financial standing (which allowed him to pay £9,125 cash for Lochwood in 1825) it was only commonsense for him to enter into the early coal leases. His undoubted ability as well as his local influence must have been invaluable to his son but it is entirely fitting that the firm was named after William and not Alexander.

It follows from this that in any discussion of the origins of industrialists it is William and his brothers who should be considered. In later life they liked to emphasise their simple start in life, and certainly for the older brothers their upbringing in the farmsteadings of Woodhead and Highcross was decidedly modest. On the other hand as the latest generation of a long line of small tenant farmers they were far from the bottom of local society. At worst they might be labelled lower-middle but certainly not lower class.

From their mother they acquired a strong attachment to the Church of

Scotland. In what seems almost a caricature, daily catechism and strict discipline were the norm. James in later life recalled without rancour that with his mother 'It was a word and a blow, the blow usually coming first'[12]. Although each child was expected to help around the farm this was not at the expense of schooling. For most of the family the elementary education provided at the local parish school was all that was possible. Indeed it was all that most of them seemed to want. Surprisingly, and despite their later support for school building they do not appear to have had that dedication to formal schooling that is often said to be a Scottish characteristic. William 'was never an expert scholar', Alexander 'was never a good scholar'[13], Douglas 'not ready in learning his lessons' and so on. Some reports claim that James attended Glasgow University for a time but there is no record of him having matriculated. John and Robert did attend but only Robert stayed for any length of time and even he did not graduate. Thus with the important exception of Robert, whose legal education proved valuable to the firm, the brothers were little indebted to formal education and not at all to business or technical training.

Their father passed on his commitment to conservatism and throughout the century the firm remained prominently identified with both the Church of Scotland and the Tory party. These characteristics were by no means typical features of the emerging industrial elite. Apart from those who belonged to the smaller denominations such as Baptists, many industrialists split with the national church at the Disruption, while in politics, at least down to the mid 1880s, they provided significant support for the Liberals. These differences undoubtedly inhibited the emergence of a united business class. Viewed from London the northern industrialists including the Scots might be seen as dissenting liberals but among themselves the position was much more subtle. The Baird brothers may have had difficulty in relating to anglican tory squires[14] but an appreciation of their own conservative values and commitment to their established church is essential to an understanding of their motives and actions.

Once embarked on a career as ironmasters the brothers worked with single minded determination. As soon as the first furnace was in blast two others each of different design quickly followed, as well as new blast-heating equipment. Development continued at a frantic pace and by 1843 the works had 16 furnaces and a capacity of 100,000 tons per annum, making them the largest single pig-iron producing unit in the world. The Scottish industry's expansion was founded on the fortuitous presence of splint coal and blackband ore and the Bairds were quick to appreciate the vital importance of adequate reserves of raw materials. They 'purchased every foot of ground which they can obtain in the neighbourhood and have likewise taken leases of what could not be bought'[15]. In the case of the crucially important blackband a contemporary calculated that they held 5/16ths of the main 4000 acre block.[16]

Still committed to expansion but with Lanarkshire at saturation point, the Bairds turned to Ayrshire. A new works was begun at Eglinton in 1845, and over the next twenty years extensive mineral leases were acquired and the ironworks at Blair, Muirkirk, Lugar, and Portland were purchased and operated as the Eglinton Iron Company. In all of this they continued to display a sureness of touch. Blair for example was bought for less than a quarter of its original construction cost. By 1870 the Bairds in just forty years had built up what was reputed to be the world's leading pig-iron producer with 42 furnaces and a capacity of 300,000 tons per annum[17], with the profit for that year alone put at £1,000,000.[18]

A number of aspects of this quite phenomenal achievement are worth noting. George and Douglas joined William, Alexander, and James in the 1830 partnership and they were joined at a later date by Robert and David.[19] The seven brothers among them actively managed every aspect of the business from raw material extraction through to sales Whether sinking pits, building furnaces, laying out railways or negotiating leases, they did not leave the responsibility to experts. They looked closely at contemporary practice but ultimately they relied on their own judgement and at times on their own physical labour. Even more remarkably they financed the entire programme from within their own resources. For almost twenty years they lived modestly ploughing everything back into the business. They formed a collective but with a definite hierarchical structure reflecting relationships worked out in childhood as well as their varied and complementary talents. The family unit provided a pool within which were found all the principal elements of entrepreneurship, but without giving rise to the disunity and factionalism to which group leadership systems are prone.

William was the unquestioned leader. James attributed the success of the company to William's 'great capacity, his almost unequalled business habits, his great power of utilising to the best advantage the means within his power'[20]. Others recognised his qualities. The Western Bank directors were thrown into consternation in 1845 when they realised that he was about to retire and was ineligible for immediate re-election. They at once created a new class of 'honorary director' and William duly served in that capacity until he could be re-elected as an ordinary director the following year[21]. James although younger than Alexander was unquestionably second in importance to William. He was primarily responsible for the construction of Gartsherrie works. With no formal training and little expert help he relied on his own practical aptitude and massive self confidence. Given the relatively unsophisticated state of iron industry technology at that time such an approach was possible. Every new furnace and each new piece of apparatus incorporated some modification[22]. Not surprisingly the results were not always what had been anticipated as in the case of the no. 3 furnace which was erected on cast-iron pillars. When it failed to achieve satisfactory production levels James simply demolished it and started again even although it was barely two years old.

David and Douglas appear to have been very competent administrators but no more[23]. The other brothers were of real importance to the firm's fortunes. Alexander earned a reputation in his youth for being able to impose his will on his brothers, which must have been a considerable achievement in such a group. Having matured in the demanding environment of Port Dundas he ran the important sales department for thirty years. Dealing in the canal basin may have honed his selling skills but it did little for his more formal communication skills and Robert, who trained in the legal offices of William Taylor, thereby making him the only brother to hold a position as an employee outside the firm, was drafted in to the Glasgow office to work in tandem with Alexander. His 'rare combination of practical intelligence with sound judgement'[24] was recognised by his fellow merchants who elected him to the leadership of the Merchant House where his personal influence was such that in less than two years up to his death he enrolled more new members[25] than any previous occupant of the office. George was, like Alexander, active in the business from his teens and a partner at twenty. He oversaw the entire Ayrshire operation and had a special interest in the negotiation of all the company's mineral leases.

William and James were clearly men of outstanding ability and the family was fortunate to have two such formidable talents. That the other brothers were less gifted was probably a source of strength, as taken together, their interests and abilities covered the whole range of activities of the company. No hint survives of even the slightest dispute and clearly the deep family loyalty was an important element in their success. Thus whether entrepreneurship is defined in Schumpeter's[26] grand innovator terms or in Coleman's[27] incrementalist terms, or indeed if it is extended to encompass what some would regard as managerial functions, the Baird brothers between them possessed all the attributes required for success.

The appropriate company records have not survived to reveal profit details for this period. However, the records of the trial caused by the dispute between Baird and J B Neilson over the Hot-blast plus some fragmentary details of production costs give some indication. Thus during the 1836 boom the selling price of Gartsherrie no. 1 pig was 338% above production cost, while by 1840 when the price had dropped by 44% from its 1836 peak the profit for the year was £54,855[28]. James provided dramatic evidence of their financial security when he settled the outstanding financial claims against them in the hot-blast dispute by writing a cheque for £106,000[29].

It seems clear that the brothers were driven by the same passion for social advancement which had raised their father from small farmer to minor gentry. Iron and coal provided the obvious source of the money required, but there was no strong commitment to the industry as such. As soon therefore as it became possible they began to penetrate the ranks of the landed elite as determinedly as they had entered the iron industry.

Starting with the purchase of part of Closeburn, Dumfries in 1848 by Douglas, the brothers over the next fifteen years spent £1,115,000 on 125,000 acres in seven counties[30]. The social status of the brides rose with the fortunes of the brothers. In 1840 William married Janet the daughter of Thomas Johnstone a local coalmaster. But when George married in St George's Hanover Square in 1858 his bride was Cecelia the daughter of Admiral Hatton of Clonard. The next generation was groomed for its new position. The educational background of five of the nine grandsons of Alexander is known. Of these three went to Eton and two to Harrow, three went on to Oxford, and one to the Royal Military College. Wills were made with an eye to promoting social advancement, but although sons were favoured over daughters, primogeniture was not practised and the wealth was widely spread. There was however wealth in abundance.

The value at death[31] of each of the brothers was as follows:

1854	Douglas	£224,864 (£225,000)
1856	Robert	£189,665 (£60,000)
1860	David	£156,000 + $65,000 (£150,000)
1862	Alexander	£631,723 + $241,170 (£120,000)
1864	William	£987,785 + $177,000 (£202,000)
[1870	John	£106,216]
1870	George	£918,457 + $279,450 (£145,000)
1876	James	£1,190,868 (£247,000)

Note: Bracketed figures are purchase prices of principal estates held.

Their wills contained elaborate provisions to keep their newly acquired estates in the family and ensure the survival of the Baird name. Robert was especially keen that Auchmedden, purchased in part because it had been the ancient seat of a Baird family, should remain their possession. Alexander stated the position clearly when he arranged for the recipient of Urie to receive a sufficient income 'so that they may be able to live in a manner more becoming and suitable to their position and rank'[32]. It is clear that far from being disappointed that none of the Baird sons opted to go into business the family consciously sought something quite different. The life stories of this generation are studded with details of membership of the best London clubs, regiments of dragoons, lancers, and hussars, deputy-lieutenancies, master of hounds, and racehorses. Commitment to the conservative cause remained strong and two of them became MPs. If anything the daughters found entry into the landed classes even easier than the sons, Douglas's twin daughters, who had no brothers, were particularly attractive 'catches', and one married the heir to the Earl of Enniskillen while the other married the nephew of Lord Clarendon.

There is no easily identifiable point at which the brothers relinquished control over the firm. Rather they gradually relaxed their almost total immersion in its affairs passing through a phase of general oversight to a position of remote supervision. This process occurred over an extended period from the early 1850s to the mid 1870s, and was governed by the choices of individual brothers as well as the exigencies of illness and death.

Although none of the sons of the brothers entered the business the opportunity to acquire some say in the running of the firm remained very clearly restricted to family members. As the brothers withdrew, control passed to the sons and son-in-law of one of the sisters. Alexander senior had two daughters Jane and Janet. Jane married Thomas Jackson, who with support from the Bairds set up a malleable ironworks on land at Coats acquired from her brothers. Their children were educated at Douglas Baird's expense[33]. Of the sons William Baird Jackson died young, Alexander Baird Jackson opted to try his fortune in the Argentine and Thomas was trained at the Gartsherrie office before taking over the Coats works where he carried out the first trials of the Bessemmer steel process in Scotland. Janet was married twice. By her first husband, Alexander Whitelaw she had two sons Thomas and Alexander, and by her second husband John Weir, she had another son William. They too were educated at Baird expense and unlike their Baird cousins they were consciously prepared for entry to the business. Alexander like his Jackson cousins was educated at the Grange school Sunderland and then studied mining before entering the Gartsherrie office. Douglas Baird directed that since William Weir had said that he would like to enter the counting house his education should focus on 'arithmetic, mathematics, speaking English correctly, French, Latin reading and pencil drawing'.[34]

Thomas Whitelaw was being trained at Gartsherrie when he died in 1850 aged 24. His brother, Alexander had by then taken on the mantle of assistant to his uncle James at Gartsherrie and when William Weir joined the firm he went to Ayrshire to assist his Uncle George. When the partnerships were reorganized in the early 1860s they were admitted together with the manager of the Gartsherrie office David Wallace. The son of an excise officer he left a Glasgow accountants office to join the company in 1846, and married William Weir's twin sister. Another key employee James Bain, later to become Sir James Bain, Lord Provost of Glasgow, was not so fortunate. Convinced that his lack of family ties to the Bairds had blocked his advancement he left taking two colleagues, Blair and Patterson, and they established their own works in the newly emerging Cleveland district[35].

That Whitelaw and Weir did enter the firm, unlike their Baird cousins, was in part a matter of timing. They were closer to their uncles than to their cousins – Alexander Whitelaw, for example, was only nine years younger than his uncle David – and they therefore grew up while the firm was still comparatively young. Moreover the indirect influence of George, who died in 1870, and more importantly James, who died in 1876, meant that their control was for long a qualified one. During the sixties and seventies Alexander was the key figure, not least because of his particularly close relationship with James, who was his wife's brother-in-law as well as being his uncle. Alexander was in constant communication both by letter and in person with James whose Cambusdoon estate was only a few miles from William Weir's Ayrshire home.

The evidence for the company's performance during the sixties and seventies is somewhat contradictory. It was hardly to be expected that the phenomenal growth of the early years could be maintained. Yet a number of significant initiatives were undertaken. In the Gartsherrie district the vital matter of raw materials was addressed. Ironstone fields were bought or leased in the Denny-Kilsyth area during the 1860s as determinedly as the brothers had earlier established their premier position in the Monklands. In 1862 alone the company sank twelve pits in the district[36], and at Gartshore where the first pit started production in 1861, no. 10 pit was being sunk in 1872[37]. By the late 1870's the district supplied 68% of the ore consumed at Gartsherrie[38]. In Ayrshire, Alexander Whitelaw's young protégé, Robert Angus, was placed in charge of the complete rebuilding of the works at Lugar. Yet although praised for being willing to innovate, by, for example, funding the development of mechanical coal-cutters, the company was criticised for conservatism in its core business of iron production, for failing to emulate even the modest initiatives of some of its Scottish rivals. Even so it remained consistently and indeed at times extremely profitable. Contemporary estimates put profits in the late 1860's at a minimum of £750,000 per annum[39] rising to over £1,000,000 in a good year[40]. At one point Alexander Whitelaw wrote to James urging him to do something about the vast sums of money he had lying in his account[41]. It is no coincidence that this period of stable but unimaginative success was presided over by Alexander Whitelaw. He was an extremely hard worker, with an astonishingly retentive memory and a legendary grasp of figures. A comment on his style as an MP is however indicative of his caste of mind. He was described as being of the 'strictest sect of tories' for whom 'when Lord Beaconsfield [Disraeli] spoke it was wisdom, when he was silent it was wisdom'[42].

Not surprisingly the company entered the late Victorian era apparently ideally fitted to supply primary evidence for the prosecution in the case against the Victorian entrepreneur[43]. The exact opposite is, however, nearer the mark. Britain's alleged failure to respond adequately to the challenge of the rising economies of the late nineteenth century has been vigorously debated. The significance of entrepreneurial inefficiency has undergone reconsideration with some writers shifting the emphasis to economic variables less amenable to control by individual firms. Even so the pioneering studies of D L Burn[44] and Burnham and Hoskins[45] led to many of the illustrations in the general debate being drawn initially from the iron and steel industry. Despite the broadening of the debate to other industries these studies have remained as powerful evidence for the justification of the hypothesis at least so far as the iron industry is concerned. On a regional front Byres' study of the heavy industries of the West of Scotland [46] has been cited as further evidence in support of this case.

In the revised edition of his pamphlet on the topic[47] P L Payne reflects the recent work in the field and underscores his original judgement that the notion of 'dissipation of an initial fund of entrepreneurialship is untenable'. Yet his one specific reference to the Bairds survives unchanged from the first edition. Drawn from Byres it condemns the firm as an expression of 'the Buddenbrook Dynamic'. 'Control of their great firm [he writes], passed out of the hands of the family after the impressive efforts of the second generation had given it a position of supremacy in the scottish iron industry.'[48] Yet the issue of family ties and the process of succession in ownership/control within the firm is much more complex than Byres and others have allowed.

David Wallace was forced into virtual retirement through illness in 1875. In the following year James Baird died and Alexander Whitelaw suffered a stroke brought on by over work. Although he remained lucid, recovery was only partial and by the summer of 1878 he was confined to Gartsherrie House, where he died in 1879. Thus for much of the 1870s only William Weir the junior partner was fully functional. It is hardly surprising that the firm was condemned as 'the most cautious and conservative firm in the industry.'[49] Nor had the next generation been groomed to take over. Both Wallace and Whitelaw had sons, but they emulated the Baird brothers in raising them to pursue a life outside business.

David's son John was educated at Harrow and Trinity College, Cambridge prior to life as a country gentleman. The four Whitelaw sons likewise received their education at Harrow and Trinity, though they went beyond the narrow life of country gentlemen to include the equally acceptable activities of bank and railway directorships and in the case of Graeme and William membership of the House of Commons. The eldest son Alexander made a particularly acceptable match by marrying Disraeli's niece.

By the late 1870s reorganisation of the firm had become a pressing concern. In February 1878 in the most dramatic change yet to occur in the control of the firm six new partners were admitted. Unfortunately no detailed evidence has survived concerning the event. Pressure for change did come to some extent from below from the senior executives who had come to play a critical managerial role as the number of active partners declined. Robert Angus went so far as to threaten to leave unless an attractive offer was made to hold him[50]. The new partners were Alexander Fleming, John Alexander, William Laird, Robert Angus, Andrew Kirkwood McCosh, and James Baird Thorneycroft. Three of them Alexander (21)[51] Laird (24) and Angus (21) had given almost as many years to the firm as Weir while Fleming (14) and McCosh (15) also had considerable experience. Thorneycroft was the obvious exception. He had joined the firm in 1869 as an eighteen year old and his assumption as a partner is an interesting example of the family link continuing through the female line as it had done in the Whitelaw and Weir cases. He was the son of Alexander Whitelaw's sister Jane.

The debate about the late Victorian entrepreneur has in recent years been clouded by criticism of the very foundation of the initial discussion by those who have rejected the core definitions of the original participants including the definition of entrepreneurship itself[52]. For the most part the earlier debate focused on a range of socio-economic criticisms of which the main social ones were, control through a family or friendship group drawn from a narrow background; an absence of or hostility towards scientific training or formal education; over-long retention of power; and excessive involvement in extra-firm pursuits. When considered under each of these headings Bairds are remarkably free from criticism.

The new team came from widely differing social backgrounds. Alexander Fleming left his father's poor West Highland farm at Ballyvain to seek his fortune in Glasgow at the age of fourteen, and is probably a real example of a Victorian tale of rags to riches. William Laird also came from a farming family, in Perthshire, but in his case it was able to provide him with the necessary education and secure him a place in a lawyer's office. Nothing whatsoever is known about John Alexander's father which suggests that he too came from a modest background. Robert Angus was usually described as the son of an engineer, though his marriage certificate describes his father James as a horsekeeper. A K McCosh by contrast was from a prominent Ayrshire legal family. His father James acted for the Bairds in their expansion into Ayrshire. J B Thorneycroft's grandfather George B Thorneycroft, first mayor of Wolverhampton, patented several inventions for the improved manufacture of iron. As owner of the Shrubbery works he was a purchaser of Gartsherrie iron in the early days and became a personal friend of the brothers. The current view is that the number of entrepreneurs who rose from humble origins has been greatly exaggerated and Erikson maintains that the middle class virtually monopolised power in the steel industry[53]. The Bairds clearly considered ability above origins even family origins when choosing and promoting men. A family link might guarantee an opportunity but the individual concerned had then to prove himself.

In the supposedly more progressive steel industry fewer than 10% of the pre-1914 owners had a technical school training or university education[54]. Four of the Baird partners concentrated on the commercial side. Weir as noted did have his schooling directed towards commerce but he went into the office straight from school as did Thorneycroft. On the other hand the Baird offices were highly regarded for the quality of the training they provided and many Scottish businessmen sought to have their sons placed with the company before they went into their own family business. Laird went into a lawyers office from school and moved to the Bairds at age 24. Of this group only Fleming had substantial experience outwith the firm but again no formal higher education, although he did attend evening classes during his rise from office boy to manager with the Monkland Iron and Steel Company.

Critics have tended to concentrate on the inadequate scientific and technical knowledge of British entrepreneurs. A K McCosh studied science at the universities of Glasgow and Edinburgh. At the former he studied under Professor Macquorn Rankine, and won the mechanical engineering prize. He then served his articles with Ronald Johnston, a Glasgow civil and mining engineer. Robert Angus qualified in the service of one of Scotland's foremost engineers, Neil Robson. At least two of John Alexander's three brothers were engineers, which lends some support to the impression that he received an appropriate education before gaining experience in the service of the Monkland Iron and Steel Company.

Far from being hostile or indifferent to science the partners both employed suitably educated personnel and fostered technical education among its own workforce. Outside scientific experts, notably analytical chemists, were used at least as early as 1853[55]. By 1880 chemists were employed at the works and far from being despised they were highly regarded. W J Dunnachie at Gartsherrie was made joint manager[56], while at Eglinton the firm so valued the expertise of their chemist Stevenson that they ignored the fact that he was a rather eccentric esperanto speaking vegetarian atheist[57]. His manager at Eglinton in the 1880's was described as 'a gentleman whose scientific attainments are not a whit less than his great practical skill'.[58]

The Gartsherrie Academy Science and Art School, financed by the firm produced many key workers for the Bairds and other firms, not least Robert Angus and his brother John, who became manager at Muirkirk. It had laboratories which were only surpassed it was claimed by Macclesfield, Liverpool, Birmingham, and Charterhouse. In 1878 it received the third largest payment by results grant of any school in Scotland. Subjects taught included mathematics, theoretical mechanics, applied mechanics, magnetism and electricity, inorganic chemistry, organic chemistry, and steam. It had a class of sixty in mining at a time when there were only two other such classes in Scotland, each with eight students. Immediately following the passage of the Technical Schools (Scotland) Act A. K. McCosh wrote to the government to try to speed up the setting up of such a school, although he had no official standing in the matter.[59] In 1890 Coatbridge Technical School, the only one created under the act was begun on land given by William Weir.

Only Fleming and Alexander who both came from the Monkland Iron and Steel Company had any substantial experience outside the firm, so the others were trained within the firm and are open to the charge of narrowness.

Against this is the fact that the company provided a quality training within a very diverse business environment. A more serious charge is that they retained control for too long, failing to give way to younger men. Certainly they tended to work until they dropped. None retired, although Fleming was of limited importance following a stroke in 1902. Alexander died in 1895, aged 70; Laird in 1901, aged 71; Fleming in 1909 aged 85; Weir in 1913, aged 78; McCosh in 1916, aged 75; Thorneycroft in 1918, aged 67; and Angus in 1923, aged 87. Nevertheless although they were reluctant to relinquish power they were willing to share it with other younger men.

The inclusion of additional executives was facilitated by the reorganisation of the partnership as a limited company in 1893. The decision to reorganise was certainly not motivated by any perceived need or intention to seek a wider public involvement in the firm. The principal motive seems to have been to end the artificial distinction between Ayrshire and Lanarkshire and facilitate the introduction of new blood. One interesting gesture of recommitment to the firm's sense of family was the acceptance of the arrangement whereby a portion of William Weir's shareholding was allocated to William Baird, son of the original founder, thereby once again giving the senior branch of the family a direct voice in the affairs of the firm.

Some of these men came from within the controlling group exhibiting the tendency for the development of a bureaucratic dynasty, and confirming in a new guise the strong family tradition within the firm. A K McCosh II and his brother William W McCosh were groomed for their future role. Both were educated at Fettes and Trinity College Cambridge where Andrew took the Mechanical Sciences Tripos in 1902[60] and William went on to train as a mining engineer. The Angus brothers were likewise prepared for their future role. Like the McCoshes they attended Fettes, rather than Eton or Harrow as favoured by the Bairds. They then entered the firm and were given practical experience. Just as with Fleming, talented outsiders were brought in if the interests of the firm required it. With the death of Laird and the illness of his lawyer son, the firm recruited Stuart Foulis, brother of William, the highly respected Gas Manager for Glasgow. One time legal partner with Cluny McPherson a former Baird employee, he was a specialist in liability and compensation cases in the coal industry. On his death in 1914 his place was taken by another Glasgow lawyer, James Morton. Capable employees were given every encouragement. J T Forgie, born at Coatbridge in 1855, served his apprenticeship with Simpson and Wilson, civil and mining engineers, before joining the company in 1879. By the 1890's he was responsible for all the firms mining interest in Lanarkshire, Stirlingshire, Dumbartonshire, and Renfrewshire. In 1901 he became a shareholder with the transfer of 590 shares from William Weir, and four years later he joined the board.

The transfer of shares to Forgie was not an isolated case and typified the willingness of the group to share power. Weir ensured the continuation of the policy after his death by making provision in his will for the transfer of shares, at the request of the board, to suitable employees, 'in consideration of the interest which I have in the continued prosperity of the business with which I have long been associated and with the view of promoting the same by encouraging capable and deserving employees engaged in the working thereof'[61]. Erickson's study suggested that at the end of the century there was a decline in the chances of a modest born individual reaching the top[62]. William Baird & Company seem to have avoided that tendency.

Byres gives the examples of Whitelaw and Laird in support of the criticism that the firms leaders were guilty of being distracted by activities outside the firm in contrast with the original partners who poured all their energies into it[63]. Thus Whitelaw was the first chairman of the Glasgow School Board and MP for the Central Division of Glasgow, and William Laird who was knighted for his services to the Conservative party was involved in a number of transport undertakings. This criticism simply cannot be sustained. Whitelaw died in 1879 and can scarcely be classed as a late-Victorian entrepreneur. Laird was only one of seven partners and their extra-firm activities do not stand in sharp contrast to the original brothers, at least after the first decade of the firm. William Baird was connected with nine railway companies, James with eight, George with two, Douglas with three, Alexander with four and Robert with five. They were also involved in the Clydesdale Bank, the Western Bank, the Forth & Clyde Canal, the Glasgow Joint-Stock Feuing Company and the Glasgow News. Alexander sat on Glasgow Town Council, Robert was for a time Dean of Guild, and William and James were successful and George unsuccessful candidates for parliament. Of the later group none stood for parliament although all except Fleming were ardent conservatives. Alexander and McCosh confined their direct activity to local politics. Only Weir and Fleming owned country estates, modest ones in both cases. Their business involvement, apart from schemes of importance to the company, was largely confined to local concerns like the Coatbridge Gas Company. Byres cites Laird's involvement in the North British Railway. the Glasgow and Bothwell Railway, the Glasgow City and District Railway, the Harbour Tunnel Company and the Glasgow Subway. With the possible exception of the Subway these were the very opposite of extra-firm business interests. These concerns always had one and frequently more than one member of William Baird & Company on the board. for example, the Glasgow and Bothwell Railway, the route of which was perfectly suited to exploit the Baird's recently acquired mineral leases, also had John Alexander on the board and James Baird as its first and David Wallace its second chairman[64].

When attention is focused on the more strictly economic criticisms of the late-Victorian entrepreneur, the analysis of the performance of the Baird partners is hindered by the absence of virtually all the key company records. Yet circumstantial evidence gives an indication of their calibre at least in the eyes of their contemporaries. As the controller of the company's marketing strategy for forty years, Fleming became the most powerful individual domestic influence on the price of Scotch pig-iron, and hence of importance in determining world prices. Slighted in love he devoted himself exclusively to the iron exchange where his dominance was legendary and he was known to all as 'Sir Oracle'[65].

The events leading to Laird's election as chairman of the board of the North British are testimony to his qualities. The opponents of the intended future election of Lord Elgin thwarted the opening moves of his campaign in March 1899. No criticism was voiced when the Marquis of Tweeddale resigned in a fury the following month, but when he wrote to the *Glasgow Herald* attacking Laird, the affair spilled out into the open. Tweeddale was dismissed as 'clay in the hands of the potter'. No sooner had the board determined on one policy than Tweeddale, at the bidding of Laird, 'his terrible Glasgow mentor' changed it. Laird, widely praised for his management of the financial affairs of William Baird & Company, was promptly elected to the board and immediately made chairman[66]. Yet these two talented and forceful men did not dominate the partnership, indeed they seem to have occupied the third rank behind Weir in first place and Angus and McCosh.

Weir's dominance was confirmed when on the transformation of the partnership into a limited company in 1893 he was allocated one third of the shares, while none of the others received more than 11%. Angus and McCosh based in Ayrshire and Lanarkshire respectively were probably equal second in the group, a position formally acknowledged in 1905 when their shareholdings were increased to place them above the others. Both were widely recognised as outstanding businessmen. Angus was described as 'a man of great ability, action and masterful mind, possessing the highest qualities of leadership'[67] and 'a typical Scot dedicated to hard unremitting work, possessing high business skill'[68], while McCosh was considered the 'presiding brains' of the Gartsherrie firm[69]. Yet Weir was no mere figurehead chairman, as McCosh confirmed on one occasion when he reluctantly abandoned a proposal because he and Angus were not agreed and unless they could present a united front 'there was no prospect of carrying Mr. Weir'[70]. The evidence seems compelling that the company was led in the closing years of the century by a team of very able men with diverse and complementary talents.

It is also impossible to reconcile the claim of a profound loss of enterprise with the evidence of the company's attitude towards investment, technical and product innovation, productivity, and marketing. Internal research and development was vigorously promoted. Alexander and McCosh set an example to their staff by the manner in which they persevered in the development of by-product recovery apparatus. Although it was well known that the furnace gases contained valuable by-products conventional wisdom held that in relation to the volume of gas given off they would be so little as to defy separation or be separable only at prohibitive cost. The Gartsherrie furnaces alone produced almost as much gas in one day as all the Glasgow gasworks could produce in one week[71]. Tests at Gartsherrie in 1877 led Dr Wallace, one of Scotland's foremost industrial chemists, to state without reserve that the by-products were not commercially recoverable[72]. Alexander and McCosh refused to accept this judgement and continued with experiments which led them to patent an apparatus in 1879. Although no substantial trials had been possible and tests in 1880 yielded results well below the theoretical maximum, they remained confident and began to erect large scale plant at Gartsherrie in 1881 quickly followed by Lugar and Muirkirk[73]. Alexander and McCosh had been forced into an early patent[74] by the intense interest of their Scottish rivals who were desperately looking for some way of responding to the low cost competition of other U K producers. The Neilson's of Summerlee patented an alternative plant in 1882[75], followed soon after by James Addie at Langloan[76] and other variants followed rapidly.

Steady improvements in the efficiency of the plant were partially offset by a rapid fall in the selling price of sulphate of ammonia, the main by-product, and this makes any assessment of the importance of the system very difficult. At Gartsherrie in 1885 the profit was equal to 30p per ton of pig iron, falling to 18p per ton in 1900[77]. The 1885 profit, equivalent to a reduction of 12.8% in the cost of production of Gartsherrie iron, would have been welcome at any time. Coming as it did in the 1880s when the Scottish industry was experiencing the most difficult trading conditions in fifty years by-product recovery saved the industry from severe contraction.

By-product recovery apparatus was not the only example of technical innovation. A coal-cutting machine patented by the company won a gold medal at the American Centenary Exhibition in Philadelphia in 1876,[78] and proved a starting point for many later American models. European demand proved so heavy that the company built an engineering works specially to make them[79]. Many of the firm's collieries were equipped with the 'Bothwell' conveyor system designed and patented by one of the company's managers, Richard McPhee[80]. The company was also quick to adopt new technology developed elsewhere. It was the first company in Britain to adopt Bauer coke ovens. Before Bauer had even appointed a commercial representative in the UK Bairds had arranged for trials to be conducted at Schneider & Co's Creusot works.[81] Similarly it was the first company in Scotland and one of the first in Britain to erect plant for the manufacture of briquettes, when the use of the furnace gases to heat the blast created a surplus of dross.[82]

In the very difficult trading conditions of the closing decades of the century the company, far from drifting along under poor leadership, reacted positively. Not only did it eagerly develop or adopt new technology to drive down production costs but it invested heavily in new plant and in new products.

While other Scottish pig-iron makers slid towards extinction, Bairds modernised. Between 1878 and 1896 all sixteen Gartsherrie furnaces, some dating back to the early years of the original brothers, were replaced in a programme which extended to 'all modern improvements for making ordinary and hematite pig'. Only partial figures survive but these show that between 1882 and 1885 £76,000 was spent on by-product plant alone, while in the early 1890's £56,000 was spent on the furnaces[83]. At Lugar and Muirkirk the furnaces were modernised, with £40,000 spent on by-product plant alone. In 1894 four of the furnaces were demolished to be replaced with larger closed-topped ones linked to by-product recovery plant, and when these were completed the remaining three were demolished and replaced. The result was more economical and more productive furnaces. At Gartsherrie coal consumption per ton of pig which had deteriorated to 42.46 cwt. in 1890–91, was reduced to 31.9 cwt in 1903–4, and 1889–90 average output of 165tons 1 cwt. of ordinary iron was raised to 296 tons 8 cwt. by 1906–7.[84]

Investment at the works was matched by large and imaginative investment to secure the necessary raw materials. That they were not the first to acquire foreign mines was partly because they had been so effective in gaining the lion's share of the domestic deposits, but when they did move they acted decisively. Mines were purchased in Santander but it was soon realised that the northern deposits were becoming poorer and difficult to work. In 1893 the company became the first foreign firm to become involved in southern Spain when it purchased the Monte de Hierro (mountain of iron) mineral field[85]. The deposit lay 10 miles from the nearest railhead, which was in turn 53 miles from Seville, thus giving the firm the doubtful honour of operating the longest land haul for exported ore in Spain[86]. Considerable capital and enterprise were required to open up the deposit and link the Pedroso mines to Seville, but within three years production stood at 266,322 tons per annum[87].

The development of their coal interests was an even more significant departure. Although coal sales were always part of the company's business the essential role of the pits until late in the century was to serve the furnaces and it was common practice to sublet coal reserves which did not satisfy this purpose. Thus in 1861–2 75% of the coal output of the Gartsherrie region was used in the furnaces. By 1910–11 however the furnaces took only 10% of the output of the pits. In the closing decades of the century the company became one of the leading coal firms in the country. Not until 1878 when output was 479,401 tons did production in the Gartsherrie region exceed the 1865 record of 475,130 tons. Thereafter output rose steadily, passing 1,000,000 tons in 1891 and 1,500,000 tons in 1906 to reach a pre-war peak of 1,737,584 tons in 1910[88]. Estimates for the Ayrshire region suggest that output rose from 750,000 tons in 1894 to 1,640,000 tons in 1913[89].

The company's rate of growth exceeded both the Scottish and UK average. As well as direct coal sales the manufacture of coke also became a significant feature of the firm. In 1878 some 50,000 tons were converted to coke in the Gartsherrie region and by 1910 this had risen to 415,315 tons[90] to which Ayrshire production would have to be added. Identifiable investment in coking plant in the Gartsherrie region for four particular ventures between 1899 and 1914 involved £227,522, some of which was for the erection of Semet-Solvay by-product recovery ovens, which put the company in the forefront of coke production technology[91].

A critical constraint on Bairds and their main domestic rivals was that their reputation lay in the production of top quality foundry iron. This in large part explains their failure to build furnaces with productivity to match that of other countries. They could of course have made a radical break with their past and, so some have argued, switched to steel production. But this was far from being the obvious way forward that it superficially appears to be. The steel industry developed in Scotland in response to the demands of the shipbuilding industry. On the supply side pig-iron makers like the Bairds knew well that their own success had been built on the base of suitable raw materials and equally that their product was unsuitable for the new industry. They were fully aware of the unsuccessful outcome of the experiments conducted by the Bairds nephew Thomas Jackson at Coats[92] and subsequently conducted a series of trials at Gartsherrie to try to find a way of using Scottish raw materials for steel production[93]. In any event the criticism ignores the essential fact that until 1914 at least Bairds was a very successful and profitable business, based upon production of the premier brands Gartsherrie and Eglinton for the forge and foundry. Far from a blinkered and timid policy of plodding on as before the firm expanded along lines which harmonised with its existing strengths, extending its range of products when this became advantageous. As early as 1868 experiments in the production of hematite iron were carried out at Gartsherrie. These continued throughout the 1870s. From the mid 1880's onwards hematite production became a standard part of the companies production particularly in Ayrshire.

Despite the absence of company accounts there is clear evidence that the company achieved continuous healthy profits over the period 1878–1914, from which their investment programme was financed. Following the 1893 reorganisation as a limited company the dividend on ordinary shares averaged 33% for the first ten years with a peak of 80.75% in 1900, and in addition the firm repaid £400,000 of debentures and built up sizeable reserves. Figures survive for eight of the ten years between 1903 and 1913 and for these the average dividend on ordinary shares was 23%.[94] Such High dividends have been seen by Chandler[95] as evidence of a failure to invest, but in the Baird case it co-incided with continuing investment as for instance the sinking of the ultra modern Barony pit in 1906[96].

In reviewing from the standpoint of 1914 the history of the 'Bairds' over the previous century it is possible to see the shifting pattern in some of the broader themes.

Rubinstein in his analysis of the relative wealth generated by industry and commerce, and its application to the purchase of great landed estates has conceded that Scotland was something of an exception to his general conclusion[97]. It would be little exaggeration to say that the 'Bairds' almost singlehandedly account for that exception. In his list of millionaires 1809–1949 he gives William Baird (£2 mil.); James Baird (£1.2mil.); William Weir (£2.2mil.); and the disputed case of Alexander Fleming (£1.3mil.). Although falling below the £1 million threshold the others did leave substantial fortunes:[98]

Name	Year of Death	Confirmed Estate
Douglas Baird	1854	£224,864
Robert Baird	1856	£189,665
Alexander Baird	1860	£631,723
George Baird	1870	£918,457
David Wallice	1877	£359,538
Alexander Whitelaw	1879	£705,307
John Alexander	1895	£198,280
William Laird	1901	£313,648
Andrew McCosh	1916	£818,546
Jas. B. Thorneycroft	1918	£509,423

Although the Baird brothers did seek to found landed dynasties[99] the others conform more closely to the Rubenstein model. Most of them did buy land but typically it was purchased relatively late in life, and was generally the modest locus of a country house, rather than the vast rural acreages of the Bairds.

Whatever the personality traits of particular individuals – and some were naturally more comfortable in the public eye than others – to be a 'Baird' automatically conferred significant public standing. As the *Glasgow Herald* said of Alexander Whitelaw 'he was born to the purple'[100]. A particularly significant aspect of their public life was their contribution to Scottish politics, both local and national. At a local level from the time of Alexander Baird's membership of Glasgow Town Council in 1841 down to A K McCosh's third term as provost of Coatbridge in 1907–1909 the partners filled numerous offices in Lanarkshire and Ayrshire. Several of the first generation of partners stood for parliament but none of the later, which is consistent with Rubinstein's more general survey, and may be explained in terms of the partners enduring commitment to the firm or the greater demands of a parliamentary career or both. Yet their staunch conservatism was an enduring characteristic and a sketch of the 'Baird' involvement in national politics reveals an aspect which the narrower focus on the company fails to bring out. William and James each represented the Falkirk Burghs (which included Airdrie in the Baird heartland), the former in 1841–1846, and the latter in 1851–57. George was outraged when he in turn stood for the seat in 1857 and was defeated by James Merry a rival ironmaster. William was the first conservative to hold a burgh seat in Scotland after the Great Reform Act. In the 1860s James Baird's influence (he was described as 'the soul and spirit of Conservatism in the West')[101] was credited with securing Ayrshire for Colonel Alexander. Lockhart's return for Lanark in 1873 was also attributed to James Baird who led by example by voting at six different polling stations[102]. In 1874 the Baird name was decisive in Alexander Whitelaw's victory in Glasgow Central which made him the first conservative to represent the city since the Reform Act of 1832. In that same election the first of a new generation entered the lists when John Baird's son Alexander stood unsuccessfully for the Falkirk Burghs. A steady stream of Baird candidates then followed. In 1885 John Baird was elected for N. W. Lanarkshire and in 1886 John George Alexander Baird was elected for Glasgow having failed the previous year. In 1892 Graeme A Whitelaw succeeded to N. W. Lanarkshire though his brother Alexander was unsuccessful in N. E. Lanarkshire while a third brother was elected for Perth.

Some writers[103] have portrayed the sons of the industrial pioneers as passing through public school and Oxbridge and into landed society where they carefully buried any trace of their industrial roots. This was certainly not so in this case. No one in the press or on either side of the political divide was in any doubt that these were 'Baird' men. The company's Glasgow office was often used as their official address. Partners shared platforms with them and used their positions as constituency officials or chairmen of constituency associations to provide support. Without them the history of Conservatism in the industrial belt of Scotland would have been very different.

In a way the national church found itself facing a problem not dissimilar to that of the Tory party. It struggled throughout the century to make its presence felt in the rapidly expanding industrial towns. From public platforms, and at the General Assembly itself Baird partners constantly urged on the Kirk the need for more churches, and they themselves were responsible for building and/or endowing a large number of new churches. James who was particularly outspoken on the subject astonished the country by giving the some of £500,000 in 1873 to promote church extension[104]. In the related field of social concern and motivated in part by the same desire, namely to christianise the industrial masses[105] the partners gave thousands of pounds to provide schools, institutes, reading rooms. and public parks. At the time of the passage of the 1872 Education Act Baird schools were educating 5,000 children[106]

It is hardly surprising that set against the main themes of the debate the Baird evidence both supports and undermines by turns. As regards origins, most of the individuals and particularly the Bairds themselves lend support to Crouzet's claim that the concept of the 'self-made man' can meaningfully be applied to movement from the lower levels of the middle class[107]. On the other hand the evidence offers little support to Erickson's point that by the turn of the century boardrooms had become closed to the lower ranks[108]. Nor does it confirm Chandler's related point[109] that British firms failed to invest in future management. Forgie, already referred to, rose to become chairman in the 1930's where he was joined on the board by men such as Mark Brand, whose father William had started as a clerk in the Gartsherrie office in the 1860's rising to become company secretary.

James Baird has often been presented as an example of the classic entrepreneur embodying 'capitalist, financier, works manager, merchant, and salesman'[110], with the company after his death providing an example of 'new model' entrepreneurship in which an association (the bureaucratic dynasty) rather than an individual performed these roles. It may be nearer the mark, and be part of the explanation for the company's success to see it as an early example of entrepreneurship by association, albeit that the association was a single family.

Nor does the study lend support to the argument that Britain's economic decline can be attributed to a closed, anti-technological, self-perpetuating entrepreneurial group which neglected investment opportunities. Only if entrepreneurship is defined in terms of radical, pro-active, mould-breaking activity could questions be raised. In the context of the time they showed drive and imagination, made rational choices and earned the profits to prove it.

Yet for all that the firm may deserve a favourable report at least down to 1914, there remains something intriguing about its position and the role of its owners in nineteenth century Scotland – the enduring legacy, perhaps, of the founding family. The very rapidity of their rise to pre-eminence, without outside assistance, and the maintenance of that position, founded on a secure raw material base, favourable transport links and pre-eminent status in the market, made Bairds a law unto themselves. Their 'apartness' was underlined by their conservatism within a largely whig establishment. They neither needed nor sought alliances with others, and on the rare occasion on which they participated in a common scheme they either created it for their own purposes[111] or gave it weak and brief support[112]. The exhaustive study by Scott and Hughes[113] confirms that as late as 1904 the firm largely stood apart from the web of interlocking directorships which bound the Scottish business establishment together, except for the important railway links. In keeping with the strict cash settlement ethos of the brothers they neither borrowed nor loaned. They were in short a remarkably self-contained enterprise.

By 1914 the company was already slipping from centre stage, though few
– least of all the directors – would have agreed with such a proposition. It
survives today having been transformed into a textile firm – the kind of radical
entrepreneurial step of which the original brothers would surely have
approved.

REFERENCES

1. For an eloquent overview of the debate and a very substantial bibliography see
   P L Payne, *British Entrepreneurship in the Nineteenth Century* (London, 1988).
2. For a general survey see F Crouzet, *The First Industrialists: The Problem of Origins*
   (Cambridge, 1985), and for a more specialist study, C Erickson, *British Industrialist: Steel and Hosiery 1850–1950* (Cambridge, 1959)
3. H. Berghoff, 'Public Schools and the Decline of the British Economy', *Past and
   Present*, No. 129 (1990), pp. 148–167.
4. W D Rubinstein, *Men of Property* (London 1981). For an alternative view see
   F. M. L. Thompson, 'Life after death; how successful nineteenth-century
   businessmen disposed of their fortunes' *Econ. Hist. Rev.* XLIII, 1 (1990), pp.
   40–61
5. M. J. Daunton, ' "Gentlemanly Capitalism" and British Industry 1820–1914',
   Past and Present No. 122 (1989), pp. 119–158.
6. F. Crouzet, *The Victorian Economy* (London 1982), p. 412
7. In the sense used by Slaven and Checkland; see A. Slaven, and S. Checkland,
   Dictionary of Scottish Business Biography, 2 vols (Aberdeen 1986–9), p. 4.
8. The outline which follows has been drawn from R. D. Corrins, 'William Baird
   and Company, Coal and Ironmasters, 1830–1914', unpublished PhD Thesis
   (University of Strathclyde, 1974), and A. MacGeorge, *The Bairds of Gartsherrie*
   (Glasgow, 1875) which is essentially the 'ghosted' reminiscences of James Baird.
9. Although such ages may seem very young they were not uncommon. Alexander senior had assumed responsibility for his first farm at 20, and in later years
   the firm placed a number of people in senior positions in their early twenties.
   cf. the analysis of the steel industry representatives in the *Dictionary of Business
   Biography* in C. Shaw, 'British Entrepreneurs in Distribution and the Steel
   Industry', *Business History*, No. 3 (1989), pp. 48–60.
10. The fact that J B Neilson accompanied William Baird when he took official
    possession of Lochwood in name of his father in 1826 raises the possibility that
    Bairds were aware of Neilsons Hot-blast experiments and encouraged to invest
    in the industry in the light of them. Scottish Record Office (SRO), General
    Register of Sasines 1424.86
11. T. J. Byres, 'Entrepreneurship the Scottish Heavy Industries 1870–1900', in P.
    L. Payne ed., *Studies in Scottish Business History* p. 268; S. Nenadic, 'Business-
    men, the urban middle classes, and the "dominance" of manufacturers in
    nineteenth-century Britain', *Econ. Hist. Rev.*, XLIV, 1 (1991), pp. 66–85
12. MacGeorge, *The Bairds*, 35

13. *Ibid.*, 45–47
14. They had if anything an even greater difficulty in relating to the traditional legal and banking elite of Edinburgh. In the 1870's James Baird recalled with bitterness that the counsel who assured them that the Gartsherrie hot-blast apparatus was not within J. B. Neilson's patent and urged them to attack it in 1842 was the same man who as judge gave the decision against them in 1843.
15. The Glasgow Herald, 28 April 1834
16. A. Miller, *The Rise and Progress of Coatbridge and Surrounding Neighbourhood* (Glasgow, 1864), p. 30
17. MacGeorge, *Bairds*, p. 38 notes that the record (pre-1874) was 298,430 tons.
18. *The Scotsman*, 21 June, 1876
19. The original partners had equal shares of $1/5$th in W B & Co but when David and Robert joined this was reduced to $1/6$th and these two each received $1/12$th; all seem to have had equal shares in the Eglinton Iron Company.
20. MacGeorge, *The Bairds*, p. 73
21. Report of the trial Liquidators of the Western Bank v William Bairds Trustees, 1873
22. *Engineer*, 30 June, 1876
23. The creation and administration of efficient office systems should not however be minimised. In the early industrial period the survival of a business was often critically affected by shortcomings in basic administration.
24. *Glasgow Courier*, 9 August, 1856
25. 240 according to notes in Strathclyde Regional Archives T-MH 41, Fleming Trust Papers.
26. J. A. Schumpeter, *The Theory of Economic Development* (1934), pp. 74–83
27. Coleman D. C., 'Gentleman and Players', *Econ. Hist. Rev.*, 2nd. ser., XXVI (1973), pp. 92–116
28. Coatbridge Public Library Archives, WB&Co MSS 'Abstract of quantities'; *Trial NvB Opening Address*, p. 62
29. Miller, *Rise and Progress*, p. 62
30. Bateman J., *The Great Landowners of Great Britain and Ireland*, 4th. edn (London 1883) according to whom the gross annual rental was £59,000; J. S. Jeans, *Western Worthies* (Glasgow, 1873); F. H. Groome ed., *Ordnance Gazetteer of Scotland*, 6 vols. (Edinburgh, 1882–5)
31. SRO, SC 15/41/10, SC 36/48/43, SC 62/44/40, SC 36/48/48, SC 6/44/30, SC 5/41/22/, SC 62/44/50, SC 6/44/39. Rubinstein gives a figure of £2 mil for William and such a figure is quite possible. The value of John's estate is included partly for the sake of completeness but also because its size, although smaller than his brothers', still placed him among the very wealthy and was derived not so much from his initially modest Lanarkshire estate as from the generosity of his brothers, and was therefore as much the product of WB&Co as was theirs.
32. Scottish Record Office, SC 36/48/48 Testament of Alexander Baird
33. Coatbridge Public Library Archives, WB&Co MSS GLB 3/572 D Wallace to Madras College, 14 July 1848
34. *Ibid* 3/572, D Wallace to Smeaton 19 Oct 1850
35. *The Baillie*, 27 Nov 1872

36. *Colliery Guardian*, 16 Aug, 1862
37. Coatbridge Public Library Archives, WB&Co MSS GLB 23, 453, A. K. McCosh to Inspector of Mines, 30 March, 1872
38. Strathclyde University Archives, WB&Co MSS 'Production Abstracts Gartsherrie'
39. J. S. Jeans, 'The Pig Iron Trade of Scotland', *Practical Magazine* vol 1 (1873), pp. 241–248
40. D. Bremner, *The Industries of Scotland: Their Rise, Progress, and Present Condition* (Edinburgh, 1869), p. 36
41. Coatbridge Public Library Archives WB&Co MSS Private Letterbook Gartsherrie, A. Whitelaw to James Baird, 18 June 1871.
42. *Glasgow Herald*, 2 July, 1879
43. For one example of the case see D. H. Aldcroft, and H. W. Richardson, *The British Economy 1870–1914* (London 1969), p. 142
44. D. L. Burn, *The Economic History of Steelmaking 1867–1939: a Study in Competition*, (Cambridge, 1940)
45. T. H. Burnham, & G. C. Hoskins, *Iron and Steel in Britain 1870–1930*, (London, 1943)
46. T. J. Byres, 'The Scottish Economy during the Great Depression 1873–1896, with special reference to the Heavy Industries of the South-west', (unpublished B. Litt. thesis (University of Glasgow, 1962)
47. Payne, *British Entrepreneurship*, p. 7
48. Payne, *British Entrepreneurship*, p. 62
49. *The Iron and Coal Trades Review*, 17 May, 1895
50. *The Scotsman*, 21 Feb., 1949
51. The numbers in brackets are the number of years service at 1878
52. B. Elbaum, and W. Lazonick, eds., *The Decline of the British Economy* (Oxford, 1986), 2
53. Erickson, *British Industrialists*, p. 24
54. Erickson, *British Industrialists*, p. 42
55. Coatbridge Public Library Archives WB&Co MSS GLB 4/*passim*.
56. Coatbridge Public Library Archives, WB&C MSS GLB 33,305, 31 Jan 1881.
57. *The Glasgow Herald*, 21 June, 1910
58. *Colliery Guardian*, 18 Jan., 1880
59. Coatbridge Public Library Archives, WB&Co MSS GLB 36,718 A. K. McCosh to Charles Buckmaster, Science and Art Department, 11 May 1885.
60. Erickson, *British Industrialists, p. 42* notes that only eight of the families already in the steel industry provided a technical or scientific education for their son
61. Codicil to Weir's will quoted in *Glasgow Herald*, 10 Oct., 1913
62. Erickson, *British Industrialists*, 13.
63. Byres 'Scottish Economy'.
64. SRO, British Rail Records BR/CBH/1/1
65. *The Baillie*, 23 Feb., 1881
66. *The Scottish Ironmerchant*, 13 April, 1899 which spoke of his 'enthusiasm, sound judgement and great business capacity'; *Glasgow Herald* 24, 25, 27, 28, March, 7 April, 1899
67. *Ayrshire Post*, 20 April, 1923

68. *Transactions of the Mining Institute of Scotland* v44, 1923–4, p. 4
69. *The Baillie*, 24 March, 1912
70. Strathclyde University Archives, WB&Co MSS Gartsherrie Private Letter Book, A K McCosh to R Angus, 28 Sept., 1888
71. A. H. Sexton, 'Bye-Products of Blast Furnaces' *Proceedings of the Philosophical Society of Glasgow* XXVII (1895–6), pp. 122–35
72. A. H. Sexton, *The Metallurgy of Iron and Steel* (Manchester, 1902), pp. 194
73. Allen, A. 'On the Utilisation of Blast Furnace Creosote', *Report of the British Association for the Advancement of Science* (1887), p. 640
74. British Patent no. 4117 (1879)
75. J. Gillespie, 'Notes on the Evolution of Blast furnace Recovery Plant' *Transactions of the Institution of Engineers and Shipbuilders in Scotland* XXXIX (1895–6), pp. 187–194
76. Wilson, A., 'On the Generation and Application of Heating Gas and the Recovery of By-products', *Journal of the Society of the Chemical Industry II* (1883), pp. 453–461
77. The profits are calculated on the basis of figures given in W. S. Sutherland, 'On the most recent results obtained in the application and utilisation of Gaseous Fuel' *Journal of the Iron and Steel Institute* (1884 part I), 72–87, I. L. Bell, 'On the Use of Raw Coal in the Blast Furnace', *Journal of the Iron and Steel Institute* (1884 part I), pp. 13–59, and J. S. Jeans, *The Iron Trade of Great Britain* (1906), p. 25
78. United States Centennial Commission, International Exhibition 1876 *Reports and Awards, Group 1*, (1878)
79. Coatbridge Public Library Archives, WB&Co MSS. GLB 24,686 J. Alexander to Miller & Anderson, 21 Feb., 1873
80. *The Iron and Coal Trades Review*, 29 July, 1910
81. Strathclyde University Archives, WB&Co MSS, EIC Leasebook no.2 folio 513
82. *Engineer*, 24 Sept., 1886
83. Strathclyde University Archives, WB&Co MSS., Abstracts of Production Gartsherrie
84. Strathclyde University Archives, WB&Co MSS., Abstracts of Production Gartsherrie
85. *Engineering*, 12 May, 1893
86. Wilson, A. P., 'The Iron Ores of the Mediterranean Seaboard', *Journal of the Iron and Steel Institute*, vol.II (1894), 182
87. Coatbridge Public Library Archives, WB&Co MSS, 'Notes of Sevillan Deliveries 1896–7'
88. Output calculated from Strathclyde, WB&Co MSS., Valuation Books Gartsherrie, and Production Abstracts Gartsherrie.
89. For these calculations and the assumptions behind them see Corrins 'William Baird', p. 228
90. Strathclyde University Archives, WB&Co MSS., Production Abstracts Gartsherrie
91. Strathclyde University Archives, WB&Co MSS., Leasebook no. 7, folio 45
92. W. Cockey, 'Bessemer's Process for Manufacturing Iron' *Proceedings of the Philosophical Society of Glasgow* vol.IV (1855–6), pp. 81–2

93. W. Gorman, 'On producing Cast Steel or Ingot Iron from crude or pig iron', *Proceedings of the Philosophical Society of Glasgow* vol.XVI (1884–5), pp. 289–296

94. Coatbridge Public Library Archives, WB&Co MSS., Agenda Book 1893–1914, *passim*

95. A. D. Chandler, *Scale and Scope: Dynamics of Industrial Capitalism* (Cambridge, Mass., 1990), p. 390

96. *Rylands Directory of the Iron Steel and Colliery Trades*, 1908

97. Rubenstein, W. D., 'Debate "Gentlemanly Capitalism" and British Industry 1820–1914', *Past and Present*, No.132 (1991), pp. 150–170

98. Scottish Record Office, SC 15/41/10; SC 36/48/42; SC 62/44/40; SC 36/48/48; SC 62/44/50; SC 44/44/23; SC 36/48/89; SC 35/31/5; SC 36/48/136; SC 35/31/15; SC 6/44/83.

99. Robert, Alexander, William, and James all made elaborate provision in an attempt to ensure the survival of the Baird name. It is ironic therefore that it was the descendent of John, who was never in the firm, who finally gained a title, as Lord Stonehaven and whose present representative had to change his name from Baird on assuming the Earldom of Kintore.

100. *The Glasgow Herald*, 2 July, 1879

101. *Edinburgh Evening Courant*, 21 June, 1876

102. *The Glasgow News*, 21 June, 1876

103. L. Stone, and Stone, J. F. C., *An Open Elite? England 1540–1880* (Oxford, 1984), 411–2; M. J. Weiner, *English Culture and the Decline of the Industrial Spirit 1850–1980* (London 1981), p. 24

104. SRO, Court of Session Register of Deeds 1478,469 'The Baird Trust'. The trust, besides establishing an annual lecture, was created to promote the building of churches, but James Baird was careful to set conditions criticised by some as introducing piece rates into religion. Feelings were so strong that several presbyteries urged that the money be rejected.

105. But also no doubt by their antipathy to organised labour

106. *Edinburgh Evening Courant*, 21 June, 1876

107. Crouzet, '*First Industrialists*', p. 142

108. Erickson, '*British Industrialists*', p. 182

109. Chandler, '*Scale and Scope*', p. 286

110. C. Wilson, 'The Entrepreneur in the Industrial Revolution in Britain' *Explorations in Entrep. Hist.*, III, (1955) p. 132

111. As for instance when they decided to kill off the scrip system in the Glasgow iron market and establish the warrant system. *The Glasgow Herald*, 25 Nov., 1850

112. As when they effectively ended a price support agreement by withdrawing. H. W. Macrosty, *The Trust Movement in British Industry* (London, 1907), p. 60

113. J. Scott and M. Hughes, *The Anatomy of Scottish Capital* (Edinburgh, 1980), p. 30

5

Tombstone Territory: Granite Manufacturing in Aberdeen 1830–1914

TOM DONNELLY

Nestling between the rivers Dee and Don, Aberdeen from the late eighteenth century down to 1914 became the main centre of the Scottish granite industry. This was caused primarily by Aberdeen's economic growth which exerted a strong demand for a durable building stone to facilitate industrial, commercial and urban expansion, and it was found that the abundant local granite was ideally suited to this purpose. At first stone was extracted in and around the city at quarries such as Loanhead, Ferryhill, Cove, Torry and Rubislaw, but over time, especially with the growth of a thriving export trade in paving setts and building stone to London, these early workings could no longer satisfy demand and so the frontier line of quarrying was pushed northwards and westwards from Aberdeen. This was eased initially by the opening of the Inverurie canal, but more importantly by the arrival of the Great North of Scotland Railway into the Alford Valley, and by the 1860s granite was being actively quarried at Corrennie and Tillyfourie on the outskirts of the Grampians.

This chapter will concentrate on examining a spin-off from quarrying, namely granite manufacturing which emerged in the latter half of the nineteenth century. This sector of the industry can be split roughly into two subdivisions, monumental and building industry, but firms frequently crossed the boundary line to take advantage of relative shifts in demand. Indeed, some of the larger concerns had a foot permanently in both camps. Granite manufacturing fitted in well with Aberdeen's industrial tradition of small firms, as represented by its engineering, shipbuilding, shipping and fishing industries. Indeed, granite manufacturing's growth and development pattern reflects the problems faced generally by small concerns and so here emphasis will be laid upon the ease of entry into the industry and its accompanying high mortality rate, the sources of capital and diversity of investment as well as the interplay between domestic and export demand, leading to a succession of booms and slumps before the industry entered the initial phase of its long term decline after 1900.

I

The monumental and building slab side of the industry did not emerge until after 1830. Granite comes in a variety of colours and quality, but only that of the highest quality is suitable for polishing and it was not until the basic techniques of polishing were developed did this branch of the industry, known as granite manufacturing, experience a significant boost. In the eighteenth century it was well known that the stone was capable of taking on a fine polish. Indeed, in 1776 an Aberdeen jeweller, Colin Allan, opened a small workshop where he polished stone but how successful he was is not known. Twenty years later, Dr James Anderson commented that although 'granite was extremely susceptible to polishing, few people did so because of the expense involved'.[2] It was not until the 1820s that serious interest in granite polishing was renewed through the efforts of Alexander MacDonald. The son of a small farmer, MacDonald was born at Foss in Perthshire in 1794 and after completing his apprenticeship as a free-stone mason, he moved to Aberdeen at the age of twenty six and opened a stonecutting yard in the city's Denburn district. There he made hearthstones, mantel pieces, Turin head-stones and other small pieces in marble.

In 1829 examples of granite which had been polished in Egypt during the reign of Ramesis II were displayed in London and MacDonald made the long journey from Aberdeen to examine them. On his return he began a series of experiments with various substances and tried to polish small pieces of granite by hand, but this proved such a long and expensive process that MacDonald turned to the idea of using machines. By 1832 he had succeeded in developing a steam-powered polishing device, driven by an engine borrowed from the Aberdeen Comb Works. What MacDonald's exact methods and early devices were like is not known, but it is unlikely that the process differed much from that used in the later part of the century. The first stage was known as *shotting* in which sea sand was rubbed onto the stone until a flat surface was achieved. After this *emery sand* was applied in a similar fashion which gave the stone a very dull polish. The third and final stage, known as *rougeing*, involved rubbing the granite with oxide of iron for about four hours after which a reflection began to appear in the stone. Throughout the whole process water was continually poured over the granite to reduce friction. MacDonald's early experiments were justified by results. In late 1832 he sent a specimen of his work to Kensal Green Cemetery in London where it was acclaimed by the local sculptors and monumental masons. Orders for similar stones were quickly forthcoming and gradually granite manufacturing began to emerge in Aberdeen's east end. MacDonald is also accredited with the subsequent invention of the three main polishing machines, the *lathe*, the *pendulum* and the *waggon* which dominated the industry until the late 1880's when the *Jenny Lind* polisher was invented and introduced quickly in the industry.[3]

Before granite can be polished it has to be cut, carved and shaped to the required size by a stonemason before being passed on to the polishers. At first MacDonald and his immediate contemporaries were content to cut and carve with the fine points and chisels which had been introduced to Aberdeen in 1818 by free-stone masons from the South of Scotland who had migrated to the North East in search of employment, but while suitable for ordinary building work, these tools, because of their lack of precision, were not entirely suited to monumental masonry. The problem of precision cutting was made much easier with the advent of the *patent-axe* in the 1830s. Originating in the United States, this tool, known colloquially as the *bush hammer*, was introduced to Aberdeen by James Hadden of Persley, a quarrymaster and one times provost of the City, who had first acquired one on a trip to New York. At some point in the early thirties, Hadden gave his axe to a local builder named Milne, who at that time was engaged in construction work in Aberdeen. Milne experimented with it, but whether through lack of skill or some other reason he cast it aside as useless. By some means it passed into Alexander MacDonald's hands and he discovered that it was ideally suited to monumental carving. MacDonald ordered more of a similar design and these proved so effective that all the City's monumental masons adopted them within a short time. The bush hammer remained the main cutting tool in monumental carving until the coming of pneumatic tools and sand blasting in the nineties and was still in common use down to the Second World War. Although the manufacturing side of the industry had its roots in monumental masonry, it very slowly acquired a small building slab section. Polished granite proved ideal for decorating the fronts of public and commercial buildings, but this sector remained small until the late nineteenth century.[4]

II

Although MacDonald's early products were successful, the growth of demand, as will be discussed in greater detail later, was slow. In 1847 there were only ten firms listed as granite manufacturers in Aberdeen and by 1855

Table 1: Imports of Foreign Granite at Aberdeen Harbour 1895–1914

Year	Tons	Year	Tons
1895	11,111	1905	26,286
1896	10,340	1906	23,717
1897	13,824	1907	24,942
1848	12,619	1908	27,396
1899	10,213	1909	27,305
1900	11,861	1910	25,467
1901	20,607	1911	30,880
1902	16,280	1912	23,740
1903	18,280	1913	22,496
1904	24,119	1914	19,735

(*Source: Aberdeen Harbour Board: Abstract of Accounts 1880–1914*)

the number had dropped to seven. Indeed, it was only with the emergence of the American market for tombstones after the Civil War, that the number of firms grew significantly, rising to forty six in 1880, to eighty one in 1894 before peaking at ninety six in 1908 by which time the industry had entered its long drawn out decline. In all, just over two hundred concerns manufactured granite between 1847 and 1914. Of these, forty two per cent enjoyed a life span of less than ten years with thirty per cent going out of business in less than five years. A further seventeen per cent endured no more than twenty years with a final ten per cent surviving more than fifty years. There appears to be little correlation between a firm's date of foundation and its longevity, but nevertheless at any one time there was always a hard core of well established firms that provided the industry with an element of stability.[5]

The absence of satisfactory business records makes it extremely difficult to estimate either the inputs or outputs of granite for the industry as a whole and more especially for individual concerns. At first the quarry masters obtained their raw materials from either the grey granite quarries of Aberdeen and its neighbouring hinterland or from the red granite quarries at Peterhead. By the 1880's it was becoming evident that local deposits of polishing stone were dwindling and to meet the immediate and growing shortage of stone, new sources of supply were sought. At first stone was brought from Orkney, Sutherland and Argyll, especially from the Ben Guachan area, but it was of poor quality and in no way solved the problem. The answer lay in importing stone from Sweden, Finland, Norway, Germany and even Russia. Initially foreign granites were imported in small quantities, the stone being carried as ballast in the cargo and timber boats that plied between the North East corner of Scotland and the Baltic. By the early nineties the import trade had grown rapidly and had fallen into the hands of two shipping firms, Davidson and

Son and Stewart and Son, neither of which had any direct connection with the granite industry[6]. It was felt by many of the manufacturers that these two exercised a near monopoly over the trade and so in 1896 a group of prominent manufacturers formed a co-operative company, for the express purpose of importing granite. The initial share capital of the Aberdeen Granite Supply Company was £20,000 in ten thousand one pound ordinary shares and an equivalent sum in preference shares, which were taken up rapidly by the granite masters[7]. The 'Supply' as the new company was called quickly drove its rivals out of the market and stocks of foreign granite were built up from imports.

So powerful did the Supply become that it was approached by several of the local quarrymasters and was invited to act as a selling agent for them. By 1914 only the Rubislaw Granite Company in Aberdeen did not avail itself of the facilities provided in the Supply's King St Warehouse[8]. The end result was that by 1901, some fifty per cent of all the granite cut in the yards came from Northern Europe and nine years later this figure stood at sixty per cent. Foreign stone came in a wide variety of colours adding significantly to the greys, reds and pinks of Aberdeenshire. From Sweden and Norway came blue, green and red granites, from Germany grey stone, from Finland a selection of blue and greys and from Russia grey, green and black stone. These could not be passed as genuine Aberdeen granite so no doubt with an eye on the market because, apart from colour, no layman could possibly detect the difference between native and foreign stone, the Aberdonians gave Scotish or Scottish sounding names to imported stone. Thus, there was 'Balmoral Red' 'Bon Accord Black' 'Birkhall Grey' and 'Glencoe Red'.[9]

From the quantity of stone imported, a very rough and crude estimate of the total input of stone can be made. Earlier it was stated that between 1901 and 1910 foreign granites accounted for between fifty and sixty per cent of all the stone used in the yards and, using the simple import figures it seems likely that the total input of stone between the turn of the century and 1914 varied between thirty and forty thousand tons per annum. Output estimates are equally difficult because of the highly individualistic nature of the final product. The wastage of stone was high, reaching up to between fifty and sixty per cent in the cutting of a Latin Cross, for example. This is an extreme case, but no matter what type of monument or slab was being cut their was a considerable wastage. On this basis though it is likely that total tonnage output for the same years hovered around fifteen to twenty thousand tons a year.[10]

The industrial tradition of Aberdeen in the nineteenth century was one of fairly small to medium sized firms: even in their heyday the local shipyards never employed more than two and a half thousand men. The decennial census are unhelpful as a source of information because they simply list all masons, failing to distinguish between monumental and building masons in the yards and those employed in straight forward building construction and repair work. Nevertheless at its peak at the turn of the century granite manufacturing employed around two and half thousand men, but with the almost immediate onset of decline the work force slowly dwindled and by 1914 it had fallen to 1,851 operatives.[11] The costs of entry to the industry varied. Until 1880 a yard could be opened for as little as £100. All that was required was a piece of ground that could be fenced off and a hand crane for lifting the stone. Indeed that was all that Alexander Robertson had when he opened his King St Yard in 1878 as all cutting, carving and polishing of stone was effected by hand. With the growth of mechanisation in the 1880's and 1890's, costs began to rise and around £300 was required to open a yard with very basic equipment. In 1912 David Morren purchased James Dunn's yard in Holland Street for £400 and in 1915 John Crichton brought James Chalmers yard for £305[12]. As yards varied considerably in size it is difficult to say what a typical granite yard looked like during this period. At one extreme there were the large yards of Alexander MacDonald, of Bower & Florence and of Charles MacDonald which each employed in excess of a hundred men, while at the other end of the spectrum there were those which struggled on with a dozen or so men. In between these was a group of firms giving work to between thirty and forty operatives. This group, around 1900, would have possessed a number of common characteristics. Their equipment was a mixture of new and second hand, consisting of perhaps one hand or steam-powered crane, one or possibly two sawing machines and two or possibly three polishing machines, chosen from the waggons, pendulums, verticals and Linds that were available to them as well as some pneumatic tools. Thus it was common to find masons relying on a combination of traditional mauls, chisels, bush hammers and pneumatic tools in their every day work. Similarly hand polishing survived because many of the surfaces were too intricate to work by machine and there was no other effective way of polishing them. Indeed many stones were polished both by hand and by machine because of their individualistic design.[13]

The impression emerging is that investment patterns in the industry were haphazard. A new saw would be acquired then a polishing machine and so on. New or second hand equipment was acquired only when firms could afford it. Indeed in many of the medium to larger sized concerns new, old and second hand machines operated alongside each other for many years. The 1890s, however, saw a high wave of investment hit the industry for the first time. This was caused by changing markets which necessitated a drive to reduce labour costs and to boost productivity in an increasing competitive situation as new entrants piled into the trade at the lower end of the market. The American market, as will be shown, with its demand for small, but elaborately carved tombstones declined, forcing many firms to look to the English and Imperial markets as alternatives. The size of stone popular in these markets was much larger than that exported to America and so took much longer to cut, carve and polish. To speed up productivity, therefore, many firms turned to pneumatic tools and sand blasting to cut costs. Similarly, the expansion of the slab trade in polished building fronts encouraged the use of powered saws and of Jenny Linds which were ideal for polishing flat surfaces. A further impetus to investment was perhaps the experience which many of the masters had gained through working for periods in the United States where the yards were highly mechanised. Arthur Taylor, Charles MacDonald, William Taggart, Robert Gibb and William Edwards were among the leaders in the mechanisation process and all had worked for periods in America, where, no doubt, they had seen pneumatic tools and Linds at work and were anxious to reap the same benefits for themselves. Lastly, the Operative Masons and Granite Cutters' Union proved most co-operative and encouraged mechanisation, provided only its members were allowed to operate the new machines. By 1900 the surge of investment had come to an end and it is fair to say that down to 1914 there was almost no new investment in the industry.[14]

There is no doubt that technological advances added to improvements in productivity levels, but differences in yard size bore little relationships to the varying levels of efficiency that existed between firms. The basic difference between the larger and smaller firms lay in the numbers and quantity of capital equipment employed, but in practice a small firm could function just as efficiently as a larger one. The basic reason for this was that in running a granite yard, layout was of prime importance.

The working area of a yard was defined as the area covered by the cranes or pulleys. The larger yards, having a greater area, usually had overhead cranes or pulleys for shifting granite, while the smaller yards, arranged in a square with sawing machines on one side, polishing on another and the stonecutting on a third could use a derrick placed in the middle to move the stone from one side to the other. Indeed it was not easy to add to the size of a granite yard without unduly increasing handling costs. Size, therefore, was not synonymous with efficiency for a small yard with strategically based equipment could operate as expertly as any of its larger rivals. Similarly, although the output of larger concerns exceeded that of the smaller, there is nothing to suggest that economies of sales were enjoyed. Regardless of size, granite yards did not carry large stocks of raw material. To have been truly effective this would have involved carrying too large and expensive a volume of too many different types of stone. Demand for stone varied so much from order to order that the masters did not want to be left holding stocks of stone which simply tied up capital. Thus stock piling of finished or semi-finished products was avoided except in times of dull trade when attempts were made to hang on at least to key workers to stop them from drifting out of the industry. Essentially the industry was dominated by craftsmen who purchased the different types of stone only when required to meet particular orders.[15]

Table 2: Exports of Aberdeen Tombstones to the United States 1880–1914

Year	£	Year	£
1880	12,343	1896	55,452
1881	14,344	1897	36,915
1882	13,745	1898	26,709
1883	18,807	1899	18,807
1884	25,930	1900	19,471
1885	27,542	1901	18,135
1886	33,040	1902	19,910
1887	41,703	1903	20,859
1888	49,950	1904	22,300
1889	54,842	1905	20,760
1890	81,767	1906	26,536
1891	71,360	1907	33,843
1892	69,098	1908	33,735
1893	89,341	1909	33,005
1894	63,938	1910	35,082
1895	60,777	1911	29,517
		1912	21,459

Source: Daily Free Press: Aberdeen Journal Annual Trade Report 1884–1912

III

As hinted at earlier, the growth of demand for polished granite was slow. During the industry's formative years demand for polished granite memorials and tombstones came primarily the local Aberdeen and London markets, but sadly there is no way of calculating either the quantities or value of the stone involved. The advent of the Bush Hammer did lead to orders for statues, but these were few and far between. The first statue cut was that of the fifth and last Duke of Gordon which was cut in MacDonald's yard and erected in Aberdeen's Golden Square. The figure was carved by MacDonald himself, Adam Mitchell, a mason in his employ and by an apprentice, Robert Ferguson, who became a partner in the firm after MacDonald's death. Other decorative works executed in this period included the sarcophagus of Prince Albert and the Fountains in Trafalgar Square[16]. The most important source of demand before 1880 was the American market after the Civil War in 1865 when the stonecutters found new outlets for their memorials in the cities on the Eastern seaboard of the United States. American demand came primarily from the wealthier classes in Boston and New York who considered it fashionable to commemorate their dead with Aberdeen headstones and, also, from Scots exiles who for sentimental or other reasons wanted to erect a Scottish monument to their departed. The level of craftsmanship in the Aberdeen stones was considered superior to its American counterpart and presumably this went some way to boosting sales. More importantly, the high cost of labour in the United States made hand-cut monuments very expensive and this gave the Scots a competitive advantage. Though the reasons why the fashion for Aberdeen tombstones spread to the United States are unclear, it must be remembered that there were considerable numbers of Aberdeen quarrymen and stonecutters working in the granite quarries of New York and Vermont during the 1860's and no doubt they helped to spread the virtues of their native product. Again nothing is known of the quantities of granite exported to America until 1880 when they were valued at £12,000 and America was considered as the main source of demand.[17]

Export to America as Table 2 shows rose until 1890 when they stood at £81,767. Shortly thereafter they began to decline and by 1901 had dwindled to £18,135. The major long term influence on the falling off in America demand was the emergence of native industry which by 1890 had reached a level of craftsmanship equal to that attained by its Aberdonian tutors. Moreover, with the greater degree of mechanisation that occurred in the American yards in the late eighties and early nineties, it was generally recognised that productivity there was so much higher than in Aberdeen it reversed the latter's previous competitive advantage. A further reason was that from the 1890s the American industry was protected by high tariffs. The first of these was the McKinlay tariff which was imposed in 1892, placing a duty of forty per cent ad valoren all imported tombstones. Fearing that this was merely the prelude to even more stringent measures, the Aberdonians embarked on an almost frantic rush to export as much as possible to the United States. A year later there was renewed speculation on the possibility of a further increase in tariffs and such was the drive to boost shipments before the new duties could be imposed that exports reached a peak figure of £89,341 in 1893. In the event it was not until 1897 that the Dingley Tariff took effect, raising the ad valoren duty on imports to fifty per cent[18]. The first tariff was a body blow to the Scots who had cut their profits to the margin just to stay in the market after the McKinlay tariff, and the second forced them to withdraw, but this was a long drawn out process.

Even before the levying of the McKinlay tariff profits in the American trade had begun to dwindle. The basic reason for this lay in the trade's organisation. There is no clear evidence on how the mechanism of the export trade evolved, but it is possible that Aberdeen masons returning home brought orders with them and that the trade developed from these informal contacts. A second hypothesis is that the Americans themselves visited Aberdeen every so often and placed orders after taking a series of estimates from different firms.

Table 3: Shipments of Polished Granite from Aberdeen Harbour 1880–1913

Year	Tons	Year	Tons
1880	2,009	1897	8,982
1881	1,883	1898	9,349
1882	2,485	1899	9,590
1883	2,607	1900	9,485
1884	2,843	1901	8,693
1885	3,488	1902	8,994
1886	3,659	1903	9,280
1887	3,787	1904	10,130
1888	3,713	1905	9,794
1889	4,547	1906	9,285
1890	4,451	1907	9,875
1891	5,333	1908	9,369
1892	6,280	1909	8,881
1893	5,915	1910	9,486
1894	6,442	1911	9,105
1895	7,494	1912	9,020
1896	8,524	1913	7,795

Source: *Aberdeen Harbour Board Abstract of Accounts 1880–1914*

Nevertheless, by 1880 control of the export trade lay almost entirely in the hands of the agents who conducted it on behalf of the American importers. The function of the agents was to secure orders at the lowest possible price for their principals. The most important of these was W. C. Townsend, who, after acting for several Boston concerns, eventually opened a yard of his own and competed in the UK market when the American trade fell off. Another was Dr John Rose, a lecturer in medicine at Aberdeen University, who had served his time as a stonecutter and had worked as a joineryman mason both in Aberdeen and Vermont. Unlike others, he did not use his American earnings to go into business for himself, but pursued a medical career and yet maintained his link with granite by acting as an agent for a Boston firm.[19] So strong did the grip of the agents become during the late eighties that they were able to dictate terms to the local manufacturers. This they could do because of the high numbers of small and medium sized firms all trying to compete in a market which was not large enough to sustain all of them. It was usual for an agent to visit a number of firms and seek estimates for cutting and polishing particular types of headstones, and as there were many firms chasing the orders, prices were cut to the bone and only the lowest tenders were accepted. Indeed, agents frequently played firms off against each other by quoting prices to enforce further competitive reductions. Furthermore, many of the small firms were extremely short of capital and agents were prepared to make advances in return for very low prices and this enabled the agents to tighten their grip on the weaker firms. Moreover, even if an order was completed it did not necessarily follow that the agents accepted it. Monuments for America were normally cut during the winter months and shipped either to Boston or New York in the spring. About the end of February the agents visited the yards to inspect the memorials and if even minor flaws were found, the stone was rejected as substandard and payment in full was refused. It was then common practice for a reduced offer to be made at a much lower price. Desperate for cash many of the stonecutters had little choice to accept and sell at a price barely covering production costs.[20]

As early as 1888 the Granite Association which had been formed to look after the trade's collective interests, was deeply concerned about the situation and invited its members to suggest ways of wresting controls away from the agents. Charles MacDonald of the Jute St Granite Works thought that a possible answer lay in setting up a 'selling agency' in America which could act on behalf of the Association. This was rejected by the others as being too expensive and impractical[21]. Undaunted, MacDonald himself set up an agency in Ohio in 1891, but with his untimely death a year later it closed. In view of the individualistic nature of the trade, it was not thought practical to control the export trade tightly. Nevertheless, in 1895 the Aberdeen Granite Association attempted to exert some degree of influence when it secured an agreement with the Boston Wholesale Granite Association, giving the latter a monopoly over exports from Aberdeen. This was achieved too late to have any appreciable impact on the situation; the trade continued to decline and the agreement was terminated by mutual consent in 1900.[22]

Gradually the Aberdonians withdrew from the American market and sought alternative outlets. In 1899 the *Daily Free Press* commented on the demise of the American market as follows:

> No one finds any great regret amongst the merchants for the profit in it was small and over the years the manufacturers have been easing themselves out of it.[23]

The main alternative markets lay within Britain with small quantities of stone being exported to Europe and the British Empire. Many of the monumental masons began to switch their attention to supplying the English market, while others took advantage of the building boom at the end of the century and began to make polished slabs of granite to decorate the fronts of buildings such as bank and insurances offices. Stones bound for East coast Scottish and English markets were normally dispatched by sea from Aberdeen harbour with only a tiny amount going from Aberdeen by rail to West coast destinations. Table 3 indicates that shipments of polished granite, inclusive of monuments and polished fronts rose steadily from the early eighties before peaking in 1904 before falling back.

Although the data available do not distinguish between monuments and slabs the *Daily Free Press* commented in 1898 that the volume of slabs shipped from the harbour exceeded that of monuments and that the growth in the frontal trade more than offset the financial losses incurred in the American market[24].

In the opening years of the twentieth century the building boom came to an end. This did not have any immediate effect on the building masons because so great was the backlog of orders that activity in the yards remained high until 1904. The subsequent decline afterwards was offset to a limited extent by a very brief inexplicable upswing in exports of tombstones to France, Belgium and above all the United States. Why the American trade revived is difficult to determine. Exports to America in 1901 stood at only £18,135, but by 1910 had revived to £35,082 before falling off again. A possible explanation might be that the likelihood of possible tariff reform in the United States, coupled with a weakening UK market, caused some of the Aberdeen mason to try to re-establish themselves in the American market despite existing tariff levels. It is perhaps significant that after the failure of the Payne Aldrich Bill in Congress to effect tariff reduction in 1909 that exports fell sharply. This second falling away of American demand left the industry dependent on the domestic market, which enjoyed a brief upswing in demand for polished fronts from 1910 to 1912 before falling back again. Finally by the onset of war in 1914, the industry was falling into deep recession.[25]

The market situation was more serious than conveyed by the above figures and market analysis. The basic truth is that from the turn of the century there were too many firms trying to compete in a market insufficiently strong to support all of them. Indeed from 1904 one can detect the beginnings of the industry's long drawn out decline as press report after report referred to the problems of continuous and ruinous price cutting and of excess capacity in the industry. The Aberdeen Granite Association was a weak body and did not even discuss rationalisation until after the First World War, choosing instead to place its faith in price control to help its weaker members. By 1910 price competition had become such a serious problem that the Association was asked to end the anarchy that existed in the industry, and so minimum price lists were issued to all members who were asked to adhere to them. The efficacy of price lists depends upon the willingness of individual firms to stick to them. This certainly was not the case in Aberdeen. The lists had little impact; between 1910 and 1912 twenty-nine firms were known to be defying the list and those included well-known firms such as Bower and Florence. James Pope and James Hadden. Fines and warnings had little impact and price cutting continued as a way of life in the industry into the post-war period. The net result was that by 1914 the industry had already embarked on a downwards path from which it never recovered[26].

IV

In general the granite manufacturers came from Aberdeen's labouring classes; some from agricultural backgrounds in the neighbouring countries and a few from other parts of Scotland. There was only the occasional entrant from the business or commercial classes. Of four main avenues of upwards mobility, moving from journeyman to master, the first was the easiest. This was for a journeyman to save the cost of opening a yard from earnings before branching out on his own. Some became yard foremen first and after gaining experience at this level proceeded to set up their own concerns. James Rust, for example, who ultimately became Provost of Aberdeen, was the son of a farm overseer at Danestone. The family moved to the city where Rust served his apprenticeship in James Milne's yard. In 1897 at the age of twenty seven he was appointed foreman and five years later he left to form his own yard with John Alexander, another stonecutter. The capital of the new firm was £300 of which Rust contributed £100 and Alexander £200. Each partner was allowed an interest of five per cent on his capital and their respective wages were not to exceed £1 per week[27]. Partnerships such as these were common and many firms such as Buchan and Anderson, Chalmers and Fleming, Robertson and Hunter, Westland and Anderson and Christie and Gordon originated through such arrangements[28].

After 1865 a common method of raising the necessary capital was for a mason to emigrate to America and earn enough through working in the granite quarries of Ohio, Vermont, Indiana and New York State. Because of their skill Aberdeen masons were in great demand during the early days of the American granite industry where they were often employed as instructors at a rate of four and a half dollars a day. In this way it did not take long to save the necessary capital before returning to Aberdeen and, according to the *Daily Free Press*, the great majority of firms entering the industry between 1870 and 1884 were financed by American earned capital. Robert Gibb, for instance, began his career as a mason in Robert Cruickshanks' yard where he became not only yard foreman, but a recognised expert in granite cutting. Like others he tried his fortune in America only to return to Scotland in 1872 and open the Excelsior Granite Works in King St which became one of the largest in the city[29]. Charles MacDonald was a native of Dyce who followed a similar pattern by going to America to join his brothers in the Barré quarries in Vermont, but came back to Aberdeen in 1872 and began a thriving trade in exporting memorials to Boston. William Edwards, too, 'crossed the pond' to work at Dix Island quarries near New York before returning to set up his own concern in St Clair St[30].

Capital from other sources was rare. There is one known case of a business-man entering into partnership with a mason. This occurred in 1870 when John Florence gave John Bower the capital to set up the firm of Bower and Florence in an alliance of technical skills and capital. Similarly, there are only two examples of professional men becoming actively involved in a firm with both becoming partners is Alexander MacDonald's. The first was the New Deer born William Leslie, who after serving an apprenticeship as a stonemason became an architect and was responsible for designing many public buildings in the North East such as Aberdeen's North Kirk end Craibstone House. It was in 1834 that he joined MacDonald and with him designed the previously mentioned statue of the Duke of Gordon. In 1852, however, he severed his link with MacDonald to pursue a political career and became Provost of Aberdeen. The second was Sidney Field who was both an artist and an architect. Field became a partner in the firm after MacDonalds death in 1867 and for many years thereafter it was he who provided the firm with artistic and aesthetic new designs in tombstones. Indeed many of Field's original designs were still being used in Aberdeen long after the firm itself disappeared.[31]

The rewards of entrepreneurship in granite manufacturing were not great and it is extremely doubtful if the switch from journeyman to master had any significant short or even medium term impact on the life style of the great majority of the masters, but this is only to be expected in an industry where the incidence of business failure was relatively high. The yards provided a steady income, but in many cases this was not much more than could be earned by a skilled tradesman or yard manager. The majority of the masters continued to live in the east end or Rosemount districts of the city for a considerable period after they had changed station, only moving to the more affluent and salubrious parts of the west end after their position had been consolidated, while some remained all their lives in the working class areas; Alexander Robertson continued to live in a tenement flat until his death in 1941.[32]

Certainly as the industry developed and became established in Aberdeen's industrial profile, the granite masters were able to enjoy a degree of social prestige through being identified with the stone which was, and still is, the symbol of the city both at home and abroad and this may have eased their way up the social ladder. Like many business men in small cities, local politics proved attractive to the manufacturers and, no doubt being a Councillor or a Ballie must have added weight to a man's prestige in what was a relatively small community. As emphasised, Aberdeen was synonymous with granite and it is possible that this source of identification acted as a spur to participate in the City's public affairs, for many of the granite masters were of the opinion that the City's reputation owed much to the efforts of the granite industry. Moreover, the masters were self made men and local politics were probably the ideal platform for gaining an enhanced position in society. From the late nineteenth century granite manufacturers were extremely prominent in the Town Council. William Taggart and James Rust both became provosts with the former achieving national fame through his recruiting drives in the North East during the First World War when he succeeded in raising an artillery brigade, known as 'Taggart's Own' for which he received a knighthood and an Honorary LL.D from Aberdeen University. Besides these others such as William Boddie, Patrick Stewart, William Edwards Jnr and Henry Hutcheon all held high office in the Council with Boddie gaining a considerable reputation as a magistrate. John Fyfe, the only quarrymaster to integrate backwards into granite manufacturing, was evident in local affairs. In 1900 he was invited to stand for Parliament as a Conservative because of his strong support for Chamberlain's policies on tariff reform, but he had to decline the offer because of his advanced age. Nevertheless, he served as a Justice of the Peace from 1899 until his death in 1906[33].

V

Granite manufacturing exhibited many of the features commonly found in small firms. It is doubtful if the industry would have emerged at all had it not been for locational factors such as the proximity of the quarries as a source of raw materials, excellent transport links from Aberdeen and a pool of skilled labour in the city. Moreover, the growth of both domestic and overseas markets and the low levels of technology required for entry encouraged men of a high level of technical competence, but with little capital to set up in business for themselves. This lack of capital or of easy access to it affected the smaller monumental masons badly, forcing them into the hands of American agents, and was doubtless an important factor in explaining the industry's high mortality rate. Similarly, it was ease of entry that exacerbated the price competition in the industry after the end of the building boom at the turn of the century which occasioned the onset of the industry's long term demise as firms fought for survival in a diminishing market.

REFERENCES

1. T Donnelly, 'The Developments of the Aberdeen Granite Industry 1750–1939', (Unpublished PhD thesis, University of Aberdeen 1975)
2. *Aberdeen Journal*, 3 Jan 1776; J Anderson, *General View of the of the Counties of Aberdeen and Kincardine*, (Edinburgh 1794), p. 31.
3. J Diack, *The Rise and Presence of the Aberdeen Granite Industry*, (Bradford on Avon 1948), p. 88.

4. *Ibid*, pp. 88–93, G. W. Muir, 'On Granite Working', *Journal of the Society of Arts* (May 1886), p. 471.
5. Post Office Directories of Aberdeen 1847–1914; *Daily Free Press*, 31 December 1884.
6. *Daily Free Press*, 31 December 1885.
7. Kings College Library: *Aberdeen Stock Exchange and Stock Exchange Association Collection*, Mss 2756/57, The Aberdeen Granite Supply Company 1896.
8. *Daily Free Press*, 28 December 1898.
9. W. Grant, *Reminiscences*, (Dotesios Press, Bradford on Avon 1948), pp. 7–9.
10. Donnelly 'Aberdeen Granite Industry', pp. 172–173.
11. *Decennial Census* 1851–1911; *Aberdeen Today 1907* (Aberdeen 1907), pp. 97–104.
12. Records of James Rust and Co; Minute of agreement between James Rust and John Alexander 1902; Private Communication Mr D. M. Morren; Title Deed referring to the sale of James Chalmer's yard to John Crichton in 1915. I am grateful to Messrs C. & P. H. Chalmers & Co, Advocates, Golden Square, Aberdeen for providing access to their records.
13. Donnelly, 'Aberdeen Granite Industry', pp. 181–189.
14. *Ibid*.
15. H. Hamilton, 'The Granite Industry' by M. Fogarty ed, *Further Studies in Industrial Organisation*, (Methuen, London 1948), p. 195.
16. Diack, *Aberdeen Granite Industry*, pp. 111–113.
17. *Daily Free Press*, 31 December 1884.
18. *Ibid.*, 30 December 1890; *Records of the Aberdeen Granite Association*: Minute Book of Directors Vol II, 24 March 1893, 28 December 1893, 25 December 1897.
19. *Ibid.*, 31 December 1884, 31 December 1885, 26 December 1904.
20. *Daily Free Press*, 25 December 1886, 26 December 1893.
21. 'Obituary to Charles McDonald', *In Memoriam*, (Aberdeen 1892), pp. 155–156.
22. Aberdeen Granite Association: Minute Book of Directors, Vol II, 15 April 1895, 31 December 1900.
23. *Daily Free Press*, 26 December 1899.
24. *Ibid.*, 28 December 1898.
25. *Ibid.*, 26 December 1904, 26 December 1905, 24 December 1907, *Aberdeen Journal*, 25 December 1910, 20 December 1914.
26. Aberdeen Granite Association, Minute Book of Directors, Vol IX, 19 May 1911, 7 June 1911, 20 Sept 1911, 11 Oct 1911, 10 November 1911, Vol X, 23 Feb 1912.
27. Records of James Rust and Co: Minute of Agreement between James Rust and John Alexander 1902.
28. Post Office Directories of Aberdeen 1847–1914.
29. *Daily Free Press*, 31 December 1884, 'Obituary to Robert Gibb', *In Memoriam*, (Aberdeen 1907), p. 57; 'Obituary to Charles McDonald', *In Memoriam* (Aberdeen 1893), pp. 155–158; 'William Edwards', *Quarrymanager's Journal*, July 1931.
30. 'Obituary to Charles McDonald', *In Memoriam*, (Aberdeen 1893), pp. 155–158; 'William Edwards' *Quarrymanager's Journal* July 1931.

31. Diack, *Aberdeen Granite Industry*, pp. 111–113.
32. Donnelly, 'Aberdeen Granite Industry', pp. 232–237.
33. Diack, *Aberdeen Granite Industry*, pp. 117–119; *Aberdeen Journal*, 19 July 1907.

6

Electricity Supply, Electrical Engineering and the Scottish Economy in the Inter-War Years

JOHN C. LOGAN

The economic development of the British economy in the period between the two World Wars has been generally observed and cyclical movements in the economy have been subject to detailed examination[1]. Scottish economic development in this same period has not been neglected, but the more acceptable and more widely read studies concerning the Scottish economy in the inter-war period have tended to be included in histories of Scotland over a much wider time-scale. Moreover, the focus of attention tends to be placed on the difficulties and problems facing the staple heavy industries of coal, iron and steel and shipbuilding and the traditional reliance of Scotland on these major industrial sectors for its economic well-being[2]. Such studies have undoubtedly made a major contribution to an understanding of the development of the Scottish economy in the twentieth century but their emphasis has tended to obscure more positive aspects within the economy including the notable achievement of the Scottish electricity supply industry and its influence on both the economy and society.

This chapter, in the following three sections examines the development and influence of this important 'new' industry from its formative years around 1880 until 1930. The first section, generally, examines the growth of the industry in Scotland during that period and in particular provides a closer scrutiny of the years between 1924 and 1930 when its progress was influenced by what was happening elsewhere in the economy. A comparative analysis is also made of the Scottish electricity supply industry in the wider British context and this indicates that until 1924 Scottish growth was clearly respectable by United Kingdom standards and that, although deceleration was evident after that year, between 1924 and 1930 the industry continued to expand and by the latter year the prospect of future growth was certain. The second section attempts to determine the influence that the growth of the electricity supply industry had on both the economy and society and in particular assess its input on major industrial sectors in the crucial period between 1924 and 1930; its impact on the coal mining industry is subjected to a more detailed examination. The final section examines the pattern of development of the Scottish electrical engineering industry between 1924 and 1930 and discusses a number of issues which explain its relative decline in a period which witnessed major growth in the equivalent industry in England and Wales.

* * *

Scotland, which had made major contributions to industrial development generally, both as a nation and through the efforts of particular individuals[3], played no significant part in the early development of the electricity supply industry. At a time when innovation in the electrical industry was taking place on an international basis,[4] Scotland remained firmly committed to the heavy industrial sector and steampower. Individuals were aware of the new form of energy. As early as 1834 J. B. Lindsay at Dundee experimented with electric lighting[5] and later Robert Davidson, an Aberdonian, between 1839 and 1842, used electricity to supply power to a small lathe, a saw mill and a printing press and also tested a locomotive powered by batteries on the Edinburgh and Glasgow railway[6]. However, the continuing profitability of traditional areas in shipbuilding, coal and iron and steel and the highly competitive provision of an excellent gas supply[7] inhibited greater exploitation of contemporary knowledge and the necessary investment in the, as yet, embryonic industry.

From the discoveries of Swan[8] and Edison[9] in 1878/79, marking the birth of the modern electricity industry, until the mid-1890s private installations underpinned the development of electricity supply in Scotland but were being overtaken by the more efficient central generating stations, and after 1900 by the establishment of power companies. Until 1930 the industry was broadly divided between local authorities and private enterprise, the former concentrated in the larger urban cities and towns and the latter in the less industrialised areas; the promotion of power companies complicated this simple analysis. Hostility between these sectors inhibited progress and lack of co-operation necessitated more positive government intervention in 1926. Generally, before 1926 the electricity supply industry lacked effective or-ganisation. A variety of voltages was in use and there was a multiplicity of large, medium and small generating stations. The Electricity (Supply) Act 1926 re-structured the industry. The Act set up the Central Electricity Board which concentrated output in a small number of base load stations and new super stations while closing down large numbers of smaller inefficient ones. The whole system was then connected by means of a national 'grid' of high tension transmission cables.[10]

Table 1: The Scottish Electricity Supply Industry 1907–1930[1]

Year	Number of Persons Employed		Monetary Value of Electricity Supplied		Total Capacity of Prime Movers Installed		Total Capacity of Electric Generators Installed	
	Total	% Increase	Total (£000)	% Increase	Total (h.p.)	% Increase	Total (KW)	% Increase
1907	2290	–	842	–	147658	–	100538	–
1924	5183	126	3993	374	621154	321	437290	335
1930	6041	17	5077	27	1005725	62	729417	67

For	Total Increase		Total Increase		Total Increase		Total Increase	
Period	Actual	%	Actual	%	Actual	%	Actual	%
1907–30	3751	164	4235	503	858067	581	628879	625

Source: Final Report on the First Census of Production 1907. p.p. 883,886,889,890.
Final Report on the Third Census of Production 1924. Part5, p.p. 344,345,347,349,350,352.
Final Report on the Fourth Census of Production 1930, Part 4, p.p. 498,500,501,503,504,505,506.

1. In Table 1 all percentage figures have been taken to the nearest whole number.

Table 2: The Scottish Electricity Supply Industry in the British Context 1907–1930

	Number of Persons Employed		Monetary Value of Electricity Supplied		Total Capacity of Prime Movers Installed		Total Capacity of Electrical Generators Installed	
	Total	%	Total (£000)	%	Total(h.p.)	%	Total (KW)	%
1907								
Scotland	2290	10.4	842	9.6	147658	9.6	100538	10.0
England and Wales	19702	89.6	7893	90.4	1,384,876	90.4	901426	90.0
Great Britain	21992	100.0	8735	100.0	1,532,534	100.0	1001964	100.0
1924								
Scotland	5183	10.0	3993	9.6	621154	11.2	437290	10.9
England and Wales	46607	90.0	37748	90.4	4920574	88.8	3558693	89.1
Great Britain	51790	100.0	41741	100.0	5541728	100.0	3995983	100.0
1930								
Scotland	6041	7.5	5077	8.3	1005725	10.0	729417	9.9
England and Wales	74130	92.5	56341	91.7	9052244	90.0	6629639	90.1
Great Britain	80171	100.0	61418	100.0	10057969	100.0	7359056	100.0

Source: Final Report on the First Census of Production 1907. p.p. 883, 886, 889, 890.
Final Report on the Third Census of Production 1924. Part 5 p.p. 344, 345, 347, 349, 350, 352.
Final Report on the Fourth Census of Production 1930. Part 4 p.p. 498, 500, 501, 503, 504, 505, 506.

Superficially electricity supply was vested in numerous autonomous undertakings. However, the private sector was governed by international holding companies. Foreign investment was substantial and aided private development; it was not benevolent and a price was exacted in financial and contractual obligations[11].

From the inception of the modern electricity industry in 1878 demand in Scotland continually grew as the market – industrial, commercial and domestic – widened; this was evident nationally. Moreover, the industry's ability to meet this expansion also improved as individual units increased in scale: greater efficiency was introduced in generation and transmission; even the adverse effects of the trade cycle could not detract from the overall growth of the industry. Reasonable data is available for the local authority sector from 1896. In that year Scotland's four major cities (Glasgow, Edinburgh, Aberdeen and Dundee) had, in total, an installed capacity of 6,322 kilowatts. By 1910 these cities had been joined by a further sixteen towns representative of both urban industrialised areas and rural more residential towns and by the latter year total installed capacity was 84,936 kilowatts – an increase of 1243.5 per cent. Evidence for the private company sector is less full and there are major gaps in statistical data but, nevertheless, the same source indicates that whereas three companies were registered in 1896, by 1910 twenty-one companies were registered including the major power companies, namely, the Clyde Valley Electric Power Company, Fife Electric Power Company and Lothians Electric Power Company, which had been set up by Act of Parliament.[12] However, from 1907, when the first national Census of Production was taken[13], full evidence which allows an assessment of overall Scottish developments is available, and, utilising the various censuses of production the progress of the industry can be chartered in the period under review with regard to employment and the monetary value of electricity supplied and also technically from the position of both prime movers and electric generators installed[14,15]. The situation is revealed statistically in Table 1 for the years 1907, 1924 and 1930; the table for the areas given also measures overall growth between 1907 and 1930.

In Table 1 the use of global figures for only three years has evident weaknesses and in particular the comparative assessment of monetary value over a fairly lengthy period tends to ignore changes in the very value of money itself. Moreover, such national statistics preclude detailed analysis of what was happening within individual sectors of the industry and within individual undertakings. Nevertheless, such statistics are a useful tool for measuring growth and achievement in the industry. In many respects the table provides no great surprises. There was an inevitability of expansion in all four sectors given in the table from 1907 when the industry was in its infancy as it became quickly realised that the provision of an electricity supply was not only beneficial and did much to improve the social environment but also enhanced the overall efficiency of industry; the use of electrical power gave greater flexibility to industry and commonly an ability to raise output, and where there was a need to offset increasing costs or diminishing returns its use was equally important. Thus the figures given in Table 1 acknowledge the rapid growth of electricity supply in Scotland between 1907 and 1924. From 1924 to 1930 progress continued but the pace had lessened as the industry was influenced by the downturn in the economy after that year.[16]

Contemporaneous with the widening use of conventional generating plant was the extensive use of water power to generate electricity. This was an attempt to utilise, mainly in the Highlands, the natural resources of Scotland. Many of these installations were purely for private use by wealthy landowners, of small unit size and had little impact on the general economic and social life of their area. However, at Fort William a public supply was given by a local private company from 1896[17]. More generally, successful schemes surrounded the activities of the British Aluminium Company at Foyers from 1896, at Loch Leven from 1909 and much later at Lochaber where the first stage was completed in 1929[18]; at these three schemes the power generated was taken mainly by the company for the production of aluminium[19]. The scheme with the longest history was probably that of the Falls of Clyde where initial proposals were made at least as early as 1886[20], but which only came into use in 1928[21]. The 1920s witnessed the beginnings of the large hydro-electric developments at Grampian[22] and Galloway[23] and, although these schemes were completed too late to be considered here, they mark increasing interest in Scotland's natural water-power resources.

Table 2 examines the Scottish industry in the wider British context and contains weaknesses similar to those already noted with regard to Table 1. Nevertheless, it does allow comparisons to be made. In both regions of mainland Britain the total number employed rose substantially between 1907 and 1930, and between 1907 and 1924 their relative positions as employers remained virtually unchanged. After 1924 a significant change occurred. During that period employment in Scotland rose by only 858 persons whereas in England and Wales the number of persons employed increased by 27,523. Thus, as Table 2 indicates, by 1930 Scotland only accounted for 7.5 per cent of direct employment in mainland Britain and England and Wales now accounted for 92.5 per cent of the total number. In percentage terms the figures for monetary value of electricity sold indicates that between 1907 and 1924 parallel development took place between Scotland and England and Wales, and taking into account the respective size of market these figures are not entirely unexpected. However, by 1930 the Scottish market, relative to that of England and Wales, had fallen to 8.3 per cent despite the fact that the monetary value of electricity sold had increased by over one million pounds. The pattern of development with regard to technical resources approximates to the trends already noted with respect to

Table 3: Number of Customers Supplied by Selected Undertakings between1896 and 1915/16

	1896	1900/1901	1905	1910	1915/1916
Glasgow	855	2,852	10,777	18,158	30,098
Edinburgh			7,129	12,252	16,156
Ayr			689	1,204	1,576
Motherwell			282	580	916
Paisley			460	915	1,691
Stirling		70	213	290	290
Perth				346	488

Source: Garcke, Op. cit. Vols. I, V, IX, XIV, XIX.

employment and monetary value of electricity sold. In the three years for which figures are available Scotland employed approximately one-tenth of the British total of prime movers and electric generators, although in percentage terms experiencing a slight relative reduction between 1924 and 1930. More generally Table 2 indicates that the development of the Scottish industry was respectable by United Kingdom standards until 1924 when, with the onset of the inter-war depression and with the greater severity with which it affected the Scottish economy because of it's particular industrial structure[24], progress in England and Wales forged ahead. Yet as Table 1 clearly indicates, despite the deceleration which took place after 1924, Scottish growth rates in the sectors examined remained positive and by 1930 the industry was firmly established. Future growth was certain.

* * *

By 1930 the growth of the electricity supply industry in Scotland was clearly respectable by British standards and the industry was geographically wide-spread. Little in the way of original research has been done on the social and economic effects of the growth of the industry on the rest of the economy. Yet the industry was obviously of major qualitative importance, and its indirect influence was potentially of great significance. This section attempts to make some assessment of the direct gains made by other sectors as a consequence of the expansion of this important industry.

Industrial interests in the West of Scotland and more widely in the country welcomed the beginning of a public supply. The Clyde Valley Electric Power Company (after this the C.V.E.P. Company), Scotland's major power company set up in 1901, had an area of supply of 750 square miles in West-Central Scotland which contained 1200 works, 600 of which were in favour of the C.V.E.P. Bill, either as promoters or supporters.[25] This company from 1902 through its market research and active sales policy

Table 4: Total Electricity Supplied by the Electricity Undertakings in Scotland for designated purposes in 1924 and 1930[1]

Electricity Supplied for	1924		%+[2]	1930	
	B.T.U.(m)	%		B.T.U. (m)	%
Public Lighting	9.2	1.5	112.0	19.5	1.6
Traction	37.8	6.1	191.0	110.0	8.8
Power and Manufact-uring purposes	312.6	49.6	118.8	683.9	54.7
Private Lighting Heating and Cooking	108.9	17.3	130.7	251.2 [4]	20.1
General Supply at Uniform Charges[3]	101.7	16.1	–	–	–
Bulk Supply to Authorised Distrib-utors	34.9	5.5	388.5	170.5	13.6
Purposes not separ-ately distinguished	24.8	3.9	–	– [4]	–
Units not accounted for	–	–	–	15.0[5]	1.2
Total	629.9	100.0	98.5	1,250.1	100.0

Source: Final Report of the Third Census of Production 1924, Part 5, p.p. 344,349. Final Report of Fourth Census of Production 1930, Part 4, p.p. 498/9,503.

1. Separate Scottish figures are not provided in the Final Report of the First Census of Production 1907.

2. The figures given in this column represent the percentage increase of the 1930 figures over those of 1924.

3. In 1930 this sub-heading was changed to Miscellaneous Charges.

4. References state that owing to the possible disclosure of information relating to individual undertakings separate figures cannot be given.

5. Because of the ommisions in the evidence it was necessary to insert this figure to allow the addition of this column to equate with the stated total.

accompanied and complemented by a vigorous policy of constructing sub-stations to accommodate its customers was quick to exploit demand from heavy industry. Extant records reveal that in 1923 and 1924 (continuous data is not available) collieries and iron and steel works were the major customers of the company accounting on average for 40 per cent of production. Other clearly identifiable sectors were engineering repair shops, shipyards and textiles which together absorbed in excess of 20 per cent of energy produced in each of the years, while an anonymous group 'general power users' who are not identified were responsible for taking a further 18–19 per cent. More generally, in both years sales for power purposes accounted for 98.7 per cent of total sales.[26] Meeting this demand

Table 5: Analysis of Power Applied Mechanically and Power Applied Electrically in Selected Industries and Trades in Scotland between 1924 and 1930.

	Applied Mechanically			Applied Electrically		
	1924 h.p. ('000)	% [1]	1930 h.p. ('000)	1924 h.p. ('000)	% [2]	1930
Textile Trades	1763.4	-14.7	1505.0	631.7	+48.3	937.8
Food, Drink and Tobacco Trades	180.8	-21.7	141.5	344.1	+51.3	520.5
Mines and Quarries	2070.0	-6.0	1945.3	1507.0	+20.0	1807.7
Iron and Steel Trades	1316.0	-8.4	1205.8	1127.8	+30.3	1469.4

Source: Final Report on the Fourth Census of Production 1930, Part 1, p. 25; Part 2, p. 24; Part 3, p. 23; Part 4, p. 370.

1. Percentage decrease between 1924 and 1930.
2. Percentage increase between 1924 and 1930.

proved profitable to the C.V.E.P. Company which between 1913 and 1930 paid £1,635,250 in dividends to its several categories of shareholders[27]. Equally, as already indicated, Scottish industrialists supported the development of a new source of energy[28]. Similarly, commercial and domestic consumers, the latter increasingly supplied by local authorities, favoured the development of the industry. This is shown by the example of selected undertakings in Table 3.

More generally the national pattern of demand in Scotland in 1924 and 1930 is given in Table 4. Clearly most sectors witnessed an absolute increase in consumption of electrical power, but particular points of interest arise and are worthy of comment. The level of demand in the industrial sector in 1924 – nearly 50 per cent of total supply – indicated the possibilities of industrial demand and, although in relative terms this category expanded slowly to 1930, it was a dynamic sector particularly considering the general state of the industrial economy. This phenomenon whereby industrialists used more electricity at a time when the economy was moving into decline will be the subject of comment later. Private lighting, heating and cooking was the next major component in demand accounting for slightly more than one-fifth of total supply in 1930. Undoubtedly, this reflected the expansion of the housebuilding sector of the construction industry in the inter-war period and the general upgrading of existing residential property as consumers moved from gas to electricity.[29] These developments were in many respects linked with the expansion in public lighting which was also an important element in local authority activity. The development of public housing was matched by the provision of new streets and street lighting, and suburban ratepayers expected the most modern service from their councils even if they lived in owner-occupied houses. Generally, expansion in both sectors reflected an improvement in living standards and an enhancement in the social environment. For example Glasgow Corporation built 50,000 council houses between 1919 and 1939 with the concept of the 'garden suburb' clearly evident in such areas as Carntyne, Mosspark and Knightwood;[30] in the latter area power was requested from the C. V. E, P. Company in October 1923.[31,32]

The category 'Bulk Supply to Authorised Distributors' was third in order of significance. This anonymous category increased in importance as a result of the growth of large power companies sufficiently sizeable to meet demand for street lighting and other socially useful purposes from burghs like Motherwell and Wishaw.[33] The implementation of the Central Scotland Scheme in 1927 was of great significance in the expansion of municipal demand measured under this category.[34]

One mystery requiring explanation arises from the figures for traction. Apart from bulk supply, this was the sharpest increase between 1924 and 1930 and yet it should be borne in mind that none of the major Scottish

Table 6: *Analysis of Power Applied Mechanically and Power Applied Electrically in Particular Industries in Scotland between 1924 and 1930.*

	Applied Mechanically			Applied Electrically		
	1924 h.p. ('000)	1930 h.p. ('000)	%[1]	1924 h.p. ('000)	1930 h.p. ('000)	%[2]
Hosiery	8.7	4.7	−46.0	15.3	25.2	+64.7
Cotton Spinning	923.6	764.7	−17.2	209.9	270.0	+28.6
Cotton Weaving	269.4	245.4	−8.9	48.0	70.0	+45.8
Spirit Distilling	5.1	4.8	−5.9	8.3	14.4	+73.5
Brewing and Malting	26.8	17.5	−34.7	58.0	82.2	+41.7
Coal Mining	1956.6	1826.2	−6.7	1428.7	1670.7	+16.9
Iron and Steel (Blast Furnaces, Smelting and Rolling)	1137.8	1058.3	−7.0	764.3	927.7	+21.4
Iron and Steel (Foundries)	12.4	7.7	−37.9	100.5	138.3	+38.1

Source: Final Report on the Fourth Census of Production 1930, Part 1, p. 25; Part 2, p. 24; Part 3, p. 23; Part 4, p. 370.

1. Percentage decrease between 1924 and 1930.
2. Percentage increase between 1924 and 1930.

railway companies conducted schemes of electrification and in the British context Hannah has indicated that the tramways 'had their heyday in the post-war boom of 1919–21.'[35] Between 1924 and 1930 the capital stock of tramcars in Britain remained static at 14,000[36] and its doubtful if there was any expansion of mileage in Scotland or greater intensification of use which would account for the increase. More likely, tramway companies found it more economic to buy electricity from the public supply and close their own private generating stations.

Of the other categories outlined in Table 4 it is particularly unfortunate that no statistics survive for 'General Supply at Uniform Charges' and the miscellaneous category 'Purposes not separately distinguished' in 1930. These two in 1924 accounted for about one-fifth of total electricity supplied. It is, of course, possible that greater care was taken in 1930 to assign precise categories to users of electricity and thus the category 'Units not accounted for' had shrunk considerably by that year.

Examining Scottish industry more widely, comparative data before 1924 suffer from a lack of continuity, thereby making analysis less meaningful, but good statistical evidence is available for 1924 and 1930. From the groups of industries and trades given in Table 5 it is obvious that there was a decline in power applied mechanically and an increase in power applied electrically between 1924 and 1930. Although the use of electrical power gave greater flexibility to industry, this cannot be the only reason for the changes. The downturn in the economy adversely affected these industries; output measured in monetary terms and also employment contracted[37].

Yet as an examination of the data in Table 6 makes clear, it was not only

Table 7: Total Number of Coal Cutting Machines in use in Scotland in the years stated.

| Year | Number of Machines Powered by | | | | Total |
	Electricity	% of Total	Compressed Air	% of Total	Number of Machines
1900	1	2.2	44	97.8	45
1905	102	47.4	113	52.6	215
1910	425	73.2	156	26.8	581
1920	1,149	89.8	131	10.2	1,280
1925	1,530	94.2	94	5.8	1,624
1930	1,582	96.1	64	3.9	1,646

Source: Inspectors of Mines Report 1900, East of Scotland Report.
p. 6; West of Scotland Report, p. 7.
Inspectors of Mines Report 1905, East of Scotland Report,
p. 8; West of Scotland Report, p. 7.
Inspectors of Mines Report 1910, General Report, p. 139
Inspectors of Mines Report 1920, General Report, p. 82.
Annual Report of the Secretary for Mines 1925, p. 145.
Inspectors of Mines Report 1930, Scottish Division Report p. 10.

industries faced with the bleak necessity to reduce costs or face collapse which were most forward in the increased use of electrical power. Spirit distilling, however, did have its share of problems, notably in its principal export markets of the United States of America where prohibition prevailed and in Canada where the depression of the late 1920s was particularly severe. The hosiery industry, established in areas where cheap local coal was not readily available, also embraced the new technology warmly and especially in the Borders where in the late 1920s the Balfour Beatty group of companies were extending their influence[38]. Cotton spinning and weaving were sectors clearly under pressure from competition in Lancashire and further afield,[39] but their decline was being fought using cost reducing techniques. The more successful brewing and malting sector was also applying the new technology, although its major markets were domestic, and there was also considerable develop-ment in the iron and steel industry. Thus, it is reasonable to suppose that in some industries electricity was being introduced to make more intensive use of resources, and the decline in employment may reflect more than a simple downturn in demand to take account of the re-organisation of production which the application of new power made likely.

One industry quick to realise the advantages of electricity was coal mining. As early as 1881 electric lighting was introduced to Earnock Colliery at Hamilton,[40] and it was for lighting that the new source of energy was most commonly deployed initially. However, by the First World War it was being more widely used for such operations as pumping, haulage and winding and for coal-cutting machinery.[41] Apart from coal-cutting operations precise information about the consumption of electricity in the pits is lacking. However, as Table 7 makes clear, compressed air ceased to be the main source of power after 1905 probably because of its many drawbacks. Pipes to carry compressed air were expensive, subject to leakages, and 'in seams of two feet or less it was of little value.'[42] Many of the best and most accessible seams in the Scottish coalfield had been exhausted by 1914, and the working of deeper and thinner seams necessarily involved greater cost. Generally in Scotland, and in particular in the Western coalfield, where thin seams were very common, electricity was introduced to offset higher costs. Moreover, electric coal-cutting equipment was particularly efficient in working thin seams because it produced a higher proportion of marketable coal — hand cut coal from similar seams was produced in minute pieces for which the market was limited. The sharp rise in the use of electrically driven coal-cutters from 425 in 1910 to 1582 in 1930, representing at the latter date over 96 per cent of all such machines, is the clearest evidence that this troubled industry was not lacking in the application of cost-reducing techniques, and it seems likely that the particular operational difficulties which normally led to diminishing returns forced coalmasters to mechanise and in coal-cutting to apply machinery powered by electricity. In the 1920s the percentage of Scottish

Table 8: Aggregate Horse-power of Electric Motors in use on the Surface and Underground in Scotland and Great Britain in the years stated.

Year	Scotland				Great Britain			
	Surface	%[1]	U/ground	%[1]	Surface	%[2]	U/ground	%[2]
1920	43,050	20.6	166,192	79.4	461,954	42.7	618,868	57.3
1925	63,574	22.3	221,207	77.7	715,834	46.0	840,401	54.0
1930	73,200	23.3	241,518	76.7	861,680	47.3	961,948	52.7

Source: Annual Report of the Secretary for Mines 1920, p. 49.
Annual Report of the Secretary for Mines 1925, p. 145.
Annual Report of the Secretary for Mines 1930, p. 143.

1. Percentage of Total Scottish Horsepower.
2. Percentage of Total British Horsepower.

114

output mechanically cut was twice as high as in Great Britain as a whole.[43]

Although there are difficulties in ascertaining precisely how electricity was used in pits and what amounts were applied to other operations than coal-cutting, aggregate figures are available for the total horse-power of electric motors used in Scottish mines and more generally for the British industry for the years 1920, 1925 and 1930 – both underground and on the surface. This information is given in Table 8 and clearly demonstrates that Scotland was mechanising underground operations more intensively than was the case elsewhere in Great Britain. Indeed, during the 1920s the gap widened in Scotland's favour, although there was a fall in percentage terms everywhere. The attempt to reduce labour costs, to increase productivity, and to offset diminishing returns was particularly acute, but it seems clear that Scottish coalmasters were more anxious than their counterparts in other coalfields to achieve these objectives. Moreover, it is worthy of note that the average selling price per ton in Scotland remained below the British average[44] partly as a consequence of improved efficiency, and partly because Scotland possessed relatively low grades of coal; in addition, the depressed nature of Scotland's other heavy industries, the major coal users, adversely influenced demand and lowered price.

The apparent paradox that between 1920 and 1930 aggregate use of electricity in the Scottish coalmining industry rose less than for Britain as a whole (just over 50 per cent as compared with 69 per cent) is readily explained by the fact that the rest of Britain had more leeway to make-up, and some other British coalfields had greater profit potential and less depressed markets. According to the 1930 Census of Production, the furniture industry was slower to change its motive power to electricity than was true of industry in Britain as a whole. Although this may be partly explained by a reluctance to change, there was a practical reason why the tendency to change from steam was slow. The generation of electricity provided no outlet for wood shavings and chippings and sawdust which with steam prime movers could be fed into the furnace.[45]

* * *

Using measures such as employment, monetary value of electricity sold and total capacity installed, the Scottish electricity supply industry represented 10 per cent of the total British industry in 1907, 1924 and 1930[46] and the unwary reader might have assumed that a similar pattern of development might have prevailed in the electrical engineering industry down to 1930.[47] This was not the case. As Table 9 makes clear the Scottish industry was small and shrinking between 1924 and 1930. Consequently, by 1930 Scotland had only 1.2 percent of the total number employed in the electrical engineering industry in Britain.[48] Table 10 confirms this impression, in this case in

Table 9: Average Number of Persons Employed in the Electrical Engineering Industry in Scotland, England and Wales and Great Britain in 1924 and 1930.

	1924			1930	
	Number	%	% (±)[1]	Number	%
Scotland	3,383	2.2	−29.5	2,385	1.2
England and Wales	150,439	97.8	+26.0	189,585	98.8
Great Britain	153,822	100.0	+24.8	191,970	100.0

Source: Final Report of Third Census of Production 1924, Part 3, p. 280.
    Final Report of Fourth Census of Production 1930, Part 2, p. 304.

1. Percentage increase (%+) or decrease (%−) between 1924 and 1930.

Table 10: Value of Goods Made and Work Done in the Electrical Engineering Industry in Scotland, England and Wales and Great Britain in the years stated

	1907		1924		1930	
	Value £ 000	*%*	*Value £ 000*	*%*	*Value £ 000*	*%*
Scotland	422	3.0	1,291	1.8	987	1.1
England and Wales	13,467	97.0	68,859	98.2	86,687	98.9
Great Britain	13,889	100.0	70,150	100.0	87,674	100.0

Source: Final Report of First Census of Production 1907, p. 191.
    Final Report of Third Census of Production 1924, Part 3, p. 280.
    Final Report of Fourth Census of Production 1930, Part 2, p. 304.

Table 11: Gross Output Per Capita in The Electrical Engineering Industry in Scotland and England and Wales in 1924 and 1930 (£)

Year	Scotland	England and Wales
1924	381.61	457.72
1930	413.84	557.52

Source: Tables 9 and 10

terms of gross output. In neither 1924 nor 1930 did Scotland's share of overall British gross output in electrical engineering exceed the 1907 figure of 3 per cent, although in absolute terms the monetary value of Scottish gross output did increase. Thus, the Scottish electrical engineering industry failed to maintain its market share during a period of growth.

Efficiency and productivity in the Scottish electrical engineering industry rapidly improved between 1924 and 1930 as measured by gross output *per capita* and indicated in Table 11.

Nonetheless, although the gap had narrowed between Scotland and the rest of the United Kingdom, *per capita* output in England and Wales was still greater.[49] A reduction in manning levels and more effective use of capital assets in Scotland had produced a closer run race, but in the process the Scottish electrical engineering industry had become more minute.

The relative decline of the electrical engineering industry in Scotland had a number of roots. Some historians have noted at length the overt commitment to the heavy industrial sector[50] and it can be suggested that this was detrimental to the accumulation of electrical engineering skills. Certainly by the middle 1930s there was difficulty in obtaining skilled electrical fitters, engineers for switch gear assembly and testing and draughtsmen.[51] Yet from the 1880s there was wide academic interest and practical training available at Dundee and more particularly in the West of Scotland at the Glasgow and West of Scotland Technical College.[52] Few firms had apprenticeship schemes and one firm indicated in 1936 that the supply of houses was inadequate to attract migratory workers and staff.[53]

However, the major problem was undoubtedly English competition and certainly Scotland no longer had wage rates which compensated for other economic disadvantages. Scottish firms needed to buy most malleable castings in England and special materials, particularly shafting, were brought from England. Practically no die-casting was done in Scotland and little extruded metal-work. Copper and brassparts and rods were also brought from England together with special steels in sheet or stamp form. England was also the source of over half the insulating materials used by manufacturers in Scotland, and fabrics for cable manufacturing, glass tubing, bulbs and rods for neon sign and light manufacture and such basic components as electric boiling rings, meters, insulating bases and arc shields and starters were also obtained outside Scotland.[54]

The composition of output was distinctly lop-sided, reflecting the comparative advantage enjoyed by English manufacturers. In particular, heavy lathes, boring and punching machines, large scale heating and ventilation equipment, air conditioning and refrigeration machinery were produced in Scotland, often to meet the demands of the heavy industrial sector but much electrical engineering machine tooling was supplied from English manufacturers, from America and Germany. In such new areas as radio manufacture there was virtually no development in Scotland and little component production. Too many sets were already being produced in England, and the growth of combines in the South, particularly Electrical and Musical Industries Limited, made any development unlikely – the small Scottish market was a telling factor. There is also some evidence that Government contracts were distributed to suit the ease of organised inspection from London, and thus Scotland suffered. Scottish firms were often too small to withstand the long delay in Government payments, and more generally were handicapped by lack of knowledge of English commercial law.[55]

Customers believed that Scottish firms did not provide them with the service provided by English companies. From their viewpoint English firms had a well organised after-sales service, they were more considerate of customers' needs and more prompt in their delivery. This group of subjective views may well confirm the weaknesses of the small Scottish firm which did not do the volume of business to enable it to provide the kind of after-sales service obtainable in England. Moreover, the larger English combines had established their reputation for an extensive range of products and could afford like the General Electric Company to spend heavily on advertising the promotion of a new product.[56]

Many Scottish electricity supply undertakings were consumers of electrical machinery and accessories. Possibly the principal cause of their buying from English firms was the financial involvement of substantial shareholders from South of the Border or even from overseas. Such shareholders and consultants were more likely to recommend the award of major contracts for machinery and parts to English companies. In this regard it is possible to cite the long-term connection between the C.V.E.P. Company and the British Westinghouse Electric and Manufacturing Company, and among others the financial and contractual relationship of the British Power Company, Edmundsons' Electricity Corporation, Crompton and Company and the National Electric Construction Company with major Scottish electricity supply undertakings.[57] This reliance on imported technology in the private sector adversely affected the native electrical engineering industry, and it should be borne in mind that relatively the local authority sector lacked the dynamism to generate a major level of demand for the industry.

The electrical engineering industry with its industrial and consumer based outlets was not unique among Scotland's 'newer' industries in finding it difficult to maintain market share during the inter-war period. In particular, the motor vehicle industry and the aircraft industry which were well-established before and during the First World War were unable to maintain momentum in Scotland during the 1920s and yet flourished South of the Border. By 1930 in Scotland passenger-car production had ceased and only the Albion Company continued to produce commercial vehicles, and all that was left of the aircraft industry – yet another potential 'growth industry' – was work on the de Cierva autogiro by W. and J. G. Weir. The reasons for the relative demise of such industries have been well-documented and are not entirely dissimilar to those offered here to explain the shrinking character of the Scottish electrical engineering industry.[58]

From the available evidence the Scottish electrical engineering industry was largely confined to the provision of electrically driven coal mining and pumping equipment. Bruce Peebles and Company of Edinburgh supplied machinery to the Fife and Lothian pits, while in the West of Scotland, Mavor and Coulson and Anderson and Boyes and Company served a similar purpose for local industry. At Alloa, the Harland Engineering Company made electrically driven pumping sets which by the 1930s were being exported in number.[59] Nevertheless, the nature of the problems of the coal mining industry in the inter-war period suggest that this market had limitations and the lack of balance within the Scottish electrical engineering industry was most marked by the absence of the mass production of consumer durables. Thus, despite the substantial foundation provided by academic institutions from at least the 1880s the electrical engineering industry in Scotland developed mainly as an adjunct to a heavy industrial sector, and where novelty occurred, as for example in the provision of refrigeration and air conditioning in ships, demand was linked with the fluctuating fortunes of the capital goods sector. The early foothold obtained by non-Scottish concerns in the provision of heavy electrical machinery for power stations and the long-term financial obligations of Scottish undertakings to alien holding companies further inhibited the diversification of the Scottish electrical engineering industry. That industry expanded narrowly until 1924 but by 1930 was apparently in decline.

* * *

The growth of the Scottish electricity supply industry in the formative years after 1878 was not smooth but by 1907 significant progress had been made in both the private and local authority sectors as the advantages of the new form of energy – economic and social – were realised by domestic, commercial and industrial consumers; the establishment of major power companies, such as the C.V.E.P. Company, was a telling factor. From 1907 until 1924, as Table 2 indicates, Scottish growth rates in this important 'new' industry were respectable and matched those South of the Border. Between 1924 and 1930 the Scottish industry was undoubtedly affected by the downturn in the economy, deceleration took place, but growth remained positive. By 1930, and aided by the 1926 legislation, the Scottish electricity supply industry was firmly established and set for future growth.

After 1924 the structural weaknesses in the Scottish economy were emphasised as traditional staple industries such as coal, iron and steel and shipbuilding together with their attendant trades floundered; even 'newer' industries like motor vehicle and aircraft production found it increasingly difficult to survive. Yet the Scottish electricity supply industry continued, despite any deceleration, to display significant growth. In this period of downturn in the economy the positive advantages of electrical power over rivals sources of energy were being clearly recognised by Scottish industry generally and not simply by those sectors most adversely affected; its use in raising living standards and in improving the quality of the social environment was also acknowledged in the local authority sector and in housebuilding. For industry, electrical power had many used and advantages. It made for greater flexibility, the more extensive use of resources, increased productivity and, more generally, improved efficiency; it was also used to reduce costs, including labour costs, and to offset diminishing returns. That industry made increasingly extensive use of electrical power is clearly evident in Tables 4, 5 and 6.

Surprisingly in a period when the Scottish electricity supply industry was showing positive expansion, its adjunct, the Scottish electrical engineering industry was shrinking; employment in this industry fell by almost thirty per cent between 1924 and 1930. Despite Scotland's long heritage in engineering and despite early academic interest and training in electrical engineering skills being made available at Dundee and Glasgow from the 1880s, the contribution of the electrical engineering industry to the Scottish economy was slight, particularly when compared with its counterpart South of the Border as indicated in Table 10. It is much too simple to explain the decline of this industry in Scotland in terms of its relationship with heavy industry, although this was a contributory factor. The larger English market and the effect of competition from companies outwith Scotland in the Scottish domestic market were of major significance. Many apparently autonomous supply undertakings in the more dynamic private sector in Scotland were from their outset virtual subsidiaries of much larger British concerns, and decisions taken in the interest of parent companies were not without influence in retarding the development and diversification of the Scottish electrical engineering industry. Thus, it is difficult to fault the Scottish electrical engineering industry and/or perceived weaknesses within this sector for its failure to maintain market share between 1907 and 1930, to the extent that by the latter year it was in apparent decline. Moreover, as Table 11 suggests, between 1924 and 1930 by reducing manning levels and making more effective use of capital assets it was most certainly increasing its efficiency and productivity.

REFERENCES

1. S. Pollard, *The Development of The British Economy 1914–1990*, 4th edn. (London, 1992); S. Newton and D. Porter, *Modernisation Frustrated*, (London,

1988) and T. May, *An Economic and Social History of Britain 1760–1970*, (London, 1987).

2. R. H. Campbell, *Scotland Since 1707*, 2nd. edn. (Oxford, 1985) and A. Slaven, *The Development of the West of Scotland 1750–1960*, (London and Boston, 1975).

3. Cambell, *Scotland Since 1707* and Slaven, *Development of the West of Scotland 1750–1960*.

4. L. Hannah, *Electricity before Nationalisation*, (London, 1979) pp. 3–4; I. C. R. Byatt, *The British Electrical Industry 1875–1914*, (Oxford, 1979).

5. *Telegraphic Journal*, Vol. XI. 16 September, 1882.

6. Strathclyde Regional Archives (SRA), General Notes Vol. 10. No. 238

7. See M. S. Cotterill, 'The Scottish Gas Industry Up To 1914,' (Unpublished Ph.D. Thesis, University of Strathclyde, 1976)

8. *Dictionary of National Biography 1912–1921*, (London, 1927) pp. 518–519; *Who Was Who Volume 1 1897–1915*, (London, 1926); *Alphabetical Index of Patentees and Applicants for Patents of Inventions*, (London, 1858–1870), Patent Number 18, 2 January, 1880 – Electric Lamps. Patent Number 250, 20 January, 1886 – Electric Lamps.

9. *Encyclopaedia of World Biography Volume 3*, (New York, 1973), pp. 518–520; *Who Was Who Volume 3 1929–1940*, (London, 1941); M. Josephson, *Edison*, (New York, 1959); *Alphabetical Index of Patentees and Applicants for Patents of Inventions*, (London, 1858–1870). Patent Number 4576, 10 November, 1879 – Electric Lamps. Patent Number 5127, 15 December, 1879, – Electric Lamps.

10. Pollard, *Development of The British Economy*, p. 44.

11. For a detailed examination of the growth of the electricity supply industry in Scotland see John C. Logan, 'An Economic History of the Scottish Electricity Supply Industry 1878–1930,' (Unpublished Ph.D. Thesis, University of Strathclyde 1983.).

12. E. Garcke, *Manual of Electrical Undertakings*, Vol. i, XIV.

13. Final Report on the First Census of Production, 1907, (Cmd, 6320, 1907).

14. *Final Report on the Third Census of Production, 1924*, (HMSO, 1924); *Final Report on the Fourth Census of Production, 1930*, (HMSO, 1930)

15. Prime Movers are defined as Reciprocating Steam Engines, Steam Turbines, Gas engines, Petrol and Light Oil Engines Heavy Oil Engines and Water Power.

16. The figures for employment and technical resources between 1924 and 1930 may have been affected by economies resulting from a rationalisation process arising from a government inspired re-organisation of the industry in 1926 which culminated in the Central Scotland Scheme adopted by the Central Electricity Board on the 29 June, 1927 and officially inaugurated on 30 April, 1930. The situation is not clear from the extant records. See Central Electricity Board, *First Annual Report 1927/28*, pp. 5–6; Central Electricity Board, *Third Annual Report 1930*, pp. 9–11.

17. *Electrical Review*, Vol. XXXIX, 4 September, 1896; Vol. XL, 5 March, 1897 and 19 March, 1897.

18. L. V. Chilton, 'The Aluminium Industry in Scotland,' *Scottish Geographical Magazine*, Vol. 66, December, 1950.

19. For a more detailed study of the aluminium industry in Scotland from its

inception until recent times see D. Turnock, *The New Scotland*, (Newton Abbot, 1979), pp. 94–102.

20. *Telegraphic Journal*, Vol. XIX, 16 July, 1886.
21. Scottish Record Office, (SRO), Records of the South of Scotland Electricity Board, SSE5,4/1.
22. Garcke, *Manual of Electrical Undertakings*, Vols. XXIX, XXXIV; SRO, Records of the Scottish Development Department, Grampian Electricity Supply Company 1922, DD11/120.
23. SRO, Records of the Scottish Development Department, Galloway Water Power Act 1929, DD 11/119
24. R. Saville, 'The Industrial Background To The Post-War Scottish Economy,' in R. Saville (ed.), *The Economic Development of Modern Scotland 1950–1980*, (Edinburgh, 1985), pp. 3–4.
25. SRA, Records of Strain and Robertson, TD 83/1/1, TD 83/6/1, TD 83/7.
26. SRA, Records of Strain and Robertson, TD 83/6/4, TD 83/6/6C.
27. SRO, Records of the South of Scotland Electricity Board, SSE5,1/1 – SSE5, 1/5.
28. For detailed evidence of the growing use of electric power in major sectors of industry, its advantages over other power sources and analysis of variation in the degree of electrification in different industries, see Byatt, British Electrical Industry 1875–1914, pp. 70–94.
29. 337,000 new houses were built in Scotland during the inter-war period, 67 per cent by public authorities. B. Lenman, *An Economic History of Modern Scotland*, (London, 1977), p. 243.
30. M. Lindsay, *Glasgow*, 3rd. edn. (London, 1989), p. 253.
31. SRO, records of the South of Scotland Electricity Board, SSE5,1/3
32. For a detailed survey of housing in the United Kingdom throughout the last one hundred and fifty years see, P. Nuttgens, *The Home Front*, (London, 1989).
33. SRO, Records of the South of Scotland Electricity Board, SSE5, 1/1–1/4.
34. See Reference 16 above.
35. Hannah, *Electricity before Nationalisation*, pp. 163 and 168.
36. B. R. Mitchell and P. Deane, *Abstract of British Historical Statistics*, (London, 1962), p. 230.
37. R. H. Campbell, *The Rise and Fall of Scottish Industry 1707–1939*, (Edinburgh, 1980), pp. 197–201.
38. In 1909 G. Balfour and A. H. Beatty formed the private company Balfour, Beatty and Company to conduct business as general and electrical engineers, contractors and operating managers for tramways, railways and lighting properties and also for the promotion of new companies. The Galashiels and District Electric Supply Company was formed in 1913. In 1928 this company changed its name to the Scottish Southern Electric Supply Company and by 1931 was negotiating the purchase of privately owned undertakings at Melrose, Jedburgh and Hawick. Garcke, *Manual of Electrical Undertakings*, Vols. XIV, XVIII, XIX, XXXIV.
39. Campbell, *Rise and Fall of Scottish Industry 1707–1939*, p. 153.
40. *Telegraphic Journal*, Vol. IX. 1 June, 1881.
41. For a detailed examination of the development of the coal industry in Britain,

including the effect of the introduction of electricity, see N. K. Buxton, *The Economic Development of the British Coal Industry*, (London, 1978).

42. Buxton, *Economic Development of the British Coal Industry*, p. 115.

43. Buxton, *Economic Development of the British Coal Industry*, p. 183.

44. Buxton, *Economic Development of the British Coal Industry*, p. 187.

45. Scottish Economic Committee, *Light Industries in Scotland*, A Case for Development, (1938), p. 39.

46. See Table 2.

47. The electrical engineering industry was a multi-product industry including the manufacture of all types of electrical machinery, batteries, insulated cables, telephones, telegraph and wireless apparatus and other electrical plant, appliances and accessories. In assessing the overall monetary value of the industry the 1930 Census of Production also included contract and constructional work carried out by manufacturers outside their own factories. The pre-1930 censuses were slightly broader in scope and included firms for example which by 1930 were defined under Motor and Cycle Trade rather than electrical engineering. However, alterations in the collation of data were not thought to affect the comparability of census results seriously, *Final Report of the Fourth Census of Production 1930*, Part 2, p. 282.

48. Employment statistics for the Electrical Engineering Industry are not provided in the Final Report of the First Census of Production, 1907

49. Although in Tables 9, 10 and 11 England and Wales have been grouped together, the Welsh contribution was negligible. In 1930 only about 0.1 per cent of gross British output came from Wales and as late as 1935 only 424 persons were employed in the electrical engineering industry in Wales. R, E, Catterall, 'Electrical Engineering,' in N. K. Buxton and D. H. Aldcroft, (eds.), *British Industry between the Wars*, (London, 1979), p. 270.

50. Inter Alia, Slaven, *Development of the West of Scotland 1750–1960* and Campbell, *Rise and Fall of Scottish Industry 1707–1939*.

51. Scottish Economic Committee, *Light Industries in Scotland. A Case for Development*, p. 208.

52. From 1881 classes, in connection with the City and Guilds examinations for telegraphy, telephony and electric lighting, were conducted at the Glasgow College of Science and Art. The Glasgow and West of Scotland Technical College (now the University of Strathclyde) incorporated the College of Science and Art in 1887 and became the venue for such courses in 1888. In 1890, 150 students attended evening classes in electric lighting and by 1891 over 90 day students entered electrical laboratory and engineering workshop courses from such diverse countries as India, China, Australia, New Zealand, Mozambique, South Africa, West Indies, Norway and from all over Britain. See *Telegraphic Journal*, Vol. IX, 1 June, 1881; Vol. XXIII, 17 August, 1888; Vol. XXVII, 31 October, 1890; Vol. XXIX, 10 October, 1891.

53. Scottish Economic Committee, *Light Industries in Scotland. A Case for Development*, p. 208.

54. Scottish Economic Committee, *Light Industries in Scotland. A Case for Development*, pp. 208–209.

55. Scottish Economic Committee, *Light Industries in Scotland. A Case for Development*, pp. 83–84, 90–91, 209–212.

56. Scottish Economic Committee, *Light Industries in Scotland. A Case for Development*, pp. 213–214.

57. For a more detailed analysis of the activities of holding companies in the Scottish Electricity Supply Industry see, Logan, 'Economic History of the Scottish Electricity Supply Industry,' Chapter 7.

58. See inter alia, Pollard, *Development of the British Economy 1914–1990*; Saville, *Economic Development of Modern Scotland 1950–1980*; Slaven, *Development of the West of Scotland 1750–1960*, and Campbell, *Scotland Since 1707*.

59. C. A. Oakley, *Scottish Industry Today*, (Edinburgh, 1937), pp. 142, 272, 273.

7

The Emergence of Edinburgh as a Financial Centre

CHARLES W. MUNN

In most undergraduate textbooks of economic history students will read about the technology of major industrial sectors and about supply and, to a lesser extent, demand factors affecting those industries. There will usually also be some useful information about economies of scale and about factors influencing the location of particular industries in a particular part of the country. Service industries, such as transport, will also receive very full treatment as will the construction industry. Yet there will be very little about financial services. Despite the importance of finance in the economic equation economic historians, especially those who write basic textbooks, tend to have very little to say about the importance of money or about the contribution of the financial sector to the process of economic growth. Most limit themselves to some carefully chosen words about the changing structure of banking and, perhaps, the stock exchange over time. Insurance, in particular, is almost always ignored.

This is disappointing for if students are to obtain a balanced view of the process of economic growth then they must be aware of the contribution to that process made by all sectors of the economy and not just by manufacturing industry. This is doubly important given the essentially service based nature of many modern economies. In the United Kingdom financial services now employ just as many people as the whole of manufacturing industry. The trend towards a service dominated economy has been evident since at least the mid-nineteenth century and has recently been the subject of some scholarly comment.[1]

In terms of contribution to economic growth, employment and the balance of payments the British insurance industry must count among the top rank of British industries. Yet students of economic history learn precisely nothing about it. It may be thought that this argument is moving towards a dangerously utilitarian view of the purpose of undergraduate teaching of economic history. Perhaps it is. But even if you do not accept that the purpose of teaching economic history is to give your students an understanding of the modern economy there must also be an argument for saying that you have a duty to them to give a balanced view of the whole process of economic development. At least in the British case it must be argued that the financial services sector has made a major contribution to growth – both as a growth industry and for the manner in which financial services contribute to growth in other sectors.

The economic development policies being pursued by many countries nowadays recognise these facts. Many countries throughout the world are currently pursuing policies aimed at creating financial centres or at enhancing centres which are already in existence. Dublin, Vancouver and Lyon fall into these categories. Large, well established, centres, such as London, are worried that their traditional business may be stolen away by these centres which are able to offer inducements to attract business from them. The major consideration in the development of these new financial centres is the creation of employment. Historically, however, the activities of financial institutions did not figure very highly on the list of development priorities. Indeed it is really only in the last twenty years that they have begun to come to prominence in programmes of economic development.

This seems somewhat strange because financial services got off to a good start in the minds of economists. The Scottish economist Adam Smith thought highly of banks.

> That the trade and industry of Scotland . . . have increased very considerably during this period, and that the banks have contributed a good deal to this increase, cannot be doubted.[2]

Thereafter many economists took a passing interest in banking but concentrated their attentions on the mysteries of the supply of money. It is not surprising, therefore, that they took a greater interest in manufacturing industry and the more visible services such as transport. These things are, after all, much easier to comprehend. Moreover it is probable that the provision of financial services, notwithstanding the importance of capital in the economic equation, were not seen as generators of growth. Perhaps for this reason most twentieth century economic development programmes, at least in the United Kingdom, concentrated their efforts on manufacturing and transport infrastructure. Only very recently has the supply of financial services assumed any importance in the plans of development economists.

In these plans the place where services are provided is a major consideration and the creation, or further development, of a financial centre is at the core of these ideas. Yet the idea of a financial centre as a place where the provision of financial services is concentrated is relatively new to the disciplines of economics and economic history. In modern times a great deal of credit for stimulating thinking on this subject must go to Charles Kindleberger whose 1974 Princeton study[3] is, I believe, the key to a greater understanding of this important subject – even if it raises more questions than it answers.

Kindleberger identified that the study of the location of financial centres falls between two stools – financial economics and urban and regional economics. Neither have taken much interest in the 'geography of finance'. The situation, however, is improving with a number of scholars looking at the interstices between these two branches of economics and discovering that financial centre location raises a number of important questions.[4]

With some honourable exceptions historians too have tended to ignore the origins of financial centres. The exceptions are N. S. B. Gras and M. Fanno both of whom wrote in the first quarter of this century.[5] More recent writers such as M. Collins capture the factors which led to the emergence of London as a financial centre without actually addressing the issue of concentration and location.[6]

In the United Kingdom there is a perfectly natural tendency to regard London as the financial centre of the country. It is, after all, one of the three largest centres in the world. Yet this is not the whole story as far as the provision of financial services is concerned. Nor is London the only financial centre in the country. By some measures Edinburgh ranks alongside the largest European centres and other cities, such as Manchester, have aspirations to be regarded as financial centres in their own right. In the nineteenth century, when the whole of Ireland was part of the United Kingdom, Dublin was certainly the locus of financial provision and that city has recently revived its claim to financial centre status. Although there is no universal agreement on the definition of a financial centre the term may be taken to mean a city where many head-quarters of financial institutions are located. The minority view is that it is the number of financial transactions in a city which define its status, rather than the number of head offices. This difference of opinion has not yet achieved the level of historical debate but it is important. In the late nineteenth century, for example, the Scottish financial centre was in Edinburgh, judged by the number of head offices but in Glasgow judged by the number of financial transactions.

The United Kingdom in the nineteenth century can provide several case studies of emerging financial centres – London, Edinburgh and Dublin as major centres and other cities such as Manchester, Birmingham, Belfast and Glasgow as less important but still significant centres. The purpose of this paper is to examine the development of Edinburgh as a financial centre but with sideways glances at some of the other cities of finance. In particular attention will be given to the rivalry between Edinburgh and Glasgow in the nineteenth century and to the Glasgow challenge to Edinburgh's hegemony.

I

One of the most interesting, but perhaps inconclusive, aspects of Kindleberger's paper was his view of world financial centres in terms of which of them were capital cities and which were not. Although politics were identified as a major contributory influence they were not, in themselves, a guarantee that a financial centre would emerge, if one was going to emerge, in the capital of a country. Yet in the United Kingdom, which is an unusual historical amalgam of countries, financial centres emerged in the three capital cities of London, Edinburgh and Dublin, but not Cardiff.

If it is assumed that there will be a close correlation between the emergence of industry and the emergence of banks and other institutions then the experience of Scotland, Ireland and England is all the more curious. In each case the centre of industry emerged in a city or region separate from the financial centre – Glasgow in Scotland, Belfast in Ireland and Lancashire in England. Inevitably this has given rise to questions about whether the financial organisations, banks in particular, have been sufficiently in tune with the needs of industry, given their geographical separation from the industrial centres.[7] It will be argued that, given the organisational form of banks in Scotland, this was not a problem.

By the end of the eighteenth-century Scotland had developed a three tier system of banking. The three largest banks, Bank of Scotland (1695), Royal Bank of Scotland (1727) and British Linen Company (1746) were based in Edinburgh. They were joint-stock companies, constituted by Act of Parliament or by Royal Charter. These were what Checkland described as the 'Public Banks'.[8] All were deposit taking, note issuing banks and all had developed a branch banking system, although the Royal Bank had confined itself to a single branch – in Glasgow, opened in 1783. It was said of this branch that it was the busiest bank office in the UK other than the Bank of England.[9]

Secondly there was a number of Edinburgh based private banks which tended to act as retailers of credit from the public banks. These banks accepted deposits and borrowed large sums of money from the public banks which they then lent to their own customers. This was a very early variety of what has since been called – round-tripping. No archives for these banks have survived so it is impossible to be precise about their activities. Only the largest of these private banks, Sir William Forbes, James Hunter and Company, issued bank notes and none of them had branches.[10] These were, therefore, very much a part of the Edinburgh financial scene and their partners often served on the boards of directors of the public banks.

The third element in the system was the provincial banking companies. These began to be formed after the Jacobite rebellion in the 1740s. They were to be found first of all in the major provincial cities, but particularly in Glasgow, where the pace of economic development was quickest. By 1770 provincial banks were to be found in Glasgow, Aberdeen, Dundee, Ayr and Perth and from there the system spread to encompass most towns of any size. One of the responses of the public banks to the formation of the provincials was to force them to join a note exchange, and thus to bring stability to the Scottish monetary system. The second response was to establish branches in direct competition with these local banks. By the 1780s most of these banks faced competition from a branch of one or more of the public banks. The Edinburgh system was, therefore, already reaching out into the provinces just as the industrial revolution was getting under way. Edinburgh bankers were determined to meet any competition head on but they also saw themselves as guardians of the system and it was their responsibility not to allow it to be destabilised by reckless banking. The note exchange became the main means by which they controlled the threat, real or imagined, from the provincial banks.[11]

Glasgow was, in the third quarter of the eighteenth century, the centre of the British tobacco industry and conducted a large entrepot trade between the American colonies and France.[12] The problem which faced the tobacco merchants was that few of them were well known in Edinburgh, a city some 45 miles distant, where the public banks were to be found. This meant that it was difficult, if not impossible, for them to obtain bank credit prior to the setting up of public bank branch networks in the 1770s and 1780s. Only the larger, and better known, merchants had credits with the Edinburgh banks. Many had no access to bank credit and even those who had access doubtless found it difficult to operate these accounts in an easy manner. There is also evidence to suggest that there were concerns about the profits from banking being earned by Edinburgh institutions, with a consequent loss of resources in Glasgow. Very few Glasgow merchants were shareholders in the public banks.

Their solution was to set up their own banks.[13] This is a classic case of the people at the centre not appreciating the needs of people on the periphery and the people on the periphery taking the matter into their own hands and producing their own response. What is remarkable in this case is the relatively small size of the country in which this happened. Nevertheless this was the pre-railway, and pre-canal, age and transport and communications problems undoubtedly contributed to the difficulties experienced by Glasgow, and other, merchants.

The provincial banking companies were, on the whole, a highly successful part of the Scottish banking system.[14] Nevertheless they were viewed with some suspicion by the Edinburgh bankers who tried to control them via the note exchange and then to court them by offering correspondent banking relationships. There was thus an ambivalence in the attitude of the public banks to the existence of the provincials. However, what was emerging in Scotland by the late eighteenth century was an efficient and price competitive banking system which was able to meet the growth requirements of its customer base. Leadership of the system was clearly with Edinburgh although there were elements in the system which would allow Glasgow banks to grow and to try to threaten the ascendancy of the Edinburgh banks.

One of the factors which made the banks so successful was the highly developed education system in Scotland where commercial subjects such as book-keeping were part of the curriculum. This ensured a ready supply of good quality clerks. Perhaps more important than this was the Scottish legal system, in many ways different from the English system, in which partnerships were recognised as separate legal entities. This brought some of the benefits, and responsibilities, of legal incorporation. All of the private and provincial banks were organised on this basis and this enabled some of them to grow into quite sizeable businesses.

There was also one accident of law which greatly benefitted the Scottish banking system. In 1708 the English banking system was encumbered with a piece of legislation which ensured that England was deprived of a banking system 'commensurate with a period of rapid economic growth'.[15] This legislation, which was designed to preserve the monopoly of the Bank of England, had the effect of limiting the number of partners in English country banks to six. It became apparent in the crisis of 1825–6 that the English banking system was weak by comparison with the Scottish where the 1708 legislation did not apply. The result was that many of the provincial banks were multi-partnered organisations. Some of them had as many as 50–60 partners and this made them the fore-runners of joint-stock banks.[16] It was the fully developed joint-stock form of organisation adopted from the 1820s that finally gave Glasgow banks the size to threaten the public banks in Edinburgh.

As a sidelight on this matter it is noteworthy that when the Bank of Ireland was established in Dublin in 1783 it was given powers and protections similar to those enjoyed by the Bank of England. This did not produce stability. Indeed most of the Irish private and country banks failed in a crisis of 1820 and it was not until the monopoly powers of the Bank of Ireland were whittled away and the Irish erected a banking system based on the Scottish model that they were able to enjoy a measure of stability and growth in their banking system and their economy. It is also significant that much of the new growth in banking came from organisations in the industrialising north, around Belfast, although none of these new banks were able to rival the Bank of Ireland in the nineteenth century.[17] As we shall see it was not just the Irish who adopted the Scottish system of banking.

There were a number of features which characterised the Scottish system of banking. Freedom from central (political) control, branch banking, note-issuing and joint-stock type organisation were the major structural elements. The ways in which Scottish bankers went about their business were also quite distinctive. The Scots pioneered lending by overdraft – a system whereby customers received an agreed borrowing limit and could borrow up to that limit, but with the flexibility of being able to repay any amount at any time, and to borrow again for as long as the account was in operation. Interest was charged only on the daily balance basis. This cash account, as it was called, was repayable on demand and was therefore a short-term credit instrument but in practice these accounts remained in operation for many years and became, in effect, long term loans. Customers could also accumulate credit balances on these accounts for which interest was credited at a rate only 1% below the lending rate.[18]

It is significant that notwithstanding the fact that there were three fairly distinct types of bank in Scotland they were quite homogeneous in terms of the lending services which they offered. Where there was a difference was in the other services normally associated with modern banking.

The Scots were very early into the paying of interest for deposits and it was not just on cash account balances. Deposit receipts were also highly popular devices. It is noteworthy that the practice of accepting deposits, and paying interest for them, began in the area of greatest economic growth in the eighteenth century, in Glasgow, but eventually spread throughout the country. Deposit banking was therefore general in Scotland before it became common in England.[19]

Significantly there is evidence to show that deposit gathering activity was more intensive in the rapidly growing industrial west of the country than in the capital city of Edinburgh. In 1827 the Edinburgh based National Bank of Scotland had to pay higher rates on deposit interest at its west of Scotland branches than it did at its other branches or at head office. The reason for this was quite simply to compete with the rates paid by Glasgow banks.[20] Some Edinburgh banks kept out of Glasgow for many years but eventually bowed to the inevitable. In 1844 the Edinburgh based Commercial Bank of Scotland decided to open branches in several west of Scotland towns because it was in that 'district the principal banking business is done'.[21] This point highlights the definition of a financial centre stressed earlier. The head offices of the major financial organisations were in Edinburgh but the bulk of the business was in the West.

The same type of thing happened in Ireland and when the Dublin based Provincial Bank of Ireland opened an office in the industrial city of Belfast in 1826 it had to pay a higher rate of interest for deposits there than at its other branches.[22] It is not clear from the available evidence, however, how long these differential rates of interest survived between the capital cities and the industrial cities in Scotland and Ireland.

By the time of the commercial crisis of 1825–6 the Scottish banking system had developed a level of sophistication which was not apparent anywhere else in the United Kingdom. The Parliamentary enquiries which were published in May 1826 began to make public the virtues of the Scottish system.[23] Indeed the pamphleteer and company promoter, Thomas Joplin, had begun the process of informing the public about Scottish banking in 1822 and there was soon a substantial pamphlet literature on the subject.[24] Legislation in Ireland and then England was brought in to reduce the monopoly powers of the Bank of Ireland and the Bank of England and to allow these countries to develop banking systems which were more in keeping with the needs of customers. In short it was clear that the banking system which had evolved in Scotland was much more closely the result of customer demand than the banking systems of Ireland or England.

Yet it too was changing. As the economy entered the railway age in the 1830s and other industries were growing apace the private and provincial banking companies found that they were too small to meet the needs of their customers. Within a few years they were gone, mostly by a process of mergers but there were a few failures. In their place there grew a series of large scale joint-stock banks some of whom, like the Glasgow based Union Bank[25] bought up a number of the smaller banks. The effect of this was that by 1845 Scotland had a structurally homogeneous banking system.[26] The same could almost be said for Ireland although the great size of the Bank of Ireland dwarfed the other organisations. The English banking system had begun to develop joint-stock banks but the process was slow.[27]

II

The years between 1830 and 1850 were, therefore a period of great change in British banking. Scotland, closely followed by Ireland, achieved a substantial change in its banking structure. England was some years behind.[28] It remains to be seen, however, where this change was taking place and from where these new initiatives were coming.

Throughout the nineteenth century there was a great and intense rivalry between the cities of Glasgow and Edinburgh. It is a rivalry which continues to the present day. It took many forms. On the banking scene the Edinburgh banks, especially the older public ones, the Bank of Scotland and Royal Bank of Scotland, took a superior view of the system and regarded themselves as its supervisors. They tended to view the Glasgow bankers as somewhat reckless and in 1832, when they had good reason to believe that the Glasgow based Western Bank of Scotland was engaging in business which was likely to destabilise it, they excluded it from the note exchange.[29] It is incidents like

TABLE 1. *Authorised Note Circulations of Scottish Banks 1845 (all figures in £000s)*

Edinburgh	£
Bank of Scotland	300
Royal Bank of Scotland	183
British Linen	438
Commercial Bank of Scotland	375
National Bank of Scotland	297
Edinburgh and Glasgow Bank (50%)	68
	1661

Glasgow	
Union Bank of Scotland	327
Western Bank of Scotland	338
Clydesdale Bank	104
City of Glasgow Bank	73
Edinburgh and Glasgow Bank (50%)	68
	910

Other Cities and Towns	
Dundee Banking Company	33
East of Scotland Bank (Dundee)	34
Aberdeen Town and County Bank	70
Aberdeen Banking Company	88
North of Scotland Bank (Aberdeen)	154
Perth Banking Company	39
Central Bank of Scotland (Perth)	43
Caledonian Bank (Inverness)	53
	514

(Source: C. W. Boase, *A Century of Banking in Dundee*, (Dundee, 1867), p. 432.

this which call the adoption of Scotland as a model by the 'Free Banking School' into question.[30]

There was therefore a clear difference of tone in the minds of bankers in the two cities. The reluctance of the National Bank to operate in the west of Scotland, mentioned above, is another example of the guarded and suspicious way in which Edinburgh bankers regarded the west.

When, in 1845, the Bank Act was passed which prevented the creation of new note-issuing banks the Scottish banks were allowed to have an 'authorised circulation' based on the average circulation in 1844. The figures which were published at that time give some indication of the strength of banking in the two cities.

These figures clearly show what a commanding position Edinburgh had established in the banking world by this stage. Nevertheless the struggle was not over and note issues are not the only measure by which to gauge a banking system. The Scottish bankers themselves thought of their strengths not only in terms of figures on their balance sheets but in terms of the number of branches which each bank maintained. These figures tell a somewhat different story.

In 1857 there were 607 branches of Scottish banks. Of these 228 were operated by banks with their headquarters in Edinburgh (average 45) but the Glasgow banks operated 281 branches (average 70). Other Scottish cities had banks with 84 branches (average 12). These figures clearly establish Glasgow in the ascendancy. Furthermore, in terms of note issues, the Glasgow banks were moving to close the gap with £1,454,000 against Edinburgh's £1,840,000 in 1857.[31] It must be remembered, however, that by this stage of their development note issues were becoming less important to the circulation of Scotland and cheques were being used increasingly in business.

Any ascendancy over Edinburgh which the Glasgow banks had been able to establish at this time was short lived. For in the commercial crisis of 1857 the Western Bank of Scotland failed. The shock was severe, for the Western had the largest number of branches and the second largest note circulation of the Scottish banks. In 1865 the Scottish banks began to publish modest balance sheets and these show that, by that date, any claim which Glasgow might have had to be a rival financial centre to Edinburgh had evaporated. The figures show that, in that year, the Edinburgh based banks controlled 61.5% of bank liabilities to the public (notes and deposits) while the Glasgow banks had only 30.31%.[32] In 1878 the City of Glasgow of Glasgow Bank failed and the Glasgow bank's share of total liabilities went down to 22.15% in 1880 against Edinburgh's 70.72%. The eclipse of Glasgow was complete and the industrial city never again rivalled the capital city of Edinburgh as a banking centre.

In Ireland the Bank of Ireland continued to dominate the system and the Belfast banks never looked like threatening the Dublin based banks[33] in the way that the Glasgow banks had threatened those in Edinburgh. In 1850 the three Belfast banks had 49 of the 174 Irish bank offices (28.2%). By 1880 they had 138 out of 415 offices (33.3%).[34]

The number of branches and the amounts of notes issued are, of course, not the whole story. Advances to customers are probably even more important but it is more difficult to obtain reliable data. S. G. Checkland ranked the Scottish banks at five yearly intervals between 1865 and 1972 based on published balance sheet information. In 1870 the five Edinburgh banks ranked 1,2,3,5, and 6 with the three Glasgow banks ranked 4,7, and 8. In 1880, after the failure of the City of Glasgow Bank, the Edinburgh banks ranked 1,2,3,4 and 5 with the remaining Glasgow banks ranked 6 and 7.[35]

Mention of bank lending raises the question of where the money was being lent. It is certainly clear from the above that the bulk of Scottish banking was controlled from Edinburgh. Yet it seems likely that most lending took place in Glasgow and the west of Scotland. This was, after all, the industrial centre of Scotland where the highest densities of population were to be found. In the last quarter of the nineteenth-century Scotland, particularly the west of Scotland, maintained a dis-proportionately large part of Britain's heavy industry and the demand for credit must have been very high. What is not clear is where the lending decisions took place. Branch managers certainly had some discretion especially where discounting of bills took place. It is much less likely that they had discretion in the granting of cash credits.[36] In these cases decisions were made either at head office or by one of the regional boards or committees which some banks operated.

The Glasgow based Union Bank of Scotland operated a regional committee system. Its historian, Norio Tamaki, discovered that in the regions of Perth, Aberdeen and Edinburgh, between 1860 and 1865, deposits exceeded advances – sometimes by a large margin. But in Glasgow the reverse was the case; advances were continually ahead of deposits.[37] The conclusion to be drawn is the obvious one that branches were not just used to gather deposits and channel them in to head office but that was their main function. It is also noteworthy that the west of Scotland branches produced the largest volume of deposits. Unfortunately none of the Edinburgh banks has attracted the same degree of careful examination from an historian so that it is not possible to see how this system operated from Edinburgh. However, the notes made by S. G. Checkland and his researchers, using board of directors' minute books, show that Edinburgh bankers made many loans to west of Scotland businesses. These would be operated via accounts in Glasgow and other west of Scotland branches. It is tempting to assume that the Edinburgh banks did the bulk of their lending in the west but there is no hard evidence to support this. The quotation from the National Bank that Glasgow was where 'the principal banking business is done' lends weight to this supposition but there is clearly a need for more research in the archives of the Edinburgh banks.

Given the dominance of the Edinburgh banks in the last quarter of the nineteenth century and the preponderance of industrial developments on the other side of Scotland it might be tempting to assume that this led to questions about the quality of the banking service which customers received. It is often claimed of England, although without much substantiation, that the physical separation of banking head offices in London from industrial head offices in the north of England led to an inferior quality of banking service. This is usually related to lending, in particular, and the argument, in its more extreme form, is that the banks turned their backs on industry. Given that there was this same physical separation of banking head offices from industry in both Scotland and Ireland might it not be argued that these countries suffered an inferior quality of banking service, especially in lending?

The evidence for such an argument is non-existent. It is possible to find a few examples of applications for loans being turned down but this is not the same as saying that the banks were blind to the needs of industry. It is just that they knew a poor lending proposal when they saw one. The branch banking system and the operation of regional boards ensured that banks, wherever their head office, were well attuned to the needs of industry. Moreover the German banking system of having bankers on the boards of industrial customers is sometimes held up as a system well worthy of imitation. Yet the Scottish and Irish practice, perhaps also the English, was to have businessmen on the boards of banks. There is an abundance of evidence to show that all Scottish banks were responsive to the needs of industry and commerce and that it was not just large well established companies who received credit from their banks.[38] Many newly formed companies, some of which were in new industries, were able to prove themselves sufficiently credit worthy to justify the faith of their bankers in lending them money.

III

The existence of a banking system is always the main element in a financial system and it is usually the most visible, especially when branch banking is part of the structure. Yet banks are by no means the whole story. In Scotland the life assurance industry has, for many years been a major element of

Table 2. Total Life Funds of Scottish Assurance Companies 1887

All figures in £000s

Name of Company	Year of Formation	Edinburgh Head Office	Glasgow Head Office	Other Head Office
Caledonian	1805	773		
City of Glasgow			1435	
Edinburgh		2119		
General	1885			899 Perth
Life Assn of Scot	1838	3081		
North Brit and Mer	1809	3645		
Northern				1960 Aberdeen
Scot. Amicable	1827		2775	
Scot. Provident	1837	5738		
Scot. Union and Nat	1878	2655		
Scot. Widows	1814	9228		
Standard Life	1825	6482		
		33721	4210	2859

Scottish financial enterprise. Unfortunately, despite its importance, it has received very little attention from historians.[39] Public sources of information about the industry are scarce and they are often unreliable.

Nevertheless a few figures will suffice to create the impression that Edinburgh's dominance over Glasgow in the banking industry was even more marked in the life assurance business. There do not seem to have been any permanent developments in the life assurance industry in the eighteenth century. Most of the nineteenth century companies were organised as mutual companies (without shareholders, although some were set up as companies and then converted to mutual status[40]) whose sole business was life assurance. There were a few composite companies who transacted all branches of insurance but the business was dominated by the mutuals.

A list in the Scottish Banking and Insurance Magazine of 1887 gives a view of the size of the industry and of the extent to which it was dominated by Edinburgh based companies.

Significantly the three largest Scottish companies – Scottish Widows, Standard Life and Scottish Provident were also the three largest British companies and several of the other Scottish companies were also significant in UK terms. The table indicates that the formative period for the industry was between 1815 and 1840. This was also the period when banking transformed itself from its eighteenth century mode into a more modern structure.

What is a little surprising is that Glasgow did not provide a greater response to the opportunities which were available. Yet whereas the development of large scale joint-stock banking was slower to be seen in Glasgow than in Edinburgh the life assurance business barely developed at all. This is not to be explained by regional demand factors for most of the Edinburgh life offices had branches in Glasgow. In the absence of primary research we must assume therefore that there was a healthy demand for life policies in the west of Scotland.

IV

The dominance of Edinburgh over Glasgow as Scotland's financial centre was evident in the eighteenth century and with the arrival of the life assurance industry in the early 19th century it was confirmed. This was re-affirmed by later developments, for Scotland came to be the home of the investment trust movement. Many of the principles on which investment trusts were established and run were developed in Scotland by people like Robert Fleming and W. J. Menzies.[41] Most of these developments were based in Edinburgh but it was Dundee, rather than Glasgow, which provided the competition.

Research on the history of investment trusts and other financial organisations is in an even less developed state than that on insurance
companies. Of the investment trust companies formed between 1873 and
1900 (and still in existence in 1932) twelve were in Edinburgh and six in
Dundee. There were none in Glasgow.[42] If the investment trusts are added
to the general category of financial, land and investment companies used by
the Stock Exchange Yearbook then the same picture of Edinburgh dominance
emerges. Of the companies formed in the nineteenth century and still in
existence in 1900 some 22 were in Edinburgh, 8 in Dundee, 6 in Glasgow
and 4 in Aberdeen. These figures simply confirm what we have already
observed.

It should be remembered too that, earlier in the century, a great deal of
Glasgow and the west of Scotland's energies were being channelled into
railways and iron companies, with banking a poor third and life assurance
barely visible. Edinburgh energies on the other hand were being channelled
into commerce, especially banking and life assurance, with comparatively
little being devoted to heavy industry. Regional specialisation may provide a
framework for describing what was happening but it does not adequately
explain why the economic development process in the two cities was so
different.

The geography of central Scotland was certainly a contributory factor in
this. The cities are only 45 miles apart and they were connected by railway
in 1841. Prior to this the canal boats had done a good trade in passenger
traffic – linking the two cities in 10 hours. Stagecoaches were even more
important. Nevertheless the pattern of development which has been described
was set before the arrival of the railways. Although railways are vitally
important to later developments in many parts of the world they certainly
do not form part of the explanation for regional specialisation in central
Scotland before the 1840s.

Clearly the development of a predominantly commercial city on one side
of the country and a predominantly industrial one on the other side is not to
be explained by a mono-causal argument. Industrial development in Scotland, as in Ireland and England, can certainly be attributed to such factors
as access to raw materials, shipping facilities and a supply of labour. These
ingredients are not so important in financial services which can be supplied
anywhere with small amounts of labour. The branch system saw to that. The
question to be posed therefore is why so many financial institutions were
head-quartered in Edinburgh rather than Glasgow.

Of course, exactly the same question can be asked of Ireland and England.
Kindleberger defined a series of factors which were important in the establishment of financial centres and to his list I have added some of my own.
These include legal stability, currency stability, location on trade route,
political centre, local demand, external economies of scale, culture, tradition,

skills, savings accumulation, information network, government policy and education.[43] Edinburgh possessed all of these attributes, with the exception of government policy. Yet Glasgow had nearly as many attributes. The only *major* difference between itself and Edinburgh was that it was not a political centre.

Ultimately the answer may be found in the eighteenth century rather than the nineteenth. The establishment of the Royal Bank's branch in Glasgow in 1783 under the management of R. Scott-Moncrieff and David Dale was extremely successful and came just at the time when Glasgow was beginning to emerge from the loss of most of its tobacco trade and to find other things to do with its energies. The Royal Bank branch soon established itself as the dominant force in Glasgow banking.[44] The fact that it was controlled from Edinburgh did not seem to matter to the Glasgow merchants who were its customers. Encouraged by this the Bank of Scotland opened a branch in 1787. The British Linen Company had a presence in Glasgow from an even earlier date. It is reasonably clear that these offices of the Edinburgh banks did excellent business and the Royal Bank in particular soon came to dominate the city's banking despite the existence of several native banks and the branches of numerous other provincial banks. Moreover the shareholdings in the Edinburgh public banks appear to have been more widely spread so that the argument about profits from Glasgow banking going to Edinburgh were no longer so valid as they had been in the 1750s.

This issue was addressed by Professor Tamaki in his history of the Union Bank. He questions why it was that in 1830 Edinburgh had five large scale banks when Glasgow had four relatively small scale organisations of its own. The answer seems to be that most of Glasgow's banking needs were being met by branches of Edinburgh banks and there was no perceived need for Glasgow to develop its own larger scale banks. What changed this situation was the sudden arrival of the railway and iron age in the 1830s. Demand for credit and other banking services grew dramatically and Glasgow, at last, produced some large scale banking initiatives of its own.[45] For a time these highly active and aggressive organisations posed a serious challenge to the Edinburgh banks but they over-reached themselves and their challenge soon faded. It may be speculated that if Glasgow business people were, on the whole, content to look to Edinburgh for their banking needs they would be equally content to look there for their life assurance and other financial requirements.

The branch and agency systems of distributing financial services proved to be a highly efficient and reliable means of collecting deposits, lending money, selling insurance policies and gathering premia. The management tasks involved in running a branch system were quite straight-forward. Basically it was sufficient to ensure that agents or managers knew their business and that there were controls on their freedom of action to ensure reasonable conformity to head-office practice. These enabled the Scottish life offices to grow to be world class financial institutions and to operate on a world scale. The banks never sought to extend their branches overseas and when they sought to move into England they were soon rebuffed by the growing confidence of English joint-stock banks.

REFERENCES

1. See especially W D Rubenstein, *Capitalism, Culture and Decline, 1750–1990,* (London, 1993). Ch 2.
2. A. Smith, *The Wealth of Nations* ed A. Skinner (Harmondsworth, 1970), p 394.
3. C. P. Kindleberger, *The Formation of Financial Centres: A Study in Comparative Economic History* (Princeton, 1974).
4. See Royal Dutch Academy of Arts and Sciences, May 1991 Conference on Financial Centre Development.
5. N. S. B. Gras, *An Introduction to Economic History* (New York, 1922) and M. Fanno, *La Banche e il Mercato Monetario* (Rome, 1913).
6. M. Collins, *Banks and Industrial Finance in Britain* (London, 1991) p. 62.
7. W. P. Kennedy, 'Institutional Response to Economic Growth: Capital Markets in Britain to 1914', in L. Hannah ed. *Management Strategy and Business Development* (London, 1976).
8. S. G. Checkland, *Scottish Banking: A History 1695–1973* (Glasgow, 1975) pp 103–4.
9. Checkland, '*Scottish Banking*', p. 146.
10. Checkland, *Scottish Banking*, p. 201.
11. C W Munn, *The Scottish Provincial Banking Companies, 1747–1863* (Edinburgh, 1981), ch. 1.
12. T. M. Devine, *The Tobacco Lords*, (Edinburgh 1975), passim.
13. C. W. Munn, *Scottish Provincial Banks*, ch. 1.
14. Munn, *Scottish Provincial Banks*, conclusion.
15. L. S. Pressnell, *Country Banking in the Industrial Revolution*, (Oxford, 1956) p. 6.
16. Munn, *Scottish Provincial Banks*, ch. 7.
17. G. W. S. Barrow, *The Emergence of the Irish Banking System 1820–1845*, (Dublin, 1975) and P. G. Ollerenshaw, *Banking in Nineteenth Century Ireland: The Belfast Banks 1825–1914*, (Manchester, 1987).
18. Munn, *Scottish Provincial Banks*, pp. 115–121.
19. Munn, *Scottish Provincial Banks*, pp 145–148.
20. C. W. Munn, 'The Development of Joint-Stock Banking in Scotland 1810–1845', in A. Slaven and D. H. Aldcroft (eds) *Business, Banking and Urban History*, (Edinburgh, 1982), p. 120.
21. Minutes of Directors, Commercial Bank of Scotland 29/4/1844.
22. Ollerershaw, *Banking in Nineteenth Century Ireland*, p. 20.
23. Munn, *Scottish Provincial Banks*, pp 80–85.

24. T. Joplin, *An Essay on Banking in England and Scotland*, (London, 1822).
25. N. Tamaki, *The Life Cycle of the Union Bank of Scotland 1830–1954*, (Aberdeen, 1983), pp 19–34.
26. Munn, *The Development of Joint-Stock Banking in Scotland* and Munn, The Coming of Joint-Stock Banking in Scotland and Ireland 1820–1845, in T. M. Devine and D. Dickson (eds) *Ireland and Scotland 1600–1850*, (Edinburgh, 1983).
27. P. L. Cottrell, *Industrial Finance 1830–1914*, (London, 1980), p. 195.
28. C. W. Munn, 'The Emergence of Joint-Stock Banking in the British Isles – A Comparative Approach', in R. P. T. Davenport-Hines and G Jones (eds) *The End of Insularity: Essays in Comparative Business History*, (London, 1988).
29. C. W. Munn, 'The Origins of the Scottish Note Exchange', *Three Banks Review*, 1975 and Checkland, *Scottish Banking*, pp. 328–9.
30. L. White, *Free Banking in Britain: Theory, experience and debate 1800–45*, (Cambridge, 1984).
31. C. W. Boase, *A Century of Banking in Dundee*, (Dundee, 1867) p. 503.
32. Checkland, *Scottish Banking*, Table 48, p. 751.
33. Ollerenshaw, *Banking in Nineteenth Century Ireland*, Table 37, p. 184.
34. Ollerenshaw, *Banking in Nineteenth Century Ireland*, Table 29, 124.
35. Checkland, *Scottish Banking*, Table 47, p. 750.
36. C. W. Munn, *Clydesdale Bank: The First 150 Years*, (Glasgow, 1988), p. 54.
37. Tamaki, *Union Bank*, Table 27, p. 89.
38. Tamaki, *Union Bank*, Ch. 5. and Munn, *The Emergence of Joint-Stock Banking*, pp. 114–139.
39. The notable exceptions are John Butt and James Treble. See J Treble 'The Performance of the Standard Life Assurance Company in the Ordinary life Market in Scotland 1850–75', in J. Butt and J. T. Ward, *Scottish Themes*, (Edinburgh, 1976) Pp 124–140 and 'The performance of the Standard Life Assurance Company in the Ordinary Market for Life Insurance 1825–50', *Scottish Economic and Social History*, Vol 5, 1985. Pp 57–77. J Treble, 'The Record of the Standard Life Assurance Company in the Life Insurance Market of the United Kingdom 1850–64' and J Butt, 'Life Assurance in War and Depression: The Standard Life Assurance Company and its Environment, 1914–39' in O Westall (ed), *The Historian and the Business of Insurance*, (Manchester, 1984. Pp 95–113 and 155–172.
40. Eg The Scottish Mutual Assurance Society which began life in 1883 as the Scottish Temperance Assurance Society Limited. See M. Magnusson, *A Length of Days: The Scottish Mutual Assurance Society* (London, 1983)
41. A. Slaven and S. G. Checkland (eds) *Dictionary of Scottish Business Biography*, Vol 2, (Aberdeen, 1990). Entry by C. W. Munn on Robert Fleming. P 401–2 and R. B. Weir on W. J. Menzies. Pp 414–5.
42. G. Glasgow, *The Scottish Investment Trust Movement*, (London, 1932).
43. Kindleberger, *Financial Centres*, passim.
44. Checkland, *Scottish Banking*, pp 146–7.
45. Tamaki, *Union Bank*, Intro. and ch 1.

Part 2

Society

8

Agricultural Change and its Impact on Tenancy: The Evidence of Angus Rentals and Tacks, c. 1760–1850[1]

PETER CLAPHAM

The transformation of the Scottish agrarian world between the 17th and 19th centuries has been a particular focus of interest for social historians. Both general texts and in-depth studies have examined various aspects of agricultural change over these two or three centuries. However, the more detailed investigations of the process have tended to concentrate either on the early modern period up to around the mid-18th century or have focussed on 19th century developments. Less attention has been directed towards the changes that took place from the mid-18th to the mid-19th century.

This paper looks specifically at this period and utilises the Airlie estate records in Angus to attempt a more detailed and penetrating analysis of developments in this period and to gauge the extent of its correlation with or divergence from current historiographic conclusions. In particular rental records are used to examine aspects of tenancy change in three parishes in which the Airlie estate held lands. However, where source material permits and other research allows comparison, reference will be made to areas and time periods outwith those of specific concern here.

There are three particular issues of interest. Firstly, the progress towards single tenancies from the older type of multiple holdings. The timing of this reduction of multiple tenancy and the concomitant rise of single tenures is one problem area of research that both historians and geographers have sought to resolve with greater precision. Most would agree, however, that regional differences were apparent and that no concerted, national timescale of change to single tenancies existed. For example, while Dodgshon found that much farm consolidation and tenant reduction occurred in the south and east in the 1730s, '40s and '50s[2] and that in some areas of the Southern Uplands no multiple tenancies remained by mid-18th century[3], Gray noted that many farms in the interior of the north-east were still jointly-held in the 1790s[4]. One of the aims of this study then, is to place at least one estate in this interjacent region on this continuum of change.

Secondly, there is the issue of tenant security or continuity of tenure. The growing incidence of written tacks in the 17th and 18th centuries is a development seen by many as increasing tenant security of tenure. The Whytes (alone so far) have examined the actual length of tenant occupancy by analysing a continuous series of rentals on one Angus estate over the period 1650–1714.[5] Their findings indicated aspects of both stability and mobility within the tenant group and these will be considered and compared to Airlie estate data in this paper. Lease lengths have been used by others as a means of assessing tenant security of tenure and again, as with tenancy change, variability across the country is apparent. In the south-east for instance, 19–21 year tacks were being introduced early in the 18th century[6] while in Kincardineshire, at least until the 1760s, most tacks were of 5–11 years duration.[7] This study makes a further contribution to the debate by delineating the change in lease lengths in the study area.

Finally, rental data are used here to construct rent profiles of the parishes in 1763 and 1846 to elucidate the extent of tenancy change and to assess what the economic and social consequences of such change may have been for the tenant class and between it and that of the landless labourers.

The Study Area

The parishes of Airlie and Alyth were selected because of their location primarily within the lowland part of the region; Airlie more particularly because of its arable specialisation and Alyth because of the existence of the growing 'industrial' centre of the village of Alyth. Cortachy, situated in the Grampian highlands, was chosen by way of comparison with the other two.

Data from the *New Statistical Account of Scotland* (N.S.A.) published in the 1840s gives a useful outline of the agrarian economies of the three parishes by this date. The most noticeable features of these parishes are, firstly the high proportion of land given over to arable cultivation in Airlie (almost 80%) and the very similar proportion (*c.* 85%) taken up by pastoral husbandry in Cortachy.[8] In Alyth, something of the order of one quarter of the land area was devoted to arable by the 1840s and most of the rest was unspecifically divided between pastoral and waste.

The First or *Old Statistical Account of Scotland* (O.S.A.) of the 1790s indicated that Airlie was producing wheat, bear and oats on a considerable scale by comparison with Cortachy in the later 18th century, which was perhaps hardly surprising when their relative acreages of arable land are considered. Despite the slant towards cultivation in Airlie however, the parish was reported to have around 700 head of cattle and 360 sheep indicating an element of mixed farming in its agriculture.[9]

The view presented by the above figures of Alyth has to be treated with some care since, despite its greater arable acreage, the comparatively larger size of the parish *vis à vis* that of Airlie dwarfed its percentage of the total. Large areas of Alyth parish were still moorish and waste by the time of the *O.S.A.* but the arable area of the parish was still capable of producing 'excellent crops of barley, oats and wheat' by the later 18th century.[10] Moreover, the importance of grass and turnip cultivation gives some impression of the existence of the pastoral sector here. In short, Alyth appears to possess something of the agrarian economies of both the other two parishes.

In Cortachy the main arable areas were, and still are to be found in the extreme south where the parish spills out into Strathmore although the alluvial soils of the valley bottom in mid-parish also produced reasonable crops. Oats, barley, pease, flax and potatoes were all recorded in the *O.S.A.* albeit qualified with the admission that even in the 'most fruitful seasons' little grain was exported from the parish. The climatic limitations imposed upon agriculture by the higher elevation of this Grampian parish meant that farmers looked to cattle and sheep-rearing to supply their rents and profits.[11]

Change in Tenancies

The work of Whyte and Dodgshon has helped to clarify what was a confusing area of discussion on the various kinds of tenancy. The three discrete types of tenure in the early modern period which they have identified and elucidated are joint, multiple and single tenancies.[12] Joint tenure involved two or more individuals who held and cultivated the land together, shared the crop and paid a single, undivided rental between them. In such communal agricultural circumstances, tenant co-operation at all levels, from the collective execution of work loads to the sharing of farming implements, would have been of the utmost necessity to maintain both the social cohesion and the economic efficiency of the fermetoun.

In this period in these three parishes joint tenancy was rare. The rentals examined at roughly decadal intervals from circa 1760 revealed only a handful of such cases. In Alyth in the 1750s and '60s, James Powrie and Thomas Mitchell held a joint possession as did John Wighton and Thomas Rattray, while almost all the other examples discovered were held by persons having a common surname.[13] As Whyte observed, this suggests that the lease 'only gave formal expression to what must have been a normal working situation. Most holdings were family units where sons and brothers would have helped in the work of cultivation.'[14] Examples of this kind of arrangement were to be found in Cortachy in the 1780s, where Euphame Whyte and her son held the farm of Wester Tarrybuckle and James Lindsay and his mother were in possession of the Mill of Rottal. The remaining instances in which common surnames were evident all appear to have been cases where fathers and sons were in possession. Almost invariably in these situations the son would take full, single possession on the death of the father, such as in the case of James and Patrick Hanton in the parish of Airlie.[15]

Multiple tenure again involved two or more tenants, but here the rents were paid separately implying that discrete holdings were involved. The vast majority of the non-single tenant farms that were studied here were of this nature. Sometimes rentals represented clear proportions such as half, third or quarter shares. In other cases there appeared to be no obvious fractional division, but simply two or more separate rentals. Dodgshon has argued that the essence of runrig tenure was the apportionment of land units of equal extent and value and further that his work highlighted a useful, though not an invariable link between share tenancy and runrig.[16] This interpretation of runrig finds clear support in the legal proceedings relating to the division of Alyth Muir in the late 18th and early 19th centuries. Alexander Robertson, a deponent in this case, said of an earlier division of the runrig lands of the farm of Balloch near Alyth, that he understood, 'the division was made between Lord Airly and Mr. Brown equally, quantity and quality considered.'[17]

To draw precise conclusions from rental data on multiple tenancy is not without its difficulties. Whyte has argued[18] that multiple tenure was most often associated with the allocation of lands under the runrig system. Tenants having equal shares in the fermetoun lands would pay equal rents so that half, third or quarter rent shares in rental data serve to identify the existence of runrig. However, where two or more tenants held a possession and paid differing rents, which did not have such clear fractional relationships, this makes for greater difficulty of interpretation. Can it be assumed, for example, that such circumstances simply indicated that the tenants had come to hold differing numbers of strips over time within the runrig system, or was it perhaps more significantly a case of an old fermetoun which had undergone division and consolidation, much in the way that Gray has recently suggested?[19] The emphasis placed on lands of equal quantity and quality under runrig seems to cast doubt on the former explanation.

Onomastic evidence has also been suggested as a means of identifying runrig. Dodgshon[20] has highlighted the relationship between runrig land allocations and certain farm names such as Easter/Wester, Nether/Over etc., though it seems apparent from the present research in the parish of Cortachy that, taken alone, nomenclature cannot firmly establish the existence of runrig tenure. For instance, an early 19th century map of Cortachy unearthed in the course of research appears to show Easter and Wester Tarrybuckle to be two, quite separate farms.[21] These interpretative difficulties need to be borne in mind in the course of the following discussion.

Rental data has been used to draw up Table 1, which compares the relative proportions of single to multiple (i.e. joint and share) tenure over the forty

Table 1. Single & Multiple Tenancies, Two Parishes, 1763–1800

(Parish) /Year	No. of Farms	No. of Multiple Tenancies	% age of Total	No. of Single Tenancies	% age of Total
(Airlie)					
1763	9	3	33.3	6	66.6
1780	9	2	22.2	7	77.8
1800	9	1	11.1	8	88.9
(Cortachy)					
1763	60	15	25	45	75
1771	59	13	22	46	78
1780	59	11	18.6	48	81.4
1790	59	10	17	49	83
1800	59	10	17	49	83

Source: SRO GD 16/30A Series

years or so before 1800. The collection and analysis of this information presented some difficulties, which need to be pointed out here. Firstly, though the majority of farms which constituted the main possessions of the Airlie estate in each parish became apparent after an initial period of familiarisation with the archive material, others were at times of ambiguous location. Secondly, in Alyth specifically, the burgeoning numbers of smaller possessions in the later 18th century made for a very confused picture of landholding and since the base number of possessions could not be accurately determined it clearly was not possible to arrive at precise percentage figures for tenancy types. Thirdly, it is important to bear in mind that of our three parishes, only in Cortachy is a complete parochial analysis provided since only here did the Airlie family possess the whole. Lastly, the small size of the dataset for that of Airlie needs to be appreciated in all the statistical information derived from it. Notwithstanding these caveats, the general trends which are indicated in Table 1 can hardly be in doubt.

Perhaps the most significant feature of the contents of Table 1 is the high proportion of single tenancies by the mid-18th century; between two thirds and three quarters in these parishes. Thereafter, the shift towards a mean value of over 85% by 1800 is, if not dramatic in scale, clear in direction.

Whyte's work relating to the Airlie estates, appears to suggest that by the late 17th century around 75% of farms were already single tenant possessions.[22] Compared to the data given above, that figure is high and would suggest, as far as tenancies are concerned, a period of relative stasis between the late 17th and mid-18th centuries, assuming that the data are comparable. However, the proportion of multiple tenancies at this point in time as represented in Table 1, correlates well with the data presented by Dodgshon for the Southern Uplands.[23] Though the Roxburgh estate had totally eradicated multiple tenancies by the 1750s, the proportion was about one third on the Buccleuch estate in 1766. By contrast, as we have already seen, Gray noted that many interior farms in the north-east were still in joint tenancy by the 1790s. Without a more precise estimate for this more northerly region it is difficult to assess rank order, but it is surely impossible to interpret the 17% of multiple tenant farms in Cortachy by 1800, as 'many', which suggests that the timescale of progress towards single tenant holdings in Angus more nearly matched that in the south-east of Scotland than that of the north-east.

In the rentals of the parish of Airlie the last indication of possessions held by two individuals paying exactly similar rents was in 1780 in the farms of Brae of Airlie and Wetfoot.[24] By 1790 the Brae had three tenants paying differing rents ranging from about £4 to almost £18,[25] which as we have already speculated may suggest *de facto* consolidation. However, if multiple tenure is to be recognised as simply the circumstance where two or more tenants were indicated in rental rolls as possessing the same farm, then the total by 1800 in Airlie was one out of nine or just over 11%. On the face of it the situation in 1846 was no different. David Davie held part of the Brae of Airlie at an annual rental of £72.12.0d, whilst Elizabeth McKillop held the other portion at a rent of £4.10.0d.[26] In 1821 the latter had held one of the two pendicles of Lundies which were subsequently let to a blacksmith and a wright by 1846. It therefore seems likely that Mckillop, who had formerly possessed a pendicle, had simply transferred to another and this suggests that the farm of Brae of Airlie comprised one large farm and a small, separate pendicle well before the mid-19th century. Thus, over these 80 or more years this part of the Airlie estate witnessed what appears to have been the gradual eradication of multiple tenancies from an original proportion of around one third of the total.

Analysis of the 19th century Cortachy data also presents interpretative problems. The proportion of farms comprising two or more tenants was about 17% by 1800 as Table 1 demonstrates. Only four possessions, however, or around 7% of these were examples of farms with rental shares which demonstrated an obvious fractional allocation of land. This had been reduced to three by 1810 and only one by 1821 with the two farms of Crossmiln and Bearfauld having been divided into several pendicles under a scheme devised in the 1810s by William Blackadder, a surveyor in Glamis. This involved the almost wholesale reorganisation of Cortachy's farms and farming community and comprised firstly, the removal of a broad stratum of poorer tenants from their possessions and their resettlement in small allotments in the Glen; secondly, the reorganisation of many farms in the middle grazing districts into farms of 50–80 acres arable and 800–1000 acres pasture; and thirdly, the introduction of newer methods of husbandry notably in the form of a five-break rotation.[27]

By 1846 then, there were five farms which still nominally had two or more tenants in possession. This represented something over 12% of the total number of holdings in the parish. But two of these were clearly pendicles as noted a moment ago (Crossmiln & Bearfauld) which thus reduces multiple tenure to about 7.5% of the total. Even those that remained were questionable as *bona fide* examples of multiple tenancies with the usually associated circumstances of runrig land division and communal endeavour. For instance, though the two nominally separate farms referred to in the rental books as 'part called Fichell' and 'part called Bank,'[28] had exactly similar rents of £66.16.0d., the early 19th century map of Cortachy already mentioned above, seems to show them as two clearly distinct and separate farms. Despite initial appearances then, it seems doubtful whether the last vestiges of multiple tenure survived the reorganisational scheme of Blackadder and by the mid-19th century, single tenancies were almost certainly all but completely dominant in Cortachy.

As already noted, Table 1 lacks data on Alyth because of the difficulties which were encountered in interpreting the landholding pattern. In a situation where individuals might hold an acre of land here, two or three roods of infield land there, where they may also be paying feu duty on other plots of land such as those that were let in Cairnleith just outside the village, it confused the calculations involved in determining the exact proportions of different kinds of tenancy to the point of unreliability. However the impression gained from examining qualitative sources is of a movement in the country part of the parish towards single tenancies by the later 18th century, while the village population swelled and the lands in and around it were further divided up to accommodate still more small tenants. 19th century rental data can be used to add statistical support to this general impression of an expanding population in and around the village. This increase in tenancies is shown in Table 2.

Table 2. Alyth Parish Tenant Numbers, 1800–46

Year	Alyth Tenants & Feuars	Cairnleith Tenants (Allotments)	Total
1800	69	24	93
1810	68	25	93
1821	78	34	112
1831	79	35	114
1846	80	44	124

Source: SRO GD16/30A/Vols. 53–111

It is interesting to see this trend of expansion in numbers in this period in strong contrast to the general, national movement towards farm consolidation and rural dispossession as was clearly the case in Cortachy. The rural industry and commerce of the village attracted individuals, both from within and outwith the parish and the county, who were accommodated by the creation of smallholdings in and around the village. The fact that in the 1840s while land rents on average throughout the parish were around £1.3s per acre, some of the lands near the village of Alyth were rented at between £3.10s and £4.10s per acre[29] lends support to this interpretation; an increase in tenant numbers would have been accompanied by an increase in demand for land and consequent rent inflation.

Quite clearly then, the weaving trade and the village's market centre functions had a distinctive influence on the development of landholding patterns in this parish over the period, a development which both contrasted with and complemented those in the other parishes. The creation of small tenancies in the vicinity of Alyth village was a consequence of the growth in demand stimulated by the general increase in population and the shake out of surplus individuals from the surrounding area by the process of farm consolidation. Furthermore, the fragmentation of agricultural lands around this growing centre represents a significant counter trend to the movement towards such consolidation. Similar processes were almost certainly occurring throughout lowland Scotland at the village centre/rural hinterland interface and must therefore serve as an important caveat to the broad generalisation that this period witnessed secular dispossession.

Continuity of Tenure

Another area of the Scottish historians' interest has been that of the continuity of tenure over this period of agrarian transformation. Lenman has suggested that the House of Airlie did not grant leases to its tenants,[30] but muniments belonging to the estate contain almost 200 tacks for the 18th century alone.[31] What proportion these written leases represented of the total granted is obviously impossible to assess and it seems likely, from comments made in the O.S.A., that certain possessions were let without written leases. For example, the minister in Kirkden reported of Lord Airlie that 'he granted but few leases to his tenants.'[32] Lenman went on to say that despite the paucity of written leases, tenants nevertheless enjoyed security of tenure. Evidence uncovered during this study is not conclusive on this point and even appears at times contradictory. On the one hand, the minister of Cortachy in the 1840s reported in the N.S.A. that,

> The removal of a peaceable and industrious farmer from this to any other parish is an event of very rare occurrence. For generations past, most of the farms have

been transmitted from father to son; and in every instance where the father has been removed by death, the greatest indulgence has been shown to his widow or fatherless children.[33]

Although written towards the mid-19th century, the impression given here is of long-established continuity of tenure. On the other hand, some of the evidence which the rental data for the latter half of the 18th century has been made to yield, perhaps suggests more in the way of change than of continuity. A statistical idea of continuity of tenure over this period in both Cortachy and Airlie has been derived from rental records but once again the confusing pattern of tenure as represented in the Alyth rentals excluded it from these calculations. Of the individuals in certain farms in 1763, the percentage of those in continuous possession was calculated at intervals up to 1790. Additionally those farms that had fallen into the possession of another individual with the same surname were also computed on the assumption that this represented continuity within the same family. The results are shown in Table 3.

There are, however, some problems involved in using the rental data in this way. Quite obviously the percentage figures in column one could be expected to show decrease over the years due to mortality and this rate of decline would have been affected by the age structure of the population in the base year. In addition, decrease might also be expected as a consequence of individuals voluntarily removing to another parish or possession. On the one hand, aspects of security of tenure are demonstrated by certain families who continued in possession of their holdings throughout the whole of the 1763–1846 period, such as the Mitchells and the How family in Cortachy and the Davie family in Airlie.[34] On the other hand, the continuity figures

Table 3. Continuity of Tenure in Cortachy and Airlie, 1763–90

Year	% age of Tenants in the same farm	% age including others with the same surname
(Cortachy)		
1763	100	100
1771	70.7	80
1780	34.7	44
1790	14.7	28
(Airlie)		
1763	100	100
1780	46.7	60
1790	20	33.3

Source: SRO GD16/30A/Vols. 2–33

Table 4. Tenant Continuity and Turnover: Cortachy & Airlie, 1800–46

Parish/ Period	No. Farms at Start of Period	No. of Tenants Continuing	% age Continuity	% age Turnover
(Cortachy)				
1800–10	63	47	74.6	25.4
1810–21	39	22	56.4	43.6
1821–31	41	29	70.7	29.3
1831–46	40	29	72.5	27.5
(Airlie)				
1800–10	8	6	75	25
1810–21	9	3	33.3	66.7
1821–31	8	6	75	25
1831–46	10	5	50	50

presented in Table 3 still appear to be quite low with a turnover rate of tenantry in Cortachy of almost three quarters and in Airlie of two thirds in this period of less than thirty years.

Since other aspects of the study tended to indicate fairly time-specific accelerations of agrarian reform in the 19th century,[35] the continuity/turn-over calculations for this period were tackled in a slightly different way. The levels of continuity and turnover of the tenantry were estimated between 1800–10, 1810–21, 1821–31, 1831–46 and not over the 1800–46 period as as whole. By this method it was thought that changes in the usual pattern or levels of turnover could more easily be narrowed down to specific decades or so.

The information given in Table 4 has been produced by the following method. The number of tenants in the final year of a survey period who still occupied the same possessions as in the first year of the same, were totalled and calculated as a percentage of the number of possessions in the final year. One preliminary methodological remark needs to be made before the more substantive points of interest in the data are discussed. This concerns the apparently fluctuating numbers of farms, particularly evident in the statistics for the parish of Airlie. It is arguable that this figure should have been ten throughout the period, since the variations occurred because of the dual leasing of the Kirktown and the Barns of Airlie only in some years and similar alterations in the leasing of the possessions of Lundies, though no evidence of physical consolidation was unearthed. But even calculated with a constant denominator of ten, the relationships of the decadal percentages is not altered as can easily be computed from the data given in Table 4. However, once again it is necessary to emphasize that the small statistical population of the Airlie data warrants a degree of circumspection when drawing conclusions from the table.

In both parishes the key period was obviously that of 1810–21. In Cortachy not only was the percentage turnover significantly higher than in the other periods in the first half of the 19th century, but the reduction of farm numbers from 63 to about 40 serves to mark out these years as ones of important agrarian reform. If this dramatic decrease is considered in our calculations for this period, then well over 60% of the tenants of 1810 had been dispossessed by 1821.

A further point of interest here is that population levels in the parish underwent a marginal increase in the years 1811–21[36] indicating either that there must have been a pronounced downward mobility of sections of the former tenant class or that there was a marked influx of farm servants to replace the former tenants. In any case, it was inevitable that a smaller tenant farming class was in possession of a reduced number of reorganised farms by the early 1820s. This was a consequence, as already noted, of the agrarian reform scheme formulated for the parish by William Blackadder in the 1810s.

The general turnover figures here may well be consistent with expected rates given mortality and mobility patterns of the tenant class, but indications from this small study are that specific periods demonstrated significantly higher levels of turnover.

Such conclusions as these are on this point must remain broad and tentative given that this sample of parishes is very small. Further studies of this nature, over different periods and places, may need to be undertaken before it becomes possible to judge the typicality of these figures.

Table 5. Changing Lease Lengths on the Airlie Estate, 1700–1800

Year	Mean Lease Length per Decade
1700–09	6.5
1710–19	6.2
1720–29	7.7
1730–39	7.2
1740–49	14.5
1750–59	12.8
1760–69	12.4
1770–79	17.6
1780–89	16.9
1790–1800	18.0

Source: SRO GD16 Airlie Muniments Inventory

Another measure of security of tenure, used by researchers, is the length of lease. An analysis of the Airlie muniments inventory provided some indication of the change in the lengths of leases in the 18th century. Table 5 shows the results of this examination of the tacks between 1700–1800 from all areas of the estate.

The Whytes' study of the Panmure estate in Angus between 1650–1714 indicated that the mean length of tenancy was 9.3 years.[37] It can readily be seen from the data in table 5 that on the Airlie estate this average tack duration was noticeably, though not markedly, smaller at something between 6 and 6.5 years over the opening two decades of the 18th century. Without a consideration of the local factors which may have caused this divergence between the two estates, it is not possible to account for it. However, the magnitude of the difference is not sufficient to suggest any real incompatibility between the two figures. From the same study of the Panmure estate, the Whyte's derived the following percentage figures for the proportions of tacks of 1, 2–5 and 11 years and over; 11.8%, 33.4% and 30.5% respectively. The comparable figures on the Airlie estate for the first half of the 18th century were 0%, 49.2% and 7.2%. Despite the complete absence of one-year tacks in Airlie, the fact that almost half the tenancy lengths were less than 5 years while conversely, those of 11 years and over accounted for well under 10% suggests a potentially greater mobility of tenantry here than on the Panmure lands. If this were indeed the reality then a much more detailed comparative study would be required to uncover the reasons behind it.

The *General View of Agriculture of Angus or Forfar* (G.V.A.), written in 1794, revealed that throughout the county, in the later 18th century, leases were anything from 15 to 38 years in length or even a lifetime, but went on to note that 'the lease most commonly given is for 19 years.'[38] Table 5 shows that by 1800, the average for the Airlie estate as a whole was very close to this common lease length. This situation was reached by incremental changes throughout the century except for a significantly pronounced increase in tack lengths from around the 1740s when mean values doubled. If these more dramatic changes in leases were related to farm land consolidation, then this would lend support to Dodgshon's contention that a 'spurt in tenant reduction and holding amalgamation'[39] occurred between 1730–50.

The much fewer numbers of tacks relating to the three parishes of study rendered a similar, decadal calculation of lease lengths there much less reliable though it was possible to draw a comparison between the two half centuries around 1750. The average lease length for the three parishes under consideration between 1700–49 was 6.1 years while that for the following half century up to 1800 was 13.4 years; again, as for the estate as a whole, the pattern is one of a doubling of lease length in the second half of the century.[40] Such figures indicate that despite general agreement between the

Table 6. Mean Length of Lease in the Three Parishes, 1775–1846

Period/Year	Airlie	Cortachy	Alyth
1775–1800	10.7	15.7	11
1821	11	12.5	13.1
1846	14	13.5	12.5

Source: SRO GD16/28 Tacks Inventory and GD16/30A/Vols. 93, 111

estate as a whole and these three parishes, the latter lagged somewhat behind in this respect.

An inventory of tacks for the 18th century together with rental data which also supplied information on lease lengths for the three parishes in the years 1821 and 1846 allowed the analysis of mean values of leases to be extended into the middle of the 19th century. The results presented in Table 6 illustrate differences among the parishes.

By comparison with historiographic orthodoxy some of these developments are predictable while others are more surprising. The Airlie figures demonstrate clear and steady increase in lease length up to 1846. However, the rise in the 1800–21 period is relatively modest and may have been a reflection of the estate management taking advantage of the quickly escalating grain prices between 1803–14[41] by restricting lease lengths and pushing up rents on expiry of tacks.[42] Such a thesis is supported firstly by the data on tenant turnover in Table 4 above and secondly by the fact that as prices dropped on trend up to the mid 19th century, so mean lease durations in the parish increased up to 14 years.

In the parish of Alyth the trend was very similar to Airlie up to 1821 but thereafter the mean value declined, which may simply be a consequence of the increase of small tenancies in and around the village as noted earlier. Such small holders, many of whom may have been tradesmen and weavers, would not have required the incentive of longer leases to take on a possession, that those tenant farmers who were engaging in costly capital outlay on farm improvements needed. The downward movement of lease lengths in Cortachy between 1800–21 was almost certainly a result of the Blackadder improvements in the 1810s when several smaller tenancies, let for significantly shorter periods, were created.

These mean values however, though useful as measures of central tendency can also conceal certain characteristics of a population or sample group. For instance, a perusal of the Airlie rental volumes which give tack length data is enough to confirm that the 14 year lease was far and away the mostly commonly granted one by the early 19th century. With this as the modal class for all three parishes in 1821 and 1846, it was possible to construct Table 7. The number of 14 year leases in all three parishes was

Table 7. 14-Year Leases as Percentage of Total, 1821 & 1846

| Year | Percentage of 14-Year Leases in Parish | | |
	Airlie	Cortachy	Alyth
1821	66.7	79.6	80.0
1846	100.0	92.3	80.0

Source: SRO GD16/28 Tacks and GD16/30A/Vols. 93, 111

calculated as a percentage of the total for which information was available
and where the tack lengths in years were specified; those recorded as 'at will'
or 'lifetime of tenant' were excluded from the calculations. It now becomes
clear that by the mid-19th century, something of the order of 90% of the
tenants of the Airlie estate in these three parishes held what appears to have
been a standard lease of 14 years duration.

Changing Rent Profiles

That rental increases occurred over the period under scrutiny is beyond
doubt. Evidence presented by others[43] and that uncovered in the course of
this study[44] confirms that rents rose from the 1760s and very steeply
thereafter until the post-war depression in the 1810s. Such rent rises are not
in question here; the point at issue is the change in rental structures within
estates and parishes. The following analysis focuses on the change in the
frequency distribution of rents on the Airlie estate within the three parishes
studied. These statistical populations have been presented as histograms in
Figure 1, in order to illustrate the developing rent profiles over these years.
It is important to note that the rentals have not been converted to a common
currency; those for 1763 being in old Scots pounds which was only one
twelfth the value of Sterling, the prevalent currency of the 1846 data. This
approach was decided upon because the point of interest here is not rent
inflation but, as already stated, but the transformation of rent profiles in each
parish between the two dates.

Table 8. Rent Profiles: Degree of Skewness, 1763 and 1846

| Year | Degree of Skewness of Rental Population | | |
	Airlie	Cortachy	Alyth
1763	+0.381	+0.844	+0.64
1846	+0.435	+1.257	+0.982

Source: GD16/30A/Vols. 2, 111

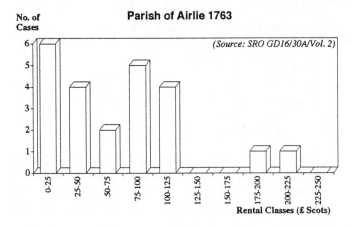

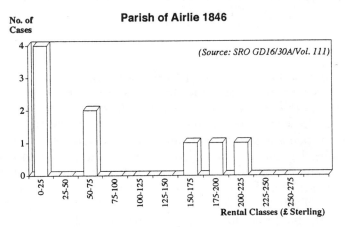

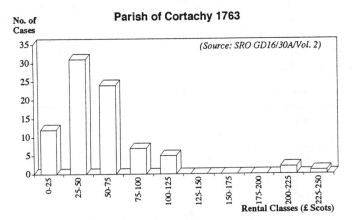

Figure 1. Rent profiles (continued on page 159)

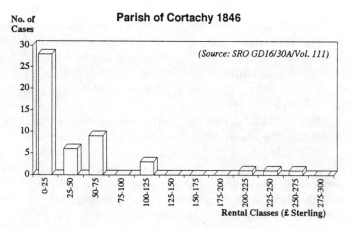

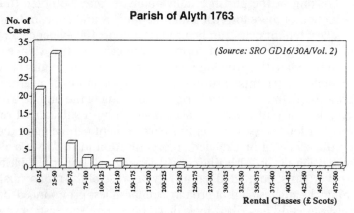

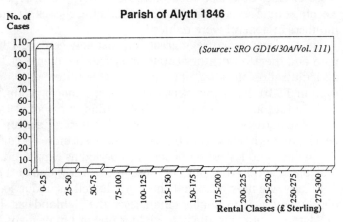

Figure 1. Rent profiles.

The first point to note is that none of the histograms represent 'normal' distributions; all six are positively skewed, which indicates a concentration of values below the mean. Secondly, the histograms for 1846, in every case, present a more simple or leaner appearance than those of 1763 with a greater degree of skewing. This visual impression of change is supported by the data in Table 8.

All these rental data have positive values and the magnitude of the skewing is indicated by the magnitude of the figure. Quite clearly then the pattern of a few highly-priced rentals and many lower-priced ones was accentuated over time. Thirdly, this change in the skewness of all three rentals over the period appears to have been effected by the reduction of a class of small tenants placed somewhat above the very lowest rent payers while at the same time, those at the base of the scale of tenancies expanded.

Looking at the parishes individually, it may be noted that in Alyth the reduction of these lower middling tenancies and concomitant growth of the smallest tenant class can be used to support the evidence already presented of the fragmentation of former tenancies on the village's periphery to accommodate the growing population in the area; a mirror reflection of the reduction of tenants in rural areas as consolidation of older fermetouns lands progressed. In Cortachy where, the doubling of the numbers of tenants in the very lowest rent class was accompanied by a substantial reduction of the three or four classes above, this development can be more readily explained by the effects of Blackadder's reorganisation in the 1810s already outlined above. Finally, in Airlie the conclusions drawn from the table and histograms as ever, must be treated tentatively because of the much smaller dataset but it may be suggested that broadly similar, if less pronounced, developments to those already described took place here too. The histograms illustrate the weeding out of several of the lower to middling classes of rent payers as tenant numbers in general were reduced.

Smout drew a picture of great contrast between the 18th century Gudeman and the 19th century capitalist farmer 'who emerged at the end of the agricultural revolution',[45] but qualified this statement with the caveat that even in 1830 the farming class was not a uniform group.[46] Clearly, on the Airlie estate in Angus, such a qualification is essential to a description of tenant structures at the end of this period of agricultural and social transition; developments here show a consistent pattern of increased differential between the highest and lowest rents over this period as expansion, not contraction, took place within the ranks of those at the lower end of the rental scales.

Finally, we may ask what these results tell us about social mobility. The absolute increase in smaller tenancies in the highland parish of Cortachy and in Alyth suggest that the potential for upward movement from the ranks of landless labourers actually increased in both cases and especially so in Alyth. Only in the predominantly arable parish of Airlie did both absolute reduction in tenancies and an erosion of the smallest holdings occur, implying a potentially greater gulf for labourers to cross in order to join the lower ranks of the mid-19th century tenantry.

Conclusion

How does this evidence relate to the national picture of tenancy change and what are the implications for general agrarian improvement? Firstly, an obvious point to emphasize is that the proportions of single tenancies by the 1760s were already high. Without tracing developments in this respect back to the 17th century, it is difficult to be sure exactly when the processes which produced this situation were operating. On the one hand, Whyte's data suggested a substantial incidence of single tenancies in this area by the late 17th century. On the other, the marked increases in tack lengths around the 1740s are very suggestive of changes other than those on paper and may well represent a 'pioneer phase' of rural change, as Dodgshon has suggested,[47] followed later by more general and sustained improvement.

Secondly, differences in the timing of change were apparent between parishes. The indications are that the arable parish of Airlie witnessed a gradual reduction in multiple tenancies and similar speed of farm consolidation. In highland Cortachy however, although a similarly gradual reduction of multiple tenancies were implied by the rent rolls, the inception of the Blackadder plan in the 1810s, marked a more deliberate and accelerated drive towards both tenant reduction and land reorganisation.

Thirdly, though Alyth tenancies increased in the later 18th century and especially in the early 19th century as peripheral lands were fragmented to accommodate an expanding population, this overall increase almost certainly concealed and helped to ameliorate the impact of a rural hinterland reduction in tenancies as farms were consolidated.

Lastly, the evidence of rent profiles indicates that certain structural changes took place. The method of analysis here is perhaps open to a number of interpretations since rent differentials and not actual holding sizes have been analysed, though these were quite obviously related to rentals. This paper has suggested that small tenancies were not completely eradicated in this period and that no significant movement towards a homogenous farming class is apparent from the rent profile analysis. Moreover, it seems apparent that even within this relatively circumscribed area, factors such as the agricultural nature of a parish and the proximity of rural industry to it, could have a significant effect upon the experience of social mobility between the tenant and labouring classes through their influence on tenancy sizes.

REFERENCES

1. I gratefully acknowledge the help and advice of particularly Professor T. M. Devine, but also of Andy Brown and Peter MacNaughton.
2. R. A. Dodgshon, *Land & Society in Early Scotland*, (Oxford, 1981), 265
3. R. A. Dodgshon, 'Agricultural Change & its Social Consequences in the Southern Uplands of Scotland, 1600–1780' in T. M. Devine & D. Dickson, (eds), *Ireland and Scotland 1600–1850*, (Edinburgh, 1983), 53
4. M. Gray, 'The Process of Agricultural Change in the North-East, 1790–1870', in Leneman, L. (ed), *Perspectives in Scottish Social History*, (Aberdeen, 1988), 126–127
5. I. D. Whyte and K. A. Whyte, 'Some Aspects of the Structure of Rural Society in Seventeenth-Century Lowland Scotland', in T. M. Devine & D. Dickson (eds), *Ireland and Scotland*, 40
6. R. A. Dodgshon, *Land and Society*, 254
7. C. E. Howlett, 'Agricultural Development and the Re-formed Rural Landscapes of Kincardineshire *c.* 1750 to *c.* 1880', Unpublished PhD Thesis, (Aberdeen University, 1987), 505
8. P. Clapham, 'Agrarian Reform on the Airlie Estate in Angus and Strathmore, 1760–1850', Unpublished MPhil Thesis, (Strathclyde University, 1990), table 2.2, 32
9. *Statistical Account of Scotland*, (O.S.A.) Vol. XIII (Edinburgh, 1791–99), 6–8
10. *O.S.A.*, Vol. XII, 19
11. This brief summary is taken from the *O.S.A.*, Vol. XIII, 119–123 and the *New Statistical Account of Scotland*, (N.S.A.) Vol. XI, (Edinburgh, 1845), 435–438
12. Most of the following is adapted from I. D. Whyte, *Agriculture & Society in Seventeenth Century Scotland*, (Edinburgh, 1979) and R. A. Dodgshon, 'Towards an Understanding and Definition of Runrig: the evidence for Roxburghshire and Berwickshire', in *Transactions of the Institute of British Geographers*, (T.I.B.G.) 64 (1975)
13. S.R.O. GD16/30A/vols. 1–2
14. I. D. Whyte, *Agriculture & Society*, 139
15. S.R.O. GD16/30A/vols, 17 & 51
16. R. A. Dodgshon, 'Understanding & Definition of Runrig', 17
17. S.R.O. GD16/27/247/184
18. I. D. Whyte, *Agriculture & Society*, 140–141 & 146–152
19. M. Gray, 'The Social Impact of Agrarian Change in the Rural Lowlands', in T. M. Devine & R. Mitchison (eds), *People & Society in Scotland*, Vol. I, (Edinburgh, 1988) 57–58
20. R. A. Dodgshon, 'Scandinavian Solskifte and the Sunrise Division of Land in Eastern Scotland', in *Scottish Studies* 19, (1975), 1–14
21. SRO RHP 5149
22. I. D. Whyte, *Agriculture & Society*, Fig. 10, 144. The figure of 75% has been

read from the map produced on this page which appears to refer to the area of the Airlie estates in Angus.

23. R. A. Dodgshon, 'Agricultural Change in the Southern Uplands', 52–53
24. SRO GD16/30A/Vol. 17, Rentals for the parish of Airlie
25. SRO GD16/30A/Vol. 33, – ditto –
26. SRO GD16/30A/Vol. 111 – ditto –
27. SRO GD16/26/Box 10, Letter from William Blackadder to the estate factor McNicoll, dated 15th December, 1813
28. SRO GD16/30A/Vol. 111, Rentals for the parish of Cortachy
29. N.S.A., Vol. X, 1124
30. See introduction to Vol. XIII of the O.S.A., xxvii
31. See S.R.O. GD16/28
32. O.S.A., Vol. XIII (new series), 421
33. N.S.A., Vol. XI, 449
34. See S.R.O. GD 16/30A series of rental volumes
35. P. Clapham, 'Agrarian Reform', 90–166 passim.
36. Ibid., table 5.1 b, 131
37. I. D. & K. A. Whyte, 'Aspects of Rural Society', 40
38. Rev. Roger, General View of the Agriculture of Angus or Forfar., (G.V.A.), (Edinburgh, 1794), 22
39. R. A. Dodgshon, Land & Society, 265
40. P. Clapham, 'Agrarian Reform', 68
41. Ibid., 91–92
42. Ibid., 97
43. T. C. Smout, Scottish People, 289
44. P. Clapham 'Agrarian Reform', 54–61 & 96–102
45. T. C. Smout, Scottish People, 287
46. Ibid., 291
47. R. A. Dodgshon, Land & Society, 273

9

Scottish Fiction and the Material World in the Early Nineteenth Century

STANA NENADIC

Introduction: Literature and the Representation of Reality

Scottish society in the first three decades of the nineteenth century was poised at a critical juncture between the old and the new worlds. This juncture was marked by political instability at home, partly arising out of decades of warfare and attendant upheaval in Europe. It was underpined by rapid changes in the economic world, which inevitable brought about change in social structure and in the relationships between rich and poor, town and country. And it was coloured by remarkable developments in the material environment in which many Scots, and in particular the urban middle classes, lived out their lives.[1]

Any period of rapid development is accompanied by social anxiety and attempts to analyse and understand the changes. Anxiety can be manifested in many ways; through political tensions and religious fundamentalism; through conscious efforts to cling to those structures of the past that are fast slipping away; and through the artistic endeavours that typify the age. There is much evidence of each of these in Scotland. Politics and religion dominated the intellectual agenda and generated conflicts of an intensity that had not be seen since the mid eighteenth century.[2] Preoccupation with the past, a phenomenon that had been gathering pace since the early enlightenment, revolved around attempts to reconcile the desire for a distinct national identity with the advantages of Union, and gave rise to mass popular involvement in a range of historical and antiquarian activity.[3] Equally striking – and notable for the ways in which they contributed to the political and religious debates of the age, and fuelled the attachment to the past – is that body of literature that flowed from the minds and pens of Scottish novelists of the first few decades of the nineteenth century. Works of literature or art are inevitably the product of the complex relationships between artists as individuals, the cultural environments in which individuals live and work, and the social norms and economic structures that give rise to those cultures. Cultural production, in what ever form it takes, feeds on the host society, recreating and reflecting aspects of that society back into itself, and thereby fueling the spiralled dynamic that characterises social change. It is the outward evidence of society engaged in the never-ending process of attempting to reinvent itself, and in certain circumstances represents a form of knowledge about that society, for both the producers and the consumers, that cannot be communicated in any other way.[4] Every age and distinct cultural grouping produces its own dominant forms of artistic expression to which it accords, by a hidden, informal but never-the-less powerful consensual process, the role of arbitrator of cultural norms and expectations and exorcisor of cultural demons. The novel occupied this role for many social groups, and particularly for the middle classes, in most western cultures from the middle eighteenth century and throughout the nineteenth century, and the novels that were produced in Scotland and refer to Scottish society as their central purpose form the subject of this essay.

Historical interpretations based on the visual or plastic arts, or music, or literary texts – sometimes known as 'discourse analysis' or 'new cultural history' – are still controversial.[5] A discourse is a many-sided debate without a predefined objective, the value of the discourse lying in the processes of discussion rather than some anticipated resolution. The medium through which the debate is conducted is vital to an understanding of its purpose or value; in effect, 'the medium itself comes to be represented as a constituent of the authority of the message.'[6] There are, of course, many different discourses conducted through many different media at any point in time. In some respects they compete – or, more accurately, they exist in a state of tension relative to one-another – and hence the information generated can be both complex and obscure. This is inevitable – 'individual discourses, because they work by exclusion, constantly evoke what they exclude, and in doing so reveal themselves as partial, and in need of other discourses to supplement and qualify them.'[7] But, if treated cautiously and with full recognition of the motives and biases of the participants and audiences, as well as the limitations of the different media of expression, there is no reason why this type of analysis should not occupy the same status as any other approach to the past, always accepting the caveat that the value of literature, music or art as history does not reside in a capacity to provide accurate accounts of events and dates, but rather as a form of representation of reality whose significance resides in the mediation of cultural identity.[8]

Scottish Fiction and the 'Audience in the Text'

Changes in material life in early nineteenth century Scotland, and in particular those broad changes that arrived with modern capitalism and the movement towards an urban, consumption-oriented society, were both reflected in and mediated by the literary production of the urban middle class. The discourse on modern capitalism was focused in Scotland on issues associated with the ownership of landed property, the acquisition and spending of money, and the accumulation of material goods. It was articulated in one of its most coherent forms through the medium of the novel, but was also evident in other types of literary output such as travel writing[9] and periodical magazines, and was manifest in the visual media of genre and portrait painting, notably in the works of David Wilkie and Alexander Carse. This was a period of great creativity in Scotland, but Scottish creative endeavour was not a narrow or parochial affair. Journals like the *Edinburgh Review*[10] and *Blackwoods Magazine*, founded in Edinburgh in 1802 and 1817 respectively, held unparalleled political and cultural authority in Britain; the novels of Walter Scott dominated the European literary landscape in the first half of the nineteenth century; and artists, notably Wilkie, enjoyed outstanding success in London. Such influence was founded in part on the dominant position of the discourse on modern capitalism within the literature and art of Scotland. Economic change and the attendant social implications were not uniquely Scottish phenomena, but they were manifested in a uniquely intense way. The speed and extent of change, coupled with the existence within Scotland – in the Highlands to be precise – of the purest European manifestation of the romantic ideals of the undisturbed, sublime landscape and primitive peoples, grasped the attention of Scots, English and Europeans alike; not least because such ideals of landscape and people, which were consciously invoked by fiction and art as an integral part of Scottish national identity, were being rapidly destroyed by advancing capitalism.[11]

The first three decades of the nineteenth century can be characterised as a period when the unifying bonds of social and intellectual intercourse, focussed on the cities and embracing most elements of a relatively small middle class, began to disintegrate. Party politics and the religious dimensions of party generated massive gulfs between the different elements that comprised the middle classes, and literary output reflected these divisions. Writing and publication had been an important feature of urban elite cultural life in Scotland for over half a century. All literate social groups make some use of the written word to articulate values and secure their cultural identity, but the use of the printed media for the encoding and transmission of ideologies had been an especially remarkably feature of the Scottish middle class for decades, and became more intense in the early nineteenth century with the development in Edinburgh of a dynamic publishing industry of a scale and influence that had no parallel elsewhere in provincial Britain.[12]

In the early nineteenth century, the Whig party in Scotland, which was closely associated with the aspirations of legal professionals for administrative and democratic reform, generated a particular form of literary endeavour that is best illustrated by the essays on moral, political and economic subjects contained in the *Edinburgh Review*. They sought a new and modern future, and their serious, utilitarian intent was commonly articulated through a rejection of fancy and creative forms of literature such as the novel, and espousal of a scientific, rational understanding of the social as well as the physical world.[13] The Tory middle classes were devoted to a different political agenda and articulated their aspirations through different literary media, espousing the role of the individual and the importance of historical processes. Few Scottish Tories sought to resist all change, but they did seek to reconcile the virtues of the past in such areas as religion, community relationships and familial values, with the advantages and benefits of the present. They did this through an evocation of personal and emotional experience rather than scientific, rational experience, and the novel, which called on the sensibilities and sympathetic engagement of the reader, was regarded as one of the primary vehicles for achieving this aim.

Compared with English writers, the novel was not a well developed literary form in Scotland prior to 1800. The age of sensibility, which had a major impact on the development of middle class values in the later eighteenth century[14], had one of its finest exponents in the Scottish novelist Henry McKenzie. But he was unique, and his fiction, notably *The Man of Feeling*, the most popular work, published in 1771, conspicuously avoided all mention of Scotland. The first Scottish novelists to employ local situations and concerns in their fiction, and to address a specifically Scottish audience, were those writing in the first three decades of the nineteenth century.[15] The years from 1814 – when *Waverley* was published – to the early 1830's were ones of unprecedented and unsurpassed literary output, with most of the fiction of Walter Scott, John Galt, James Hogg, Susan Ferrier and John Gibson Lockhart finding publication during this time. These were all writers with a Tory political orientation, middle class and urban but with strong connections with the rural world, who used their fiction to explore changing social relationships in the wake of rapid modernisation. They were also well-known to one-another,[16] being part of a relatively small literary subgroup based in Edinburgh, and had close connections with *Blackwoods Magazine* – the Tory establishment response to the *Edinburgh Review* – which from time-to-time, in acts of conscious self-parody, played a part in the narrative dynamic of the novels.[17] This was the first generation of writers in Scotland to have a strong commercial connection with the publishing world,[18] and, with the exception of Susan Ferrier – the daughter of a wealthy Edinburgh lawyer – they were all professional writers, acutely aware of the pressures of the market place, and dependent on their writing for their principal source of income.

The audience for whom this group of novelists were writing encompassed people of a similar background. All works of literature or art are produced within the context of audience creation and exclusion, which is not an overt process, though, in practice, most writers and artists do have a good notion of what their audience will comprise. Understanding the character of the implied reader, or the audience in the text, is an important factor in interpreting the cultural and historical implications of works of literature. There was certainly an audience for this fiction beyond Scotland, particularly for the work of Walter Scott, who explicitly sought to use his novels to educate an English elite audience on the virtues of Scotland.[19] This was a period of experimentation and innovation in fiction writing. The gothic novel, the 'silver fork' novel, or novel of elite social life, the historical novel, and the *bildungsroman* or novel of the individual's education into adulthood, were all developed at this time, and Scottish novelists made major contributions to each of these genre.[20] But the principal audience was Scottish, and the early nineteenth century saw both a significant growth in the groups who were the major consumers of this type of fiction – middle class and urban for the greater part, literate and skewed towards women – and the development of new opportunities for gaining easy access to published literature.[21]

Middle class expansion was the product of commercial modernisation and the attendant demand for professional services and the manufacture and supply of goods.[22] The existence and fortunes of the middle class depended on economic change and the replacement of older, protective market structures with free-market capitalism. In the eighteenth century this group had espoused the ameliorative virtues of modernisation, and were major advocates of the utility of beneficial luxury, a theory of economic growth and national prosperity based on the encouragement of demand for luxury goods and services that was especially popular in Scotland.[23] But in the early nineteenth century, and especially in the years following the end of the Napoleonic Wars – years of post-war collapse followed by the speculative vicissitudes of the 1820s, mass unemployment and political instability – anxiety replaced the former confidence, beneficial luxury was questioned and faith in the advantages of new wealth and economic modernisation gave way to doubts. Delight in the potential of wealth and luxury to bring happiness and order, and to act as a civilising influence on the poor, was tempered by a growing anxiety that the traditional Scottish virtues of religion, community and paternal loyalty were being undermined, and that this would ultimately compromise the future of Scotland. John Galt provides one of the best accounts of this new ambiguity in the narrative and experience of the Reverend Miciah Balwhidder, in his novel, *Annals of the Parish*, first published in 1821. Over a period of fifty years between the 1760s and 1810, Balwhidder

charts the emergence of commercial society as it imposes on the quiet
backwaters of his own rural lowland parish, representing Scotland in microcosm, and has a major influence on the life of his own family. After an early
widowerhood he marries for a second time and his new wife, Lizy Kibbock[24],
the daughter of an improving farmer, soon transforms the manse dairy into
a commercial venture, selling her cheeses in the nearby town and 'just a
coining of money, insomuch that after the first year we had the whole tot of
my stipend to put untouched into the bank.'[25] This industry is certainly to
his own and the village's economic benefit. The second Mrs Balwhidder sets
an example for the local women and encourages the opening of the first
village shop. But the minister has reservations, recorded on her death, which
were typical of the broader concerns seen in Scotland:

> Her greatest fault . . . was an over-earnestness to gather gear [wealth]; in the doing
> of which I thought she sometimes sacrificed the comforts of a pleasant fire-side,
> for she was never in her element but when she was keeping the servants eydent
> [diligent] at their work. But, if by this she subtracted something from the quietude
> that was most consonant to my nature, she has left cause, both in bank and bond,
> for me and her bairns to bless her great household activity.[26]

Landed Property as a Metaphor for Social Relationships

Property was at the heart of economic development in the eighteenth and
early nineteenth centuries. It was the primary source of wealth for the great
elite and the principal mark of status. Land was a safe and reliable asset, and
hence sought by those with wealth from less reliable sources, but it also had
major implications for leisure and the capacity to exert political influence.[27]
Remarkable in a relatively backward country, the market in property in
Scotland had been heavily commercialised since the later seventeenth century, and in the wake of collapsing agricultural prices and numerous
bankruptcies there was a significant turnover among land owners in the
second and third decades of the nineteenth century. This theme – the loss of
an estate and the damage wrought by legal strategies for retaining land in
family ownership – is central to John Galt's second great novel, *The Entail*
published in 1822.

Though few were able to possess their own property, the urban middle
classes had a close interest in the affairs of the landed. Preoccupation with
property and with the landscape was a characteristic feature of literary output
in Scotland at this time, seen in travel and tourist literature and in the review
magazines.[28] Such preoccupation was not new to the early nineteenth
century – the *Scots Magazine* in the later eighteenth century had also been
concerned with the issue of landownership.[29] But the new forms of literature,
and especially fiction, brought these issue to a much wider audience. Many
novels use fictional landed estates as their central metaphor for the

modernisation of Scotland, and as indicators of changing social relationships. Walter Scott did this most coherently through the account in *Waverley*, published in 1814, of the estate of Tully Veolan at the time of the second Jacobite rebellion. The novel tells the story of Edward Waverley, an English aristocrat with romantic attachment to the Stuart cause, who finds himself in Scotland as the guest of a minor landowner of ancient descent. Located on the margins between the Highlands and Lowlands, when first introduced the estate of Tully Veolan is economically backward, the local hamlet is squalid and the people are poor. The hereditary proprietor, the elderly Baron Bradwardine, is preoccupied with matters of antiquity and scholarship, but has little interest in either farming or commerce. Relationships between the Baron and his only child Rose, and the people who service the estate and live on the land, are of a traditionally paternal and feudal character. Similarly, relationships with neighbouring landowners and with adjacent clansmen operate according to feudal norms. During the course of the novel the estate encounters many vicissitudes arising out of the owner's involvement in the uprising. The land is pillaged and the house is sacked. As punishment for his treason, Bradwardine's property is seized and sold on the open market to be purchased by a friend of Edward Waverley – a Captain Talbot, English officer and nobleman who has fought against the Jacobites – and is then 'lawfully and justly acquired'[30] by the young hero, now the son-in-law of the Baron Bradwardine. Under the new political and legal regime that Walter Scott describes as emerging in Scotland in the wake of rebellion, Tully Veolan is quickly restored to the glory of it's former antiquity, but now on the basis of capitalist prosperity. The fortunes of the estate, acting as metaphor for the fortunes of Scotland at large, are shown as being built on the harmonious union of Scottish and English interests – symbolised by the marriage of Waverley to Rose Bradwardine – and an optimistic future is the outcome of traditional virtues, including paternal responsibilities and concern for rights and customs, coupled with the new prosperity that is offered by the world of commerce.

Susan Ferrier constructed a similar extended metaphor in *Marriage*, a novel of elite social manners, written in the didactic tradition and published in 1818 to high critical acclaim in Scotland.[31] The Glenfern estate, the property of a laird and his family, like Tully Veolan, conveys in miniature both the virtues and weaknesses of traditional rural Scotland. The Highland estate is not altogether backward – the Laird's favourite reading is improvers' pamphlets – but the values and relationships exemplified by the older members of the Glenfern family are set in the past and fall far short of the ideals of refinement and sensibility espoused by Ferrier. The new generation, represented by the heroine whose education for 'marriage' is at the heart of the narrative, successfully unite the virtues of the past with the advantages of the modern present, which again are tempered through relationships with England.

The Breadland house and lands described by John Galt in the *Annals of the Parish*, provides a third illustration of the use by a Scottish novelist of an elaborate estate metaphor to symbolise change. At the opening of the novel, the estate is held by the Laird of Breadland, the principal heritor and patron to the Reverend Balwhidder. On his death, the laird's widow and children move to Edinburgh, where his son is training to be an advocate, and the estate is leased to Major Gilchrist, a wealthy returned nabob, described as a 'narrow' man, and his spinster sister. In their hands the 'pretty policy [grounds] of the Breadlands, that had cost a power of money to the old laird . . . fell into decay and disorder.' But worse than this:

> the old men [of the parish], that had a light labour in keeping the policy in order, were thrown out of bread . . . and the poor women, that whiles got a bit and a drap from the kitchen of the family, soon felt the change, so that by little and little, we were obligated to give help from the Session . . . [and] I was necessitated to preach a discourse on almsgiving, specially for the benefit of our own poor, a thing never before known in the parish.[32]

A few years later the estate undergoes another dramatic change when the house is burned to the ground and the Gilchrists perish in the flames. The young laird, 'by growing a resident at Edinburgh' decides against rebuilding, and rents the land and steadings as a commercial farm to an improving farmer who had 'got his insight among the Lothian farmers, so that he knew what crop should follow another.' This in the eyes of the parish minister is a boon to the parish, and 'tended to do far more for the benefit of my people than if the young laird had rebuilded the Breadland house in a fashionable style.'[33]

The fortunes of another great house, that of Lady Macadam – 'which stood in a pleasant parterre, inclosed within a stone-wall and an iron gate, having a pillar with a pineapple head on each side' – brings fewer advantages according to the values of the minister, but provides a similar index of commercialisation and modernisation. On Lady Macadam's death the house is leased to Mr Cayenne, a Virginia planter who builds the first cotton mill in the district. When the Cayenne family leave the house for a home of their own it lays empty for a while, the gardens overgrown and 'wearing the look of a waste place'. But gradually, in the wake of urban expansion and the siting of the new road, the house 'came to be in the middle of the town' and was eventually leased by the change house keeper, for use as an inn, and renamed the 'Cross Keys'.[34]

These and other novels of the period collectively suggest that the heart of Scotland was rural when viewed through the eyes of the urban middle classes. Novels did incorporate situations in towns, but the essence of Scottish values and virtues was conceived by most writers of fiction to be derived from simple people and the localised relationships that belonged, in an ideal world, to the country parish or estate. The idealisation of rural life was also a dominant theme in the visual arts of the later eighteenth and early nineteenth century, but though manifested with a particular intensity at this time, it was part of a longer tradition in Scotland. The most popular and widely read literary work of the eighteenth century was without doubt Allan Ramsay's dramatic pastoral verse *The Gentle Shepherd*, first published in 1724, reproduced in numerous published editions and stage productions throughout the century, and illustrated by all the major Scottish artists. Ramsay portrayed the Lowlands of Scotland, setting his poem of love and courtship, described by one early nineteenth century admirer as a 'truly Scottish picture of real rural simple nature', in a shepherd community in an area to the south of Edinburgh.[35] By the early nineteenth century the simplicity and traditions of the Lowlands were all but gone, swept aside in the broad march of commercialisation, but these ideals were still to be found in the Highlands, or so it was believed, which had the additional attractions of sublime landscape, romantic isolation and antiquity. Nostalgic regret for the passing of the old ways and in particular for the loss of the presumed simplicities and certainties of the rural past is a typical feature of the European bourgeois response to modernisation. In Scotland, however – and certainly when compared with England – that regret was made more acute by the rapid speed of change and attendant human tragedy, especially in the Highlands, and by the linking of the rural past with attempts to construct a modern national identity.

The Individual and the World of Goods

In additional to the preoccupation with property and landscape, Scottish novels of the early nineteenth century are acutely sensitive to the material world and make extensive use of descriptions of goods and artefacts to represent the inner life of the individual and establish the dynamics of social relationships. The acquisition and enumeration of possessions is a major preoccupation. Even those novels that deal with historical subjects, such as Scott's *Waverley* or James Hogg's *The Private Memoirs and Confessions of a Justified Sinner*, published in 1824, create a narrative environment that evokes clear images of clothing and household furnishings in a manner that is peculiarly distinct to this period of fiction writing.[36] Such concerns mirrored the interests of a society characterised by urban anonymity and fluidity, in which status and group identity were articulated through the semiotic codes contained in possessions. Several of the novelists were themselves conspicuous consumers, notably Walter Scott, who spent a fortune in the building and furnishing of Abbotsford, a country house in the neo-gothic baronial style that signalled his own attachment to Scotland's idealised past.

Detailed descriptions of clothing abound, often employed for comic effect, but with a more serious underlying purpose emerging out of the broader discourse on economic modernisation and its damaging implications. Susan Ferrier's account of the dress of Highland gentry women compared with that of a young English lady, draws a striking picture of the backwardness of much of traditional Scotland and the foolishness of contemporary fashion. The Glenfern ladies, described in *Marriage*, preparing for a walk outdoors, dress in their practical if homely 'shrunk duffle greatcoats, vast poke-bonnets, red worsted neck cloths and pattens,' and gaze with horror on the 'lace cap, lilac satin pelisse and silk shoes' of their London visitor, a choice of clothing that is not only ill suited to the weather and terrain, but one they fear will 'frighten our stirks and stots'.[37] Accounts of the clothing worn by women is something one might expect to find described in fiction, but what is striking in this body of novels is the richness of detail on male dress and physical appearance. James Hogg, in *Justified Sinner*, makes extensive use of descriptions of antique clothing to draw his chilling portraits of individual mutation and disguise.[38] Walter Scott's involvement in the development of Highland dress as a contemporary male fashion is reflected in *Waverley*, particularly in the description of a picture in the restored house of Tully Veolan – a 'large and spirited painting, representing Fergus MacIvor and Waverley in their Highland dress . . . Beside this painting hung the arms which Waverley had borne in the unfortunate civil war.'[39] Galt is especially alert to the implications of male dress as an index of character and motivations. Our impression of the elderly and penurious Laird of Auldbiggins in *Last of the Lairds*, published in 1826, is partly based on his ancient clothing, the fashion of a previous age:

> His coat and waistcoat were of the same snuff colour; the latter with flaps after the manner but of greater amplitude than the style of the court dress. His breeches of black silk rather short and scanty were adorned at the knees with heir-loom buckles of Bristol stones set in silver – his stockings were also silk of a bluish tinge and a cottonial dimness, the effect of many lavations . . . He wore his best wig well powdered, a demi-forensic structure of a middle and anomalous architecture between the prim tye-wig, with Ionic volutes over the ears of a snug and debonair citizen, and the wig of wisdom, luxuriant with Corinthian curl, which distinguishes the upper end of a Lord of Council and Session.[40]

Galt in particular employs aspects of male dress and associated behaviour to indicate social and political relationships, notably in the *The Provost*, published in 1822. The chapter titled the 'Wig Dinner' describes a meeting of the town dignitaries in the council chamber that, following a good dinner, and the usual practice of toasting the King's health with punch, degenerates into drunken carousing. Ridicule descends, quite literally, on the heads of the town's elite when they collectively, as an act of inebriated patriotism, throw their wigs – an important sign of office and status in the later eighteenth century – into the fire, and are obliged to return home in their night caps. Only the wily politician Provost Pawkie has a second wig and is saved from public disgrace.[41] The chapter titled 'The Clothing' details another incident with political implications, this time arising out of the choice of uniform for the newly formed volunteer regiments during the early years of the Napoleonic Wars. Galt tells us that initially many of the 'doucer sort of the men' were unwilling to appear in public in scarlet and gold lace, preferring instead a more modest blue uniform. But, in the words of Provost Pawkie, a shopkeeper by trade:

> In the end, when the eyes of men in civil stations had got accustomed to military show and parade, it was determined to change the colour of the cloth from blue to red, . . . in the accomplishment of which change, I had (and why should I disguise the honest fact) my share of the advantages which the kingdom at large drew, in that period of anarchy and confusion, from the laudable establishment of a volunteer force.[42]

It is no coincidence that the novel in which these details appear is concerned with urban life, and with the making and breaking of urban fortunes. In exploiting accounts of clothing, Galt implies an intimate and inevitably judgemental connection between towns and excessive preoccupation with appearance and fashionable display. The damaging influence of urban fashions on rural relationships is suggested in *Annals of the Parish* in the tale of Miss Betty Wudrife's 'gay mantle' from Edinburgh,[43] and the theme of conspicuous display is especially notable in John Gibson Lockhart's first novel *Peter's Letters to his Kinsfolk*, published in 1819, in the lengthy descriptions of Glasgow's status-seeking business elite:

> Here was to be seen the counting house dandy, with whalebone stays, stiff neckcloth, surtout, cossacks, a spur on his heel, a gold-headed cane on his wrist and a Kent on his head, mincing primly to his brother dandy some question about pullicat handkerchiefs.[44]

The acquisition and display of other types of material goods are also richly enumerated in early Scottish fiction. Accounts of the conspicuous consumption of food and drink among the middle classes are given by Galt and Lockhart. In *Peter's Letters*, Lockhart provides a minute description of the elaborate great dinners and drinking rituals that were commonly associated with the Glasgow Atlantic merchant community.[45] Status objects are also detailed, such as the 'handsome leather covered library chair' and framed map acquired on a trip to Edinburgh by the Laird in *Last of the Lairds*,[46] or the dinning room press, filled to overflowing with glassware and china, the property of the widow Mrs Sourocks who appears in the same novel.[47] In providing an annual account of his own life and times, the Reverend Balwhidder in *Annals of the Parish* also gives an insight to the motives behind the acquisition of a range of consumer goods. Early in his ministry he aspires to own a 'mahogany scrutoire' or writing desk, which was probably the most important status object sought by middle class men in the second half of the eighteenth century.[48] A few years later, he and his wife visit Edinburgh together to attend the General Assembly, and,

> It was in this visit to Edinburgh that Mrs Balwhidder bought her silver tea-pot, and other ornamental articles; but this was not done, as she assured me, in a vain spirit of bravery, which I could not have abided, but because it was well known that tea draws better in a silver pot, and drinks pleasanter in a china cup, than out of any other kind of cup or tea-pot.[49]

New Money and the Volatility of Wealth

Walter Scott believed that Scotland was the most dramatically changed country of the modern world, and much of his literary endeavour was directed toward the preservation of a lively awareness of Scotland's past.[50] He praised the rational and progressive virtues of the new age, but for Scott, as for the other novelists of the period, the suddenness of many of the changes wrought anxiety. Men of new wealth were significant figures in the literary landscape of the early nineteenth century, and close descriptions of their sources of wealth, their conspicuous consumption and their impact on Scottish society preoccupied novelists in ways that were not apparent in England.[51] This was especially true of Galt, who provides several accounts of the 'get rich quick' strategies commonly employed by ambitious Scots. *The Provost* is a remarkable treaties on one man's rise to great riches through trade and the acquisition of property – a process smoothed by patronage and facilitated by a corrupt manipulation of positions of power on the town council.[52] The novel also gives an account of the career of Bailie McLucre, 'naturally a greedy bodie' who has 'set up as an o'er-sea merchant, buying beef and corn by agency in Ireland, and having the same sent to the Glasgow market', from which he makes a considerable speculative fortune, only to loose it all in the following year. He next tries his luck in London, to see if patronage connections can 'get a post in Government', and finds himself a clerk of customs, a poorly paid post, but, in his own words:

> Luckily . . . a flock of fleets and ships frae the East and West Indies came in a' thegither; and there was sic a stress for tidewaiters, that before I was sworn in and tested, I was sent down to a grand ship in the Malabar trade frae China, loaded with tea and other rich commodities; the captain whereof, a descreet man, took me down to the cabin, and gave me a dram of wine, and, when we were by oursels, he said to me . . . [53]

In short, he takes a vast bribe to turn a blind eye to excise abuses, and quickly returns to Scotland where the different legal system provides protection from prosecution.[54]

The Last of the Lairds provides another illustration of new wealth derived from overseas sources in the person of the appropriately named Mr Rupees, a 'Nawbub' who 'came hame frae Indy, and bought the Arunthrough property frae the Glaikies, who, like sae mony ithers o' the right stock o'legitimate gentry, hae been smothered out o' sight by the weed and nettle overgrowths o' merchandise ane cotton-weavry.'[55] Rupees is a conspicuous consumer, and the novel is laden with descriptions of his new-built house, fine possessions and exotic food. The threat of such men in the eyes of social critics was that their riches allowed them to buy the estates of traditional small landowners, a class then feeling the pressures of the new commercial age.[56] Nabobs had no commitment to the land other than as a commodity for generating status and profit, and they were disconnected from rural society and its norms. The narrative dynamic of Last of the Lairds is built on the tensions between Mr Rupees and a Lowland Laird who finds himself in debt to the 'Nawbub'. In order to clear the heritable bonds that are held against his property, the Laird has ambitions to write a book – 'a book o' soleedity, showing forth the wastrie of heritages by reason o' the ingrowth o' trade and taxes'[57]; in effect the book that Galt was writing himself. Eventually he manages to outwit Mr Rupees, but is still forced to sell the estate, and ends his days as a 'landless Laird' living the life of one of the 'Athenian gentry' in Edinburgh's New Town.

Susan Ferrier, in her second novel The Inheritance, published in 1824, also uses a nabob as a central character. Major Waddell, 'a gentleman of large fortune lately returned from India',[58] along with his social climbing bride, exemplify the emptiness of new consumerism:

> Mrs Waddell had so much to look at, and her things were all so new, and so rich, and so fashionable; and India muslin, and India shawls, and India chains and lace and trinkets were heaped upon her with such an unsparing hand, that it was quite a feast to sit and scan each article individually.[59]
> . . . she talked much and well of curry and rice, and old Madeira, and the livery, and the Company – which did not mean the present company, but the India Company. Her silver corners were very handsome, and she had to take off some of her rings before she could carve the grouse.[60]

Running parallel with concerns for the character and impact of the nouveau riche was a pervasive anxiety arising out of the volatility and instability of fortunes in Scotland. This concern was not unique to the early nineteenth century; indeed, the middle classes in many periods have feared the consequences of sudden reversal of fortunes, and express that fear through the situations and narratives that dominate their favoured forms of art.[61] But the age was notable for speculation, war-time boom and post-war collapse, and it is not surprising that the volatility of wealth should be a dominating theme of fiction, especially in light of the fact that the two leading novelists of the period, Walter Scott and John Galt, both experienced the personal tragedy of bankruptcy and James Hogg lived with parlous financial reversals.[62] Galt's

West of Scotland novels provide numerous illustrations of collapsed fortunes and descent into penury. In some instances this is the consequence of poor business judgements, as in the case of Mr Speckle, the cotton manufacturer with 'owre many irons in the fire', whose career is described in *Annals of the Parish*. Others are more tragic and sympathetic such as Mr Dwining, Speckle's overseer – 'an Englishman from Manchester where he had seen better days' – who looses his job, his only source of income, and, together with his wife, commit suicide.[63] Or the worthy Mr Maitland, a philanthropist and once Lord Provost of Glasgow, an 'old respected merchant', who fails in the spate of bankruptcies of 1793 and did not 'long survive the mutation of his fortune, but bending his aged head in sorrow, sunk down beneath the stroke, to rise no more.'[64] The Calvinist minister, Balwhidder, – representing in many respects the strong strand of Calvinist thinking in Galt himself[65] – attributes these failures to the broader workings of providence and preaches the message 'that commercial prosperity, flush as it might be, was but a perishable commodity'.[66] Such thinking is echoed in Ferrier who points to the disappointments that accompany wealth – 'the numerous evils inseparable from extensive property, and which not unfrequently embitter the peace of the possessor, such as bad tenants, bad crops. . . .' – and warns how 'difficult is it to form an estimate of worldly enjoyment by the symbols of outward prosperity.'[67]

Conclusion: Calvinism, Taste and the New Restraint

Though the literary concern with the material world, and with the social implications of the new commercial age, forms part of a broader European discourse on modern capitalism, the Scottish preoccupation with property, money and goods revealed in early nineteenth century novels has many unique features. The preoccupation was born out of rapid and dramatic changes in the economic fortunes of the nation, coupled with attempts to reconcile the past with the present in a type of literary endeavour that held a special place in the political agenda of the Tory middle classes. The distinct character of the Scottish response to the material world was conditioned in part by the religious traditions of Scotland. Calvinist themes of fate and predetermination are threaded through many of the novels, and Calvinist ideologies have always been associated with moral anxiety arising out of wealth and an abundance of possessions. In a country that is poor, and where even the relatively rich live lives of material simplicity – as was certainly the case in Scotland before the mid-eighteenth century – it was easy to accommodate the spiritual virtues of poverty. But the country, or at least certain parts of the country, was no longer poor, and the relatively rich were able to satisfy the 'urge to possess' in ways that had not been possible before.

Scotland's Calvinist traditions gave rise to paradoxical thinking and behaviour in response to new wealth. This accounts in part for the idealisation of the pastoral and the passion for the romantic landscape. A retreat into pastoral simplicity was neither possible nor desired in the real, everyday lives of the mass of the middle classes – though elite indulgence in the rural idyll did prevail[68] – but it was possible to reconcile some of the moral ambiguities of material abundance through a different approach to possessions. There was in Scotland, present in a modest way from the later eighteenth century, but more apparent from about 1810, ample testimony to a recoiling from the extremes of consumption and material display towards a new restraint; a form of conspicuous parsimony that within the British context was especially associated with the Scottish professional classes.[69] This restraint was not the product of poverty – household objects in such domestic regimes were still valuable – but arose from the explicit characterisation of opulent display as evidence of plebeian vulgarity, and the parallel endeavours among those in possession of wealth coupled with another form of capital – sometimes described as cultural capital[70] – to establish a second yardstick, called 'taste', by which status could be measured. Good taste – which was a rare and ephemeral commodity, born out of a classical education, which unlike wealth could not be acquired overnight, and the cultivation of appropriate aesthetic values – dictated simplicity and restraint in clothing, particularly in male clothing, austerity in architecture and in furniture design, and temperate hospitality. This was a way of engaging with the material world that was more consistent with Calvinist precepts, and it is not surprising that in describing such domestic regimes through fiction, Church of Scotland ministers provided the models. The most important of these was Adam Blair the eponymous hero of John Gibson Lockhart's second novel, published in 1824. John Galt, ever sensitive to the visual impact of possessions, also provides us with a telling description of this form of restraint in his account of the home of a young clergyman in *Last of the Lairds*:

> On entering the house I was shown into the parlour . . . I have always thought that the sitting room of a gentleman afforded no equivocal index to his character, and certainly the parlour of Dr Lounlands tended to confirm me in this notion. It was in all respects well-ordered, everything was suitable, but a degree of taste pervaded alike the distribution and the style of furniture, producing something like fashionable elegance on the whole, notwithstanding the general Presbyterian simplicity of the details.[71]

REFERENCES

1. S. Nenadic, 'A More Extravagant Style of Living? Consumer Behaviour and Domestic Culture in Edinburgh and Glasgow, 1720 to 1840'. Paper to the

Consumption of Culture Seminar, University of California Los Angeles, May 1991. S. Nenadic, 'Household Possessions and the Modernising City: Scotland 1720 to 1840', *Proceedings of the 11th International Economic History Congress, Milan 1994.* (forthcoming). S. Nenadic, 'Middle Rank Consumers and Domestic Culture in Edinburgh and Glasgow, 1720 to 1840', *Past and Present,* (forthcoming).

2. C. Brown, *The Social History of Religion in Scotland since 1730* (1987).

3. I. Gordon Brown, *The Hobby-Horsical Antiquary: a Scottish Character, 1640–1830* (Edinburgh, 1980).

4. For a close exposition of this approach to literature as history, see, S. Nenadic, 'Illegitimacy, Insanity and Insolvency; Wilkie Collins and the Victorian Nightmares', in A. Marwick, ed. *The Arts, Literature and Society* (1990).

5. For background see, P. Bourdieu, *The field of Cultural Production: Essays on Art and Literature,* edited and introduced by Randal Johnson (Cambridge, 1993).

6. J. Barrel, 'Visualising the Division of Labour: William Pyne's Microcosm' in A. Marwick, ed. *The Arts, Literature and Society* p. 97.

7. Ibid. p. 98

8. T. Dunne, 'A Polemical Introduction: Literature, Literary Theory and the Historian', in T. Dunne, ed. *The Writer as Witness: Literature as Historical Evidence* (Cork, 1987).

9. S. Nenadic, 'Land, the Landed and the Relationship with England: Literature and Perception, 1760 to 1830' in R. J. Morris et al, eds, *Conflict and Identity in Scotland and Ireland,* (forthcoming).

10. See B. Fontana, *Rethinking the Politics of Commercial Society: The Edinburgh Review, 1802–1832* (Cambridge, 1985).

11. On the cultural creation of the Highland myths see, P. Womack, *Improvement and Romance: Constructing the Myth of the Highlands* (1989).

12. A. Murdoch and R. Sher, 'Literary and Learned Culture', in T. M. Devine and R. Mitchison, eds. *People and Society in Scotland, Volume 1 1760–1830* (Edinburgh, 1988).

13. Novels were accepted by the *Review* as light reading, but 'every sensible person will look elsewhere for solid information. He turns to the novel for amusement, and hates to be cheated by a homily in disguise. Division of labour is a principle scarcely less commendable in literature than in manufactures: and the attempt to combine many objects often is productive of a failure in all.' *Edinburgh Review* July 1830 p. 444.

14. See, J. Dwyer, *Virtuous Discourse: Sensibility and community in Late Eighteenth-Century Scotland,* (Edinburgh, 1987).

15. The eighteenth century exception was Tobias Smollet's *Humphrey Clinker,* published in 1771, which was set in part in Scotland. The first nineteenth century novels to use Scottish settings were the now long-forgotten Elizabeth Hamilton's *Cottagers of Glenburnie,* published in 1808, and Jane Porter's, *The Scottish Chief* published in 1810.

16. Scott was the father-in-law of John Gibson Lockhart, and a personal friend of Susan Ferrier's father and of James Hogg. He also knew Galt. See, *The Journal of Sir Walter Scott 1825–32 From the Original Manuscript at Abbotsford* (Edinburgh, 1891).

17. See, for example, the final sections of the 'Editor's Narrative' of James Hogg's *The Private Memoirs and Confessions of a Justified Sinner* (1986) p. 230.
18. Walter Scott was a partner in the publishing firm of Ballantyne and Co. and J. G. Lockhart was editor of the London journal the *Quarterly Review*.
19. In this he claimed to be following the example of Maria Edgeworth in her writing on Irish subjects, see, W. Scott, *Waverley*, (1988) ch. 72 'A postscript, which should have been a preface', p. 493.
20. Scott discusses the different types of popular novel in Chapter 1, 'Introductory', to *Waverley*.
21. Notably, of course, through the development of subscription libraries such as the Stirlings Library in Glasgow, which was founded in 1791, with an annual subscription of £3 3s, and by 1800 had about 400 members. In 1854, the first year for which there is a detailed breakdown, fiction was by far the dominant area of reader borrowing, accounting for 30 per cent of all book issues, followed by history texts at 14 per cent. See, Minutes of the Glasgow Public Library (Stirlings Library), Mitchell Library, Glasgow: MS 274629.
22. For a survey, see S. Nenadic, 'The Rise of the Middle Class', in T. M. Devine and R. Mitchison, eds. *People and Society in Scotland Volume 1, 1760–1830* (Edinburgh, 1988); S. Nenadic, 'The Middle Ranks and Modernisation' in T. M. Devine and G. Jackson, eds. *The History of Glasgow Volume 1* (Forthcoming).
23. S. Nenadic, 'Consumerism and the Scottish Economy in the Age of Enlightenment'. Unpublished paper presented as a Public Lecture, National Museum of Scotland, February 1993.
24. The name is that of a type of Scottish cheese. Galt's innovative use of comic names prefigures the same in Dickens.
25. J. Galt, *Annals of the Parish* (Oxford, 1982) p. 33.
26. Ibid p. 152–3.
27. L. Timperlay, 'The Pattern of Landholding in Eighteenth Century Scotland', in M. L. Parry and T. R. Slater, eds. *The Making of the Scottish Countryside* (1980); J. Sinclair, *General Report on the Agricultural State and Political Circumstances of Scotland* (Edinburgh, 1814) Volume 1.
28. See, for example, *Blackwood's Magazine* for October 1818, on 'Ricardo and the Edinburgh Review' which discusses the role of landed proprietors in Scotland.
29. J. Dwyer, *Virtuous Discourse: Sensibility and Community in Late Eighteenth-Century Scotland* (Edinburgh, 1987), pp. 42–44.
30. W. Scott, *Waverley* (1988) p. 485.
31. Ferrier was the spinster daughter of an Edinburgh advocate who had been agent to the Duke of Argyle. She was a popular author of day, often described as the 'Scottish Jane Austen'. As testimony to her success with *Marriage*, her second and third novels received publishers of advances of £1000 and £1500 respectively. See S. Ferrier, *Marriage* (Bampton, 1984). Introduction p. ix.
32. Galt, *Annals* p. 18–19. The problems of returning nabobs was discussed in the *Scots Magazine* in the later eighteenth century. Dwyer, *Virtuous Discourse*, p. 43.
33. Galt, *Annals* p. 37.
34. Ibid. p. 122.
35. *The Gentle Shepherd, A Pastoral Comedy with Illustrations of the Scenary* (Edinburgh, 1808) p. xi.

36. English fiction of the eighteenth century, notably the work of Daniel Defoe at the start of the century and Samuel Richardson mid-century, also reveals a striking concern for material details, particularly of clothing, but this was less true of English fiction of the early nineteenth century.
37. Ferrier, *Marriage* p. 45.
38. See, in particular, the descriptions at the very end of novel when the body is exhumed. J. Hogg, *The Private Memoirs and Confessions of a Justified Sinner* (1986) p. 238–9.
39. Scott, *Waverley* p. 489.
40. J. Galt, *The Last of the Lairds* (Edinburgh, 1976) p. 109.
41. J. Galt, *The Provost* (Edinburgh, 1982) ch. 22.
42. Ibid ch. 20.
43. Galt, *Annals* p. 76.
44. J. G. Lockhart, *Peter's Letters to his Kinsfolk* (Edinburgh, 1819) Vol. 3, p. 169–70.
45. See discussion in S. Nenadic, 'Businessmen, the Urban Middle Classes and the Dominance of Manufacturers in Nineteenth-Century Britain', *Economic History Review*, 2nd Ser. XLIV (1) 1991 pp. 66–85.
46. Galt, *Last of the Lairds* p. 6.
47. Ibid. p. 137.
48. Galt, *Annals* p. 15. This was also one of the principal objects acquired by James Boswell on his first extended trip to London. *Boswell's London Journal 1762–3*, edited by F. A. Pottle (1950) p. 81.
49. Galt, *Annals* p. 100.
50. Scott, *Waverley* 'A Postscript' p. 492. – 'There is no European nation which, within the course of half a century, or little more, has undergone so complete a change as this kingdom of Scotland.'
51. See, for example, Jane Austen who was muted in her criticism of new wealth. This is less true of Francis Burney in the later eighteenth century.
52. E. Gauldie, *One Artful and Ambitious Individual: Alexander Riddoch 1745–1822* (Dundee, 1989) provides a good account of a real-life provost.
53. Galt, *Provost* ch 6 & 7.
54. Such behaviour, and the belief that patronage abuse was widespread among Scots in London, contributed to the Scotophobia that was characteristic of English society in the second half of the eighteenth century. See, L. Colley, *Britons: forging the Nation, 1707–1837* (New Haven, 1992) pp. 113–118.
55. Galt, *Last of the Lairds* p. 25.
56. The primary source of Nabob wealth was involvement with the East India Company, to which Scots had privileged access through the patronage of Henry Dundas. The fortunes accumulated by such men could be vast. Robert Clive left India in 1760 with *c.* £400,000, the largest fortune ever made in India. One James Johnstone was thought to be worth £300,000 when he returned to Scotland, where he proceeded to purchased three estates and accompanying parliamentary interests. See, M. Edwardes, *The Nabobs at Home* (1991) p. 31.
57. Galt, *Last of the Lairds* p. 24.
58. S. Ferrier, *The Inheritance* (Bampton, 1984) p. 123.
59. Ibid. p. 611.
60. Ibid. p. 425.

61. This was true, for instance, of the 'sensation' novels, dominated by the work of Wilkie Collins, in the 1860s. See, Nenadic, 'Illegitimacy, Insanity and Insolvency.' in Marwick, ed. *The Arts, Literature and Society*.
62. Scott's *Journal* gives the best account of his bankruptcy in the 1820s. On Galt see C. A. Whatley, *John Galt 1779–1979* (Edinburgh, 1979). Introduction.
63. Galt, Annals, p. 196–200.
64. Galt, *Annals* p. 145 and ch. 49.
65. J. MacQueen, 'John Galt and the Analysis of Social History', in A. Bell, ed., *Scott Bicentenary Essays* (1973).
66. Galt, *Annals* ch. 49.
67. Ferrier, *Inheritance*, 891–2.
68. Satirised, for instance, in Ferrier's *Inheritance* in the building of a cottage orne.
69. This transition is discussed in the works cited in footnote 1.
70. See, P. Bourdieu, *Distinction: a Social Critique of the Judgement of Taste*, translated by R. Nice (Cambridge, Mass., 1984).
71. Galt, *Last of Lairds*, p. 43.

10

Urbanisation and the Civic Response: Glasgow, 1800–30

T. M. DEVINE

In the early nineteenth century Glasgow was a city of contrasts, exhibiting dynamic economic growth on the one hand and increasing social misery on the other. A major centre of textile production with trading connections which stretched from the Americas to Europe and to Asia, it had experienced a revolutionary rate of urban expansion from the 1760s.[1] The number of Glaswegians had risen by over 350 per cent in the space of four decades after 1801. The city's population increased from 77,385 at that date to 274,533 in 1841. Some Glasgow commentators waxed lyrical at the achievement. In 1810 one observer reported fulsomely that the city was now 'one of the principal seats of literature and commerce in British dominions and at this instant inferior in these respects to few cities in the world'.[2] It was in this period too that Glasgow first came to be described as the 'second city of the Empire', subordinate in size and status only to London.[3]

Yet there was a much darker side to Glasgow's reputation which was given less attention and prominence by the city's governing classes. Put simply, Glasgow's extraordinary transformation over the space of a few years from provincial burgh to industrial metropolis had been achieved at considerable human cost. As the city's growth accelerated, so the urban environment became more lethal. While material progress was being sustained, social dereliction was intensifying. Scotland's most successful urban economy was also enduring the nation's most acute human problems. Mortality rates had fallen on trend in the later eighteenth and early nineteenth centuries. However, from 1821 this process of improvement was reversed. Crude death rates (annual averages per 1000 living) which had declined to 17.1 in 1801 reached 26.8 between 1825–9, and climbed further to 33.0 in the years 1835–9.[4] In the same period, epidemics of typhus became more frequent and menacing and a major outbreak of cholera took place in 1832.

In one sense, there was little exceptional in this evidence of growing urban crisis. Most expanding Victorian towns were unhealthy. The combination of huge increases in migration from the countryside, primitive social and sanitary amenities and the limitations of contemporary medical science made this inevitable.[5] But the depth of Glasgow's social problems was greater than that of most other cities. No town in Scotland and few in Britain could equal its mortality levels. W. P. Alison's analysis of 'fever' during the 1837 typhus epidemic produced a league table of deaths among the big cities in which Glasgow was ranked clearly in the unenviable first position.[6] As Edwin Chadwick's Report on the Sanitary Condition of the Labouring Population of Great Britain of 1842 concluded in magisterial fashion: 'It might admit of dispute, but, on the whole, it appeared to us that both the structural arrangements and the condition of the population of Glasgow was the worst of any we had seen in any part of Great Britain.'[7] The city which boasted it was the second in the Empire, was apparently the first in human degradation.

Historians have long speculated on the reasons for this.[8] Some contend that the speed of urban growth was such that social crisis on a massive scale was inevitable. Others stress that the nature of the city's low wage textile economy was likely to produce widespread and endemic poverty and hence further aggravate the demographic pressures. Much less attention, however, has been given to the attitudes, responses and strategies of those who actually governed Glasgow in this period. It is often simply assumed that the city's rulers were hidebound by the political and economic orthodoxies of the time and did little or nothing to alleviate the crisis which was intensifying in the years after the end of the Napoleonic Wars.[9] Yet detailed evidence of élite responses does exist in the records of the Glasgow Police Commission, established in 1800, which was responsible for paving, lighting, cleaning, the control of crime and public order. The Minute, Letter and Sederunt Books of the Commission together with its accounts are preserved in Strathclyde Regional Archives.[10] They provide a fascinating insight into the assumptions, attitudes and priorities of the civic authorities at a time of unprecedented urban expansion, political turmoil and social crisis. Invaluable for the history of Glasgow in the early decades of the nineteenth century, they also cast considerable light on the whole question of the response of the ruling classes of the Scottish towns to the first phase of urbanisation.

I

The passage of a Police Act for Glasgow in 1800 was the response to a series of pressures which had been building up in the second half of the eighteenth century. The Town Guard, on which the city had previously relied for policing duties, was an amateur force and was found wanting in a period of major social and economic change.[11] The limitations in the traditional arrangements were exposed with the increasing incidence of public disorder associated with the anti-popery riots of 1779 and the weavers' disturbances in Calton in 1787.[12] These led to the introduction of a more professional system of policing under a chief superintendent. Not, however, until 1790 did a meeting of 'heritors and burgesses' put forward formal proposals for an elected Board of Commissioners to administer policing arrangements in Glasgow. It is possible that an earlier initiative by Edinburgh, which had established a Police Board in 1771, may have influenced Glasgow.[13] More probably, however, the decision was an attempt to improve the city's response to the growing problems of public order and deterioration in urban amenity. It is significant, however, that a separate body, quite distinct from the Town Council, was regarded as the most appropriate form of organisation. An extended police authority would have to be funded, yet potential ratepayers were unwilling to concede financial control and responsibility to an unelected and unrepresentative municipal authority. Equally, however, the Town Council was for some years reluctant to accept the need for a rival organisation which would absorb some of its traditional powers. Yet, by 1799, the civic leadership had finally responded to the growing public pressure for an elected Police Board and this created by Act of Parliament the following year. The legislation applied to the lands or 'royalty' of the original burgh together with a further ninety six acres of territory including Ramshorn and Meadowflat. Further Police Boards were created for Gorbals, Calton and Anderston in 1808, 1819 and 1826 respectively.[14]

These initiatives in themselves demonstrate that the 'unreformed' burghal system was not as devoid of enterprise, flexibility and initiative as some accounts suggest. Clearly there were those among the Glasgow oligarchy who were not opposed to administrative change and who saw the need for a more creative response to the growing problems of the city. But the establishment of the Police Board was also of considerable significance for other reasons. It has been described as an 'epoch making statute'.[15] For the first time it imposed a rate on the assessed rental of urban property while declaring that the income which accrued should be used ' . . . for the convenience and health of the inhabitants who have greatly increased in number'.[16] In addition, it allowed citizens some voice in the election of their representatives, in a way that the existing Town Council did not, while conceding the principle that rating and representation were inseparable. Finally, the Act recognised the cleaning of the streets of the city as a public duty to be financed from public funds. Before 1800 the civic authorities had tried to ensure the removal of filth by decree, but now there was a clear affirmation that effective action depended on the city itself assuming collective responsibility for this and charging its citizens through taxation for carrying out the cleansing services. It was a strikingly modern concept and reflected the burgh's acceptance that the scale and speed of Glasgow's expansion demanded new institutions and fresh approaches.

Among the most innovative features of the Police Act was the manner in which it opened up wider access to political power long before the reforms in municipal government of 1833. In addition it established a clear link between civic authority and local representation. As one scholar had concluded: ' . . . the Glasgow Police Act became a model for the future organisation of local government . . . and served as an important bridge between the old burgess dominated municipality and the open system which prevailed after 1833.'[17] The *ancien regime*, in the form of the existing burgh council, did have a role to play. The Lord Provost, the Magistrates, the Dean of Guild and the Deacon Convener of the Trades were all represented on the Board of Police. But there were also 24 commissioners chosen by ballot by ratepayers within the city's 24 wards. The Board was empowered to assess rents with rates varying from 4d per £ on rentals of £14 to £6 to 1/- on rents valued at £15 and upwards.[18] All this implied a degree of real local representation which was notable by its absence in such existing burghal institutions as the Council, Merchants House, and Trades House. It also established a tradition which has been a cardinal feature of local government down to the present day. Moreover, over time, the social composition of the Police Board began to differ from that of the Town Council. In the former, merchants and wealthy manufacturers remained dominant. In the latter, professional men, shopkeepers and small traders were much more common by the 1830s. Symptomatic of its more open political complexion was the fact that the Board was attracting Chartist and even Roman Catholic members by the early 1840s.[19] Local influence and control were also strengthened in an Act of 1821 which provided for the election of two additional representatives in each ward. These 'Resident Commissioners' were given executive functions. Under the authority of the magistrates they were empowered 'to exercise a general superintendence of their several districts'. Originally the office of commissioner was confined to electors who possessed a house, shop, warehouse or other building to the value of £15 per annum. However, from 1837 every voter became eligible, provided his property was in the assessable police area, thus consolidating still further the link between local interest and police administration.[20]

The Police Commission's activities depended on three sources of finance: its own rating, a grant from the Town Council and income from the Statute Labour Act of 1807. The Council was bound to contribute no less than £800 annually in compensation for the relief to the burgh's Common Good of all the police responsibilities now assumed by the Commission. Under the Statute Labour Act of 1772 the Town Council had the duty of calling on individuals within the burgh for labour service relating to the repair of roads. The Police Act of 1800 converted this service into a monetary sum which was finally fixed by an Act of 1807 which made the income available to the Commissioners.[21] On the basis of these sources of revenue the Commission quickly became an important civic institution in Glasgow. Its income stood at £5,135 in 1801 and had almost doubled to £9,324 in 1813. The entire revenue of the Town Council itself in that year was £13,161.[22] Originally, there was a Master of Police with a staff of 3 sergeants, 9 officers and 88 watchmen. By 1815 the establishment had risen to 98 watchmen and 19 officers. In 1833 total numbers of officers and men had expanded further to 318.[23] Their duties included lighting, cleansing, firefighting and law enforcement.

II

The Act of 1800 had set up an agency which possessed considerable potential in the regulation and control of urban amenity and there can be little doubt that the Commission did contribute positively in a number of ways. The 1800 legislation made provision for the complete foot-paving of the sides of all the streets of the city at the expense of the owners of facing property. The Minute Books of the commission in the years after this date are full of references to numerous applications for this purpose.[24] These regulations were still in force in the early twentieth century. Equally significant were developments in lighting. To a very large extent the illumination at night of the streets of central Glasgow was the achievement of the Police Commission. In 1767 the Town Council had stated that more public lighting would be beneficial, not least in the detection and prevention of crime.[25] However, because of revenue constraints it was only in 1780 that lamps were placed in the Trongate, one of the burgh's main thoroughfares. The Act of 1800 made the lighting of the public streets a statutory duty and gave the Police Commissioners the power to affix lamps to walls. During the first decade of its existence this was probably the primary function of the Commission with the lighting of lamps the major responsibility of the watchmen.[26] It was also due partly to the initiative of the Commissioners that coal gas was introduced as an illuminating material to Glasgow, making the city only the second after London to be lit by gas.[27] This had the most important side effect of freeing men to undertake other duties because gas was supplied directly by pipe from the works of the Glasgow Gas Company in Townhead. Lighting the streets with oil lamps was very laborious. Oil, however, had to be carried through the streets, lamps filled and wicks trimmed. This was one reason, it was alleged, why the watchmen were not regarded as very effective in the control of crime. They were often too busy lighting and trimming lamps![28]

Glasgow's first effective fire service also developed out of the Police Commission. An Act of 1807 transferred responsibility for fire control from the Town Council to it. In that year 18 firemen were employed. Each '. . . shall have a harn frock and leather cap with a brass place upon which shall be engaged "City Firemen".'[29] One Basil Aitchison was appointed 'superintendent of fire engines' and by 1816 152 fire-plugs had been distributed throughout the city. Ten years later Glasgow possessed five fire engines.[30]

Perhaps, however, the construction of an extended sewer system was the most remarkable achievement of the Commissioners in the first three decades of the eighteenth century. Until 1790 Glasgow had no public sewers. Surface water flowed to the river through ditches and open water-courses. The Council only possessed the spare funds of the Common Good to build what were comparatively costly structures.[31] The Police Act of 1800 gave the Commissioners formal powers to construct sewers. Not, however, until the Statute Labour Act of 1807 did funds become available through the conversion monies allocated to the Commission by that legislation. Immediately, there was a veritable boom in sewer construction. James Cleland, writing in 1816, described the rapid expansion of 'common sewers, large enough to admit adult persons to clean them'.[32] By that year they already extended over four miles. In 1832 they had reached seven miles and covered 45 streets.[33] It should be remembered, however, that the burgeoning suburbs were mainly outside the radius of this network and that the system itself was not connected to house drains. The sewers of this period were designed to dispose of surface street water not domestic effluent or human waste. Indeed, the Commission actively prohibited such uses and prosecuted those who were found to be offending.[34] This seriously diminished the value of the new sewer system as an effective control on the deterioration of the urban environment in Glasgow.

The Police Commission was, therefore, an innovative body whose initiatives did much to create a new range of public services in the expanding city. In several ways, its policies point forward to the post 1833 period of municipal reform and later systematic action on sanitary regulation. The Commission was a body committed to intervention. Many of its activities are in conflict with the conventional historical picture of moribund unreformed burghal authorities impotent and irresolute in face of unbridled urban growth. On the other hand, the evidence considered earlier in this chapter shows that despite the Commission's efforts the urban environment did become steadily more dangerous in the 1810s and 1820s. Death rates increased dramatically. Typhus epidemics became more common. Conditions in the central districts of the city around the Cross sunk to unprecedented levels of acute destitution and human misery. In part, this was because the sheer scale of growth was outside the control of the contemporary authorities. During these decades Glasgow's population was expanding faster than that of any other city of its size in western

Europe.[35] As M. W. Flinn has put it: 'Some towns expanded during the early nineteenth century at rates that would bring cold sweat to the brows of twentieth century housing committees.'[36] In Glasgow, however, the civic authorities were not blameless. There is evidence that in the crucial area of cleansing policy and control of environmental nuisances, the Police Commission was not very effective. Other aspects of its activities, much less important to the health of the community, were given greater priority. Indeed, as death rates increased the urban environment became of less significance than it had been in the years immediately after the foundation of the Commission. More and more, concentration focused on the growing problems of public order in the two decades after the end of the Napoleonic Wars.

III

The cleaning of streets and the removal of filth was a statutory responsibility of the Police Commissioners enshrined in the foundation Act of 1800. The watchmen were employed 'both to watch and to cleanse the closes and streets'.[37] Throughout the records of the Commission these duties were constantly reiterated. Moreover, by the second decade of the nineteenth century, the connection between poor sanitary conditions and the menace of disease seems to have been recognised. This became clear during the typhus epidemic of 1817–18. The Commission consulted 'medical gentlemen' on the origins of 'the fever at present existing in the city'. They reported that the disease was primarily caused by 'the unclean state of the closes and by lanes in different parts of the town and stagnate (sic) water contained in the dunghills in these closes and lanes'.[38] Here was an unambiguous statement that the deterioration of the urban environment and increasing mortality were very closely linked. Yet, significantly, the Board of Police concluded that the Commission 'cannot compel the proprietors of closes to remove these nuisances.' However, the Master of Police was directed to instruct the ward officers 'to be more active than they have hitherto been in summoning persons who fail to clean their closes in terms of the Act.' They were also ordered to compile lists of streets which were not properly paved and of 'dungsteads' which were not effectively constructed.[39]

The Board was clearly inhibited by the terms of its governing legislation from interfering directly with the rights of private property but it obviously still possessed the powers to improve sanitary practices if it decided to enforce them. The evidence suggests, however, that it did not often do so. Indeed, during the three decades covered by this study energetic efforts to remove filth only took place during the 1817–18 typhus epidemic.[40] In other periods it was rare for individuals to be summoned for failing to keep closes or streets clean. Between April 1818 and July 1819, in response to the Board's injunction stated above, 261 persons were summoned for these offences. However, only 69 (or 26.4 per cent) were actually fined.[41] Even this purge was short-lived and did not last for much longer than the epidemic itself. The normal annual pattern was for only a handful of people to be summoned with the vast majority having their cases dismissed with no further action taken.[42] Other offences had much higher priority. For instance, in September 1819 only two individuals were summoned for 'dirty closes' or 'not emptying dungsteads' compared with 67 who were apprehended for begging and 24 for profaning the Sabbath.[43]

The Commission also received repeated complaints about the inadequacy of cleansing carried out by its own officers. In 1804, it was stated that 'the streets are not kept as clean as they ought to be' and similar concern was shown in 1802, 1807, 1811, 1817 and 1818.[44] Moreover, even if the Board of Police determined to enforce its responsibilities for cleaning it was by no means certain that the decisions would have a real impact because of the poor quality of its staff. The Commission itself doubted whether they were up to the job. In 1810, one Commissioner argued that 'an examination should be made into the state of all the watchmen and to determine whether they are all fit for doing the duties of their office as a number of them appear old and infirm'.[45] Specific complaints about members of the Watch abound in the Commission's records. Individual watchmen were accused of theft and allegations of intoxication were commonplace.[46] Even, therefore, if the Board of Police had taken a more serious interest in sanitary regulation it is doubtful if it could have much effect until a more professional inspectorate was established. The Board's staff had increased in numerical terms but its ethos still to a very large extent reflected the amateurism of the Town Guard of the period before 1800.

But this was not the root of the problem or the fundamental reason why the potential of the Commission of Police in the area of sanitary control was not realised in the decades before 1830. A major factor was the profound ideological and practical opposition to the substantial increase in compulsory taxation which was necessary in order to extend proper services to the community as a whole. The rise in the Commission's income and expenditure over time has already been noted. However, persistent efforts were made to control this and reduce costs despite the ever-expanding need. In 1822, for instance, the summer squad of scavengers was cut to only sixteen men and one superintendent. Scavengers' wages were also reduced.[47] The following year, the construction of a new police station was postponed.[48] In 1833 'greater economy' was being sought and a strategy put in place to pare costs further.[49] Indeed, by the 1820s and 1830s one senses more a concern with controlling expenditure than with tackling the huge problems of a rapidly growing city.

Nor is this surprising. By the 1820s committed Evangelicals were consolidating their grip on the Town Council and probably also on the Commission of Police.[50] These men were powerfully influenced by the social gospel propagated by the Rev. Thomas Chalmers who had become minister of St. John's Parish in central Glasgow in 1819. Amid the incipient social chaos caused by radicalism and disaffection in the years after the end of the Napoleonic Wars, Chalmers seemed to offer a simple and compelling solution which had wide appeal among the city's evangelically-minded middle classes.The way back to social order and hierarchy lay in spreading the Christian message among the urban population through church building and education. In addition, however, the affluent in society should assist the poor by means of charity, which enriched the Christian virtues, rather than through taxation which destroyed them.[51]

A statement published by the Board of Police in 1842 reveals how thoroughly its membership had become imbued with Chalmersian values. The Board remarked how it had not adopted the clauses in the Town Council's legislation for improving the wynds and lanes and the cleaning of the Molendinar Burn at public expense. It also opposed the clauses for constituting a Board of Health and raising funds by assessment 'for defraying the expense of erecting buildings as hospitals, dispensaries . . . and for appointing medical officers, district surgeons, apothecaries, inspectors, etc.' The Board admitted that it would be to the advantage of the proprietors in the affected areas to have their properties improved 'at public expense'. However, no burden 'should be imposed on the general community'. It may be desirable to provide for public health but, the Board stressed:

> . . . not by a *compulsory assessment*, to supersede and dry up, as it were, those sources of public beneficence which have ever readily flowed, when required for such purposes. Besides, this Board is convinced that the tendency of such as assessment would be to affect very materially *all* voluntary contributions for charitable purposes especially for the Infirmary, rendering it necessary perhaps in course of time to resort to other compulsory assessments for other objects – and this Board, therefore, cannot see any necessity for, or propriety in, the introduction of such assessments at all.[52]

As evangelical values became dominant in the Commission of Police it became more and more evident that the organisation was more interested in cleansing the moral rather than the physical environment. The city's rulers were alarmed at what they perceived as the threatened disintegration of urban society as shown by an increase in crime, rampant political disaffection and growing irreligion. As early as 1810, the Commission referred to 'these dangerous times' and decided that rewards should be paid to informers for the prevention of crime.[53] By 1817 reference was being made to 'the increasing mass of vice and profligacy and the Board recommended the appointment of a specialist criminal officer who would have no other duties but the detection of crime.' A 'dexterous thief-catcher or a known detector of stolen goods' was required![54] This action seems to have had little effect on changing perceptions because in 1819 it was admitted that 'this city has continued to increase every year with so much rapidity and perhaps the profligacy and delinquency in a much greater proportion.'[55] A year later, the Commission gave the impression that Glasgow was being steadily engulfed in an irresistible tide of rising crime. It was reckoned that the criminal department would have to be substantially increased in size because the number of 'Thieves, Rogues, Vagabonds and Depredators of every description' had grown to an alarming extent.[56]

Of equal concern was the perceived menace of political radicalism in the years after the end of the Napoleonic Wars culminating in the 'Radical War' of 1820. Historians disagree about the significance of these events, with some suggesting that the radicals did not really present a major threat to the existing political establishment.[57] It is clear, nevertheless, that the Glasgow Police Commission had a different view. A 'Secret Service Committee' was set up in 1816 to enable the recruitment of special constables.[58] A year later 700 new constables were appointed.[59] By October 1819 'the machinations of the disaffected' had become so menacing that the Committee was attempting to establish 'regiments' for 'the protection of the lives and property of the community'.[60] The Commission's officers who had been in the army were to be issued with arms and in 1820 a further 200 men were recruited.[61] The 'Radical War' itself broke out in April, 1820 but long before that the city's rulers had been in a state of acute foreboding and anxiety. In December, 1819, for instance, the Commission was dreading 'an open insurrection' and the police were armed in anticipation.[62]

It was hardly surprising, therefore, given the perceived twin menaces of rising crime against property and the spectre of revolution from below that reform of the urban environment should take much lower priority in the policies of the Police Commission. It was not so much the physical health of the community which was seen to be in danger (except during serious epidemics) but rather its social order, hierarchy, morality and religion. These were the most pressing concerns. The belief was that a root cause of moral decline was intemperance which, as one report put it, 'seems likely to undermine the whole fabric of society'.[63] This was linked to profanation of the Sabbath when alehouses and taprooms were open. These were held responsible for 'those disgusting and obnoxious scenes' which were common on the streets on a Sunday.[64] Such was the force of evangelical values within the Commission that from 1809–10 it was transformed into a guardian of public morals, acting almost like an arm of the Church in its determination to maintain the sanctity of the Sabbath. The Watch was instructed to sweep the main streets thoroughly on the Saturday in preparation for the Sunday church services. Publicans who opened on a Sunday were condemned and summoned. In the middle of the typhus epidemic of 1817–18 the Commission's attention was as much concentrated on this problem as on the potent threat to public health.[65] In June, 1819, the Board of Police adopted more stringent measures. Twenty men were appointed to 'range the streets and lanes on the Sabbath and Saturday evenings and to apprehend idle and disorderly persons'. On Sundays, 14 officers were employed specifically to report on any house open for the sale of spirits.[66]

An even more pressing problem was that of vagrancy. This also began to absorb an inordinate proportion of the Commission's time and energies because it concerned its members at several levels. Most obviously, the increasing beggar problem could provide one explanation for the seemingly inexorable rise in Glasgow's poor law assessments. It was argued that there were so many beggars in the city because natives of the country districts and of Ireland came there to gain a legal settlement.[67] Beggars were also blamed for petty crimes against property and represented a potential source of disaffection since they were not subject to the discipline and control of masters and employers. It is, of course, likely that the number of vagrants would increase in a period of rapid urban growth. Migrants did not have a legal residence in the city and hence no legal right to poor relief. The operation of the trade cycle and its impact on Glasgow's industries could lead to dramatic increases in short-term unemployment. During the winter months also many were laid off, especially in the casual labour sector, and some of these would be forced to take to the streets as beggars.

To the Commission, however, the problem was not economic or social in origin but moral and financial. The assumption was that vagrants had fallen into difficulties through their own fault and had then become parasites on the benevolence of others. A punitive and rigorous approach was therefore adopted. Concerns about vagrancy surfaced as early as 1801. The rapid increase in the poor rate led to the Police Commission establishing a census to discover the length of time the population had lived in the city.[68] In 1809 a joint committee of the Town Council and the Police Commission met to draw up plans to prevent public begging.[69] Finally, two years later, in March 1811 all public begging was prohibited in Glasgow. The police were ordered to arrest any beggars found after that date. Those who had a legal residence within the city could be provided for through the existing poor law. The rest were

> . . . to be ordered from the city and repair to the parish in which they have a legal claim for support. Those who are able to labour for their subsistence but refuse to work may be committed to Bridewall and detained therein at hard labour for such period as may be found just and proper.[70]

From that point on the officers of police were much more concerned to trace and arrest vagrants than initiate prosecutions relating to nuisances and filthy streets. During the period 1811 to 1820 the overwhelming majority of those summoned by police for offences under the Act of 1800 were beggars. This was part of a broader switch in the policy of the Commissioners away from environmental issues and towards social problems. In December, 1822, for instance, only 3.2 per cent of summonses concerned dirty closes and streets, the rest all dealt with assault, begging, prostitution, theft and profanation of the Sabbath.[71] Essentially, the term 'police' was rapidly losing its original general meaning and taking on the specialist association with 'criminal police' which it has retained ever since. Given the growing problems of public order in a rapidly growing city this was perhaps an inevitable development. But it was one which also helped to undermine a potentially important agency for amenity and environmental control.

REFERENCES

1. A new large-scale study of the city in this period is T. M. Devine and G. Jackson, eds., *Glasgow*, volume one *beginnings to 1830* (Manchester, 1994).
2. Anon., *A Project for Erecting Public Markets within the Barony of Gorbals addressed to the Heritors of that Barony by an Heritor* (Glasgow, 1810), p. 158.
3. Strathclyde Regional Archives (SRA), E1/1/14, Police Minute Book, 27 October, 1825.
4. M. W. Flinn, ed., *Scottish Population History from the Seventeenth Century to the 1930s* (Cambridge, 1977), p. 377.
5. A. S. Wohl, *Endangered Lives: Public Health in Victorian Britain* (Cambridge, 1983).
6. W. P. Alison, *Reply to Dr. Chalmers' objections to the Improvement of the Legal Provisions for the Poor in Scotland* (Edinburgh, 1841), p. 1.
7. *Report on the Sanitary Condition of the Labouring Population of Great Britain by Edwin Chadwick*, ed. M. W. Flinn (Edinburgh, 1965), p. 99.
8. For an examination of the various views see T. M. Devine, 'Urban Crisis' in Devine and Jackson, eds., *Glasgow*.
9. See, for example, A. Gibb, *Glasgow: the Making of a City* (Beckenham, 1983), pp. 104–110.
10. SRA, E/1/1, Police Sederunt Books; E1/7, Statute Labour and Cleansing Minutes and Accounts; E1/1/3, Police Minute Books; E2/1, Clerk of Police Letterbooks.
11. J. Ord, *Origins and History of the Glasgow Police* (Glasgow, 1906).
12. Irene Mavor, 'The Guardianship of the Community: Civic Authority to 1833' in Devine and Jackson, eds., *Glasgow*.
13. *Ibid.*
14. Sir James Bell and James Paton, *Glasgow: its Municipal Organisation and Administration* (Glasgow, 1896), pp. 113–114.
15. *Ibid*, p. 112.
16. R. Renwick, ed., *Extracts from the Records of the Burgh of Glasgow* (Glasgow, 1913) (*Glasgow Burgh Records*), p. ix (1796–1808), p. x.

17. Mavor, 'Guardianship of the Community' in Devine and Jackson, eds., *Glasgow*.
18. Bell and Paton, *Glasgow: its Municipal Organisation*, pp. 113–114.
19. Irene E, Sweeney, 'The Municipal Administration of Glasgow, 1833–1912', unpublished Ph.D thesis, University of Strathclyde, 1990, pp. 113–122.
20. Bell and Paton, *Glasgow: its Municipal Organisation*, pp. 114–115.
21. *Ibid.*
22. SRA, E/1, 7 Sept., 1801; 31 August, 1813; *Glasgow Burgh Records*, 24 February, 1813.
23. SRA, E2/1/3, Statement of Superintendent of Police, 16 October, 1833.
24. SRA, E1/1, 1801–14, *passim*.
25. Bell and Paton, *Glasgow: its Municipal Organisation*, p. 157.
26. SRA, E1/1, 7 September, 1801; 1 September, 1805; E1/1/3, 19 October, 1802.
27. SRA, E1/1/9, 17 October, 1816; E2/1/1, Clerk of Police to Superintendent of Lighting of the Streets of Manchester, April, 1819.
28. SRA, E/1/1, 25 August, 1817.
29. *Ibid*, 13 November, 1807.
30. Bell and Paton, *Glasgow: its Municipal Organisation*, p. 137.
31. A. McGeorge, *Old Glasgow* (Glasgow, 1819), p. 169.
32. Quoted in Bell and Paton, *Glasgow: its Municipal Organisation*, p. 137.
33. James Cleland, *Description of the City of Glasgow* (Glasgow, 1840), pp. 79–94.
34. SRA, E1/7/1, 29 June, 1809; E1/1/6, 27 February, 1812.
35. J. de Vries, *European Urbanisation* 1500–1800 (London, 1984).
36. *Report on the Sanitary Condition of the Labouring Population of Great Britain*, p. 4.
37. SRA, E1/1, 1 December, 1800.
38. SRA, E1/1/10, 2 April, 1818.
39. *Ibid.*
40. *Ibid*, 10 April, 1818 – 15 July, 1819.
41. *Ibid.*
42. SRA, E1/1, 1801–24, *passim*.
43. *Ibid*, 16 and 23 September, 1819.
44. SRA, E1/1/3, 1802–1818.
45. SRA, E1/1/6, 25 January, 1810.
46. See, for example, SRA, E1/1/6, 25 January, 1810; E2/1/1, Clerk of Police to J. Peddie, 8 November, 1817; E1/1/3, 24 January, 1804. In this last report it was stated that 'there were daily complaints from the public of the drunkenness and sleeping of the watchmen while on duty.'
47. SRA, E1/1/12, 5 April, 1822.
48. *Ibid.*, 6 June, 1822.
49. SRA, E2/1/3, Clerk of Police to Superintendent of Police, 16 October, 1833.
50. Sweeney, 'Municipal Administration', pp. 113–122.
51. Stewart J. Brown, *Thomas Chalmers and the Godly Commonwealth in Scotland* (Oxford, 1982), pp. 122–4.
52. *Notes explanatory of the Heads of a new Police Bill for Glasgow* (Glasgow, 1842), pp. 14–15.
53. SRA, E1/1/6, 13 December, 1810.
54. SRA, E1/1, 25 August, 1817.
55. SRA, E1/1/10, 27 August, 1819.

56. *Ibid.*, 3 February, 1820.
57. See, for example, T. C. Smout's descriptions of the events of 1820 as 'a pathetic outcome'. T. C. Smout, *A History of the Scottish People, 1560–1830* (London, 1969), p. 447.
58. SRA, E1/1/9, 16 May, 1816.
59. *Ibid.*, 9 January, 1817.
60. SRA, E1/1/10, 7 October, 1819.
61. *Ibid.*, 30 March, 1820.
62. E2/1/1, Clerk of Police to Mr. John Vickery, Police Office, Bond Street, London, 14 December, 1819.
63. SRA, E1/1/9, 6 February, 1817.
64. SRA, E1/1/13, 16 October, 1823.
65. SRA, E1/1/10, 1818–1819, *passim.*
66. SRA, E2/1/1, Clerk of Police to Robert Tennant, 26 June, 1819.
67. SRA, E1/1/2, 13 March, 1801.
68. *Ibid.*
69. SRA, E1/1/6, 21 February, 1809.
70. *Ibid.*, 15 April, 1811.
71. SRA, E1/1/12, December 1822.

11

Employment Opportunities and Migrant Group Assimilation: the Highlanders and Irish in Glasgow, 1840–1860

WILLIAM SLOAN

Introduction

In an attempt to describe and explain the assimilation of migrants into urban, industrial society entry and participation in the economy of the host society has figured prominently in studies carried out by historians and social scientists. It has been recognised that the economic position of migrants although only one aspect influencing migrant assimilation has a fundamental part to play in that process.[1] Scottish historiography has produced studies which have given considerable emphasis to the types of employments taken up by different migrant groups. The employment of quantitative methods, using the census data from the period 1841 to 1891, has enabled historians to consider in detail migrant involvement in the economies of these urban, industrial centres in the nineteenth century. A common approach in these studies has been to examine a specific migrant group, either Irish or Highlander and, as a result of this research, there is now a better understanding of the socio-economic position of the Irish and Highlanders in such towns in the nineteenth century.[2]

There remain, however, many aspects of the economic assimilation of these two migrant groups to urban, lowland society that require further investigation. There has been a lack of any systematic *comparative* research into the positions of these migrant groups in the largest urban centres of lowland Scotland at a time when the industrial base was rapidly expanding and transforming and, as a result, creating many new employment opportunities. Through direct comparison of the Irish and Highland migrants in Glasgow in the period 1840 to 1860 the relative performance of the two groups in penetrating the occupational hierarchy of the growing city economy can be assessed. In particular, a study of the migrant groups in Glasgow would provide an opportunity to compare the success of the Irish and Highlanders in gaining access to the new skilled employment opportunities emerging in the expanding industrial enterprises of metalworking, engineering and shipbuilding. The work of Campbell on the Lanarkshire miners and metalworkers, for instance, has revealed a more complex penetration of these occupations by the Irish than the earlier work of Handley had suggested.[3] Such a study can also provide a comparative measurement of the plight of the two migrant groups in the highly congested slums of the old central areas of Glasgow perhaps adding to the knowledge gained in other studies which have placed a considerable reliance on the impressionistic evidence.[4] Crucially, the comparative approach adopted in this study may provide a better understanding of one major factor promoting and retarding migrant group integration into mainstream society.

In this study, then a *systematic comparative* examination is made of the entry and participation of Highland and Irish migrants in two distinct types of local economy within the city: the riverside western suburb of Anderston which was rapidly expanding and transforming its industrial base and the parishes of Outer and St Andrew areas containing some of the most highly congested slum areas of inner Glasgow. In selecting particular districts for detailed study it was recognised that no exact representation of the wider experience of the migrant groups across the city could be accomplished. However, given the proposed research method and level of analysis it was not possible to examine the migrant experience throughout the entire city and by concentrating on two such contrasting areas in the social geography of Glasgow a broad picture of migrant assimilation into the city economy could be attempted.[5]

At the mid-century, Glasgow had a population largely composed of migrants and their offspring. Although Highland and Irish migrants were but two groups in a more general influx of migrants the presence of two groups was large and distinct. At the census of 1851 the proportion of the city's adult population who were Irish-born was 23.3 per cent while 5 per cent of the adults in Glasgow were from Highland counties.[6] Before considering the types of employment the Irish and Highland migrants were able to find on arrival it is necessary to give at least a brief account of the economic development of the districts chosen for detailed examination.

Employment Opportunities in Anderston

The eclipse of handloom weaving would appear to have occurred in Anderston far earlier than in the Glasgow area as a whole.[7] Textile activities still remained an important form of male employment at the mid-century in Anderston (Table 1 below) and a sizeable element of the employed males were still engaged in the moribund handloom trade. Most males working in the textile sector by the mid-century worked in the spinning and power loom factories, in the local printwork and as calendars.

The major expansion of male employment opportunities from the 1820s was however a result of the growth of engineering, metalworking and iron shipbuilding in the district. The village of Anderston proved an attractive location for many entrepreneurs and soon such industrial activity was extending westwards in the burgh to the localities of Lancefield and Finnieston. Although the district eventually proved incapable of providing the space and infrastructure needed by the companies of exceptional growth and many of the major firms established their major works elsewhere, the owners of firms generally retained their Anderston works as an integral part of their overall investment strategy. Thus, the largest establishments in the district, though eventually dwarfed by the yards and workshops built downriver and elsewhere, still employed in this period workforces in excess of 500 men. A wide range of smaller metalworking, engineering and other businesses sprung up around the major works extending and diversifying the employment opportunities in the district.[8]

Table 1: Distribution of Occupations in Anderston Household Sample, by sex, 1851

	Males	Females
Occupational group	(N=775)	(N=469)
Agriculture	1.8 %	0.0 %
Construction	8.5	0.0
Metalworking	15.7	0.0
Machinery	12.5	0.0
Shipbuilding	2.3	0.0
Gas and fuel	1.3	0.0
Glasswork and pottery	3.9	0.4
Textiles	13.4	52.5
Clothing	2.2	18.3
Shoemaking	3.6	1.7
Woodworkers	2.5	0.0
Printing	0.6	0.0
Food	3.0	0.2
Transport	12.1	1.5
Service	0.5	23.7
Commerce and finance	3.0	1.1
Shopkeepers and publicans	6.7	0.2
Labourer (trade unspecified)	1.0	0.0
Professions	1.0	0.0
Other and unknown	4.3	0.4

Note: For information on sample data and groupings see Appendix.

Source: Census of Scotland, 1851.

The new male employment opportunities to be found in the metal, machine and shipbuilding industries consisted largely of work for skilled men or their apprentices. New trades and job categories reflecting the new production materials and techniques were being created in the yards and works of the district in addition to the demand for the older trades of wright, joiner, blacksmith, painter and plumber.

The building of residences, roads, industrial sites and harbour improvements also created employment in this industrial suburb. In addition, work in transport, as labourers, porters, carters and warehouse workers were also important local employments as were the local pottery and glassworks, wood and saw mills, cabinet making, cooperage, food processing industries, retail trades, clothing and shoemaking industries. By the mid-century the industrial suburb with its factories, foundaries, engineering works and shipyards also boasted a diverse industrial and commercial base offering a wide range of employment opportunities for incoming male migrants.

In marked contrast to their male counterparts, female migrants attracted to Anderston were confronted with employment conditions in which the textile and clothing activities, along with domestic service, accounted for the overwhelming proportion of paid employment. The textile sector provided just over half, 52.5 per cent, of all female jobs (see Table 1). The spinning mills, a major source of employment since the early 1800s, remained a large employer of female labour throughout the period. A more dynamic feature of the local economy in the 1830s, however, was the growth of power loom weaving with this work predominantly taken up by young females following the eclipse of the male-dominated handloom weaving sector.[18] The 1851 data indicate that one quarter of the gainfully employed females in Anderston, and almost one-half of all female textile employees in the district, were powerloom workers. A much smaller but still significant aspect of the textile industry was printing. However, with most of the printworks jobs undertaken by males, only about one in sixteen female workers in the district were so engaged, and these were largely very young girls.

The 1851 census data indicate that the next major form of employment for women was service, which accounted for 23.7 per cent of employed females. In addition to those employed as domestic servants, there was work as charwomen, washerwomen and other forms of servicing more affluent households. The development of middle – class housing in the lands west and north of Anderston in the 1840s and 1850s ensured that there would be a considerable increase in the demand for domestic servants in the area.

At mid-century, 18.3 per cent of employed females in Anderston were working either as dressmakers, milliners, sewers, seamstresses or some other activity making or repairing clothes. Although there were other significant forms of paid employment for women in Anderston (Table 1), it was essentially the clothing and service industries, and most especially the textile industries, that held out the prospect of gainful employment for female migrants arriving in the district.

The Occupations of Highland and Irish Migrants in Anderston

It is possible to discern both broad similarities and differences in migrant group positions within the male sector of the Anderston labour market. The data presented Table 2 indicate the occupational distribution of the Irish and Highland males.[9] Compared to all males employed in Anderston, the data would suggest that the Irish and Highlanders were only slightly under – represented in the metal, machinery and shipbuilding industries with 29.3 per cent of the Irish males and 29.2 of the Highlanders engaged in these industries. However, whereas about two-thirds of all males employed in this sector were in the skilled category, only one – third of the Irish working in this area were recorded as tradesmen.[10] The Irish performance in acquiring skilled work would appear to have been better than one might expect on the basis of contemporary assessment or other studies of Irish penetration of skilled metalworking occupations.[11] Yet, closer examination of the non – labouring positions taken up by the Irish migrants reveals them to be over – represented in tasks such as hammermen, caulkers and rivetters which offered low pay and status, and which relied on strength as much as skill. Information gathered from the Catholic marriage registers of St. Patrick's RC Church, Anderston for the period 1855–1870 provides evidence specifically on the first and second generation Catholic Irish. [12] Of the 146 men engaged in metal, machine and shipbuilding, excluding labourers, 28.1 per cent were hammermen and 10.4 per cent were rivetters. The better – paid trades in these industries were also, however, well represented. Men describing them-selves as boilermakers accounted for 16 per cent of the total and 8.7 per cent were entered as moulders. In all, 28 different occupations of this sector were registered which would suggest that small numbers of first and second generation Catholic Irish were gaining access to a wide range of skilled occupations within this expanding sector even if the great majority found only unskilled work.

In contrast, about two – thirds of the Highlanders returned as employed in these industries in 1851 were skilled workers and these migrants were overwhelmingly engaged as ship carpenters and joiners, as blacksmiths and boilermakers and as engineers and shipwrights. The census data would suggest that they were rarely engaged as hammermen or rivetters. Highland migrants were very successful in gaining access to the most skilled and lucrative forms of employment in the metal, machine and shipbuilding works of the district.

The movement of goods and people was another important source of employment for both migrant groups but especially for the Highlanders: 22.2

Table 2: Distribution of Irish, Highland and all male employed in Anderston, 1851

Occupational Group	Irish %	Highland %	Total popn %
Agriculture	2.5	0.0	1.8
Construction	11.5	15.6	8.5
Metal/machine/shipbuilding	29.3	29.2	30.5
Pottery and glassmaking	6.4	0.4	3.9
Textiles	13.1	3.5	13.4
Clothing	6.4	2.3	5.8
Transport	12.7	22.2	12.1
Commerce and finance	2.5	7.0	9.7
Police	0.4	6.2	0.5
Labourer (unspecified)	1.9	0.8	1.0
Others and unknown	13.7	12.8	12.2
	100	100	99.9

Source: Census of Scotland, 1851.

per cent of the employed male Highlanders as against 11.8 per cent of the Irishmen. In this riverside district and in the adjacent harbour area of the Broomielaw the ability of the menfolk among the Highlanders to find employment as sailors, firemen and stewards largely accounts for the unusually large proportion of Highlanders who were transport workers. Very few Irishmen gained employment as sailors though a small number managed to find places as fireman on boats.

About half of all adult male Irish transport workers were dock labourers. Information contained in the 1851 and 1861 census enumerators' books would indicate that these Irish dock labourers labourers lived in the tenements in the streets running off Anderston Quay and were predominantly migrants from the north – west of Ireland, particularly Donegal, with the eastern counties of Antrim, Down, Armagh and Monaghan barely represented. It would appear that there was a quite distinct migration stream in operation with migrants being pulled in from the north – west of Ireland to take up the poorly remunerated and irregular dockside labour. Few Highlanders sought employment of this kind and only one – in – ten of the Highlanders engaged in the transport sector worked as a dock labourer. It was as porters or carters that Highlanders were to be found around the docks and indeed in other parts of the city. Highlanders were traditionally over – represented in the ranks of the city porters, accounting for a third of the city licenses granted in 1834.[13] The Irish made serious inroads into this form of employment in the 1840s and 1850s capturing four out of every ten city licences as compared to the Highlanders one – in – ten.[14] The strong presence of the Donegal men at the docks was not repeated amongst the Irish porters who to a far greater extent were drawn, it would appear, from the more industrialised counties of the north – east of Ulster.

In both Anderston and the quayside district of the Broomielaw the Irish presence among the ranks of carters was very small. An additional survey, employing the data contained in the 1861 census, and concentrating on a part of the city traditionally a residential stronghold of carters, tends to confirm the almost total absence of Irish carters in the 1851 sample. Only 4.5 per cent of the 200 carters found were Irish – born.[15] Highland migrants appear to have possessed the necessary funds or connections to enter the carter business. In the 1861 survey mentioned above, there were three times as many Highland carters as there were Irish.

It is evident from the 1851 census data that the Irish who had found skilled employment in the cotton mills of Anderston and elsewhere in the West of Scotland as spinners still remained in that skilled occupation and were also securing other skilled positions in the textile industry as calico printers, warpers and tenters.[16] Young Irish males, however, were prepared to seek employment as power – loom weavers, not work likely to lead to a better paid 'adult' occupation. Young Highland males do not appear to have found it necessary to seek employment in this dead-end activity. Indeed only 3.5 per cent of employed Highland males, compared to the 13.1 per cent of employed Irishmen, were engaged in textiles, and the Highlander males represented by that figure were largely maintaining the Highlander tradition in finishing.

There was a disproportionate number of Irish males working in the local pottery and glassmaking works, 6.6 per cent in 1851, and many of these migrants were able to secure skilled positions. Data contained in the 1861 census books covering an extensive area of Anderston and the lands to the west, revealed that 53.4 per cent of the unskilled males were Irish – born while 38.5 per cent of the skilled pottery and glass workers were Irishmen.[17] In marked contrast, men from the Highlands, on the basis of this evidence, rarely sought employment at the local pottery or glasswork establishments.

Evidence from the 1851 sample would indicate that Highland – born and Irish – born females were taking up fundamentally different positions in the local economy of Anderston. In the local pottery and glassworks, Highland girls were almost entirely absent while these works were an important source of employment for Irish girls as they were for Irish males. In the 1861 survey of pottery workers, 62.5 per cent of the females employed in this industry were Irish born.

Both the employed Irish and Highland females were under – represented in the clothing sector, although a greater proportion of Irish females, 15.1 per cent as against 10.7 per cent of Highland females, were in this sector which included dressmaking, sewing and millinery. Shoemaking, also included in this grouping, was an activity in which a small element of the Irish females was involved. In the 1851 sample, Highland females were not represented in this trade.

It was the textile industries, however, which provided most of the female employment in Anderston and over half the employed Irish females worked in textiles. In contrast, only 9.1 per cent of the employed Highland – born females were working in the local printworks or as steam – loom weavers. There was no evidence of Highland girls entering the spinning mills. In contrast, the spinning mills of Anderston proved an attraction for Irish female migrants. Power – loom weaving was another major textile occupation for Irish females, unlike the Highlanders, and the Irish had also taken jobs in the local printworks. Earlier in the century employment in the printworks had been the preserve of Highland females but by the mid-century substantial numbers of women employed in these works were Irish – born.

If Irish girls were increasingly able to procure employment as printfield operatives in the area there may have been a parallel infiltration of domestic service in what was a burgeoning sector of the local labour market but one to which, traditionally, Irish women had not been granted entry. In the mid – 1830s it was confidentially stated that there were 'a great many Highland but few Irish domestic in Glasgow'.[19] The views of Norman Macleod, the Gaelic minister, in the early 1840s, confirm this testimony.[20] Yet it is possible that such comment did not truly reflect the position of Irish females by the 1850s and 1860s. In other major population centres Irish girls had little difficulty in gaining such employment, as Lees work on the London Irish has shown.[21] It was also recognised that the hiring of domestic servants on a monthly basis in Glasgow had, by the mid – century, made recruitment in the city different from the practices adopted in other lowland towns. More-over, when allowance is made for the numerical size of the two migrant groups, the data from the 1851 sample suggest that Irish women were finding jobs as domestic servants in significant numbers. Furthermore, although there may have been a general disinclination to employ Irish girls in the 1830s and 1840s, after the mid – century scarcity of alternative sources of labour might have compelled employers of domestics to hire Irish women. Some contemporaries contended that in the 1850s the demand for servants in Glasgow was outstripping the supply of suitable females. Speaking of that decade, John Strange, the city's statistician, asserted that 'of all the classes belonging to our community, who depend upon wages, this class (domestic servants) has been perhaps the one who has obtained the far greatest rise in the remuneration for service during the last ten years'.[22] If Strang's opinion is correct, then with such a growth in demand for domestic servants households may have been compelled to seek servants among the previously excluded Irish.

Evidence gathered from the 1861 census provides reliable information on which to base an assessment of Irish penetration of this form of employment. If we concern ourselves only with those servants returned in the census as residing in the largely working class district of Anderston proper, then there would be grounds for asserting a greater Irish presence in the ranks of domestic servants than the comments of contemporaries would suggest. For in this area 13.5 percent of the domestic servants were Irish born compared to the 16.5 per cent of servants who were Highland born. There were no major differences in the occupational groups or social strata the different migrant groups served or in the streets where they found employment. However, whereas the Highland servants were predominantly young women, 76 per cent were under 27 years of age, only a minority of the Irish servants were between the ages of 18 and 27. One-quarter of the Irish servants were over 42 years old and almost a quarter were widowed or married. Female Irish servants in Anderston proper were, by age and marital status, a more heterogeneous group than their Highland counterparts.

If the survey, however, is extended to the large middle class area to the west and north of Anderston then a quite different picture emerges. Irish servants were rare in these middle class households, with only 52 (or 2.7 per cent) of the 1919 total number of servants of Irish birth.

Ten of these servants were employed by a fellow native of Ireland. Of the nine Irish servants whose birth place was recorded, three were natives of Dublin and one was from Belfast. The evidence is slight but it might just hint at a quite specific pattern of migration for the Irish entering domestic service in middle class homes. Again, surname taken on its own is admittedly a crude indicator of a person's religious group, but comparing the names of Irish servants in these middle class dwellings with those located in Anderston it would seem that a greater proportion were Protestant than was the case in the working class zone.

If the Irish proportion of the servant population dropped dramatically in the more affluent areas, the Highland proportion rose substantially. In this prosperous district 469 or about one – quarter of the servants were Highland born. Only 7.7 per cent of these Highland females were in 'Highlander' households so this presence cannot be attributed to Highland migrants employing their own kind. Moreover, Highland servants were hired by every social strata residing in this predominantly affluent district. For instance, in the wealthy and prestigious Park Circus area, Highland servants accounted for 23.1 per cent of the 978 servants. Highlander servants were acceptable to families in the highest strata of Glasgow society.

Thus, despite the growing demand for domestic servants, the Glasgow middle class do not appear to have been willing to employ Irish girls in their homes. There were sufficient numbers of female migrants from other parts of Scotland to avoid the necessity of employing Irish women even if the scarcity of such Scottish women contributed to the apparent rising wage

Table 3. Distribution of Occupations in Central Zones, 1831 (Cleland data) and 1851 (sample of census households)

Occupational group	1831	1851
Construction	3.8	7.9
Metal and machinery	4.5	5.6
Glass and pottery	0.3	0.7
Textiles	18.8	18.2
Clothing	10.5	12.1
Leather	3.1	6.1
Wood	2.9	1.9
Printing	2.2	2.4
Food	6.2	5.0
Transport	6.2	6.9
Service	12.2	12.4
Labourers and miners	4.2	1.2
Commerce and finance	6.4	7.9
Professions	5.4	1.0
Others and unknown	13.3	10.7
Per cent	100	100
Numbers	8229	694

Note: For discussion of data and groupings see Appendix

Sources: J. Cleland, *Enumeration of the Inhabitants of the City of Glasgow and the County of Lanark, 1831,* (Glasgow, 1832), pp 109, 111; Census of Scotland, 1851.

rates. The Highlands remained throughout the mid-century a major source of such domestic staff.

Employment Opportunities in the Old, Central Districts of the City

The changing economic characteristics of the old, central districts of Glasgow in this period have received considerable attention from historians.[23] The diverse economic activity of the early decades of the century remained a characteristic of employment opportunities during the mid-century but the decreasing economic significance of the central zone of the city has also been documented.[24] Information gathered from Cleland's census of 1831 and a sampling of households in selected central zones taken from the 1851 census enumerators' books provides a crude indication of the changing employment opportunities over the period. These data presented in Table 3 below suggest that the occupational distribution of the inhabitants of these old, central areas did not substantially alter in the 1830s and 1840s. The textile sector remained the most important source of employment in these districts despite the more general changes occurring in this sector of the economy. The other major sectors in 1831, clothing, service, transport, commerce and finance, continued as the major sources of employment and retained their relative positions and strengths. In the case of the generally low – paid clothing, service and transport sectors, this is hardly surprising. The rapid increase in population densities in the old, central districts, the deteriorating housing, sanitary and environmental conditions and the departure of the middle – class have been well documented. Perhaps the clearest measure of the changes in the social character of these districts is the decline in the 'Professions' category from 5.4 per cent to 1.0 per cent in 1851.

Within the general context of stability and continuity in the economic activity of the population there were adjustments within sectors. Even in those sectors which would appear to evince no significant change, there was reorganisation of industry and new job opportunities. The biggest single sector, textiles, for example, was experiencing a process of change as a range of enterprises, including embroiderers, starchers, cotton waste dealers and wadding manufacturers were established. There was also in this period the growth of the sweating system in clothing manufacture. Increasing numbers of tailors and shoemakers were to be found in the inner city operating within the sweating system. Thus, if the data in Table 3 suggest continuity in the distribution of occupations they also fail to reveal the many changes in employment, pay, status and conditions within the various sectors. The massive influx of migrants into the old inner city districts was not, as was the case in Anderston and other suburbs, the result of developments in the new dynamic sectors of Glasgow's economy.[25] The higher wages to be found in those sectors were far less in evidence in the more traditional trades followed in the old, central districts of the city. An investigation of the Irish and Highland penetration of these quite different local labour markets, therefore, should complement the findings on migrant involvement in the suburban economy.

Migrant Group Employment in the Old, Central Districts

The data on Highland and Irish male employment in the central zones has been set out in Table 4 below. It can be seen that for both the Irish and Highland migrants the construction industry was an important source of employment. The census data indicate that the Irish immigrants were over – represented in the building industry, with the great majority engaged as labourers. This reflects the findings for Anderston and would tend to confirm contemporary comment about the status of the Irish in the building trade. Although the size of the sample does not allow for any more detailed comment about the positions taken up within the industry it is perhaps worth noting that a sizeable element of the Irish building workers – one – quarter in Anderston and near one – fifth in the central zones – were tradesmen. Interestingly, however, the Irish were largely concentrated in those trades, particularly as painters and slaters, that yielded less pay, security and status. It would appear, however, that the Irish were not entirely excluded from working as masons, joiners and carpenters but the small element of Irishmen in the building industry who were tradesmen were largely concentrated in in the least rewarding and secure trades.

In contrast, the 1851 sample data would suggest that the vast majority of Highland – born building workers in the central zones, and in Anderston, were tradesmen. Only one in twenty of the Highland building workers included in the sample were labourers and those who were tradesmen were largely in the better paid and more exclusive trades of mason, carpenter and joiner. The building industry, then, was a major source of employment for both migrant groups but their distribution within this sector was markedly different.

The clothing industry was also a major source of employment for both migrant groups accounting for one in ten male jobs for both groups in the central zones. Far fewer Highland – born males (3.3 per cent) found

Table 4. Distribution of Male Occupations in Sample of Households in Central Zones, 1851.

Occupational group	Irish	Highlander	Total Population
Agriculture	2.8%	2.2%	0.7%
Construction	16.8	12.2	13.2
Metal and machinery	5.6	12.7	8.7
Textiles	4.4	6.6	8.0
Clothing	10.0	10.5	8.3
Shoemaking	14.4	3.3	7.3
Wood	1.2	3.9	3.1
Printing	0.8	1.1	3.4
Food	0.8	5.5	7.3
Transport	7.6	7.2	10.8
Shops and pubs	1.2	4.4	4.5
Dealers, hawkers etc	9.2	0.6	4.7
Office workers	1.2	1.1	3.1
Police	1.2	10.0	1.4
Professions	0.0	3.3	0.7
Labourer (unspecified)	10.8	4.4	1.7
Others and unknown	12.0	11.0	13.2
Per cent	100	100	100
N	250	181	288

Note: 1. For breakdown of occupational groupings, see appendix.

Source: Census of Scotland, 1851.

employment as shoemakers than was the case with Irish males (14.4 per cent). The census data, however, fail to offer any indication of the position of the migrant groups in these largely unprotected sectors of the labour market which saw wide variations in work experience and remuneration.[26] However, a spatial configuration of the migrant participation in these trades may offer a crude indication of the respective positions held by the Irish and Highland – born. In both tailoring and shoemaking, the best – paid class of work was centred on the shops towards the west – end of the city in and around Buchanan Street. It was in the High Street area and other old, central zones that the 'sweating system' operated by small manufacturers had become prevalent. In 1850, it was estimated that two – thirds of the working tailors of the city received their work from sweaters.[27] Also, much of the shoemaking undertaken in the old, central areas of Glasgow was done in apartments by sweated labour.[28]

Evidence gathered from the 1861 census on these two distinct localities would suggest that although Irish tailors and shoemakers were to be found in both areas they appear to have been far more concentrated in the district where these trades were conducted within the sweated system. Whereas 41.5 per cent of tailors and 53.3 per cent of the shoemakers in the High Street area were Irish, only 8.8 per cent of tailors and 18.8 per cent of shoemakers in the Buchanan Street area were Irish immigrants. In comparison, the much smaller number of Highlanders who were working in these trades were more likely to be found in that area of the city where the 'Honourable' sector was largely located.

One sector of the economy in which the Irish were clearly under-represented was in the production of food. Whereas Highland born males found employment as bakers, fleshers and confectioners, Irishmen almost entirely failed to penetrate such occupations. The Irish immigrants in the central zones, however, were able to specialise in a range of activities which provided goods and services in demand in the city and elsewhere. About one – in – ten of the Irishmen in the sampled households earned a living as dealers, hawkers, brokers or in other forms of peddling. At this period Irish immigrants almost monopolised the used clothes trade of the city. The rewards of such trading were variable but probably most involved in the trade barely earned a living out of their activities, with some having to combine it with other sources of income. The growth of the old clothes trade is perhaps a good illustration of the expansion of commercial operations within the city which, far from being a response of the indigenous commercial elements to trading opportunities, were largely the enterprise of Irish immigrants with very limited resources. These forms of trading were sometimes a temporary expedient for many immigrants who could not find other employment and, as a way of earning a living, it was 'surrounded with continual hardship, difficulties and privations'. It was also one of the few alternatives open to those who through age, failing health or physical incapacity were unable to procure even the most casual wage employment.[29]

Some of the more enterprising among the Irish immigrants, however, were able to start up and consolidate more substantial businesses. As early as the 1830s the Rev. John Murdoch, Catholic bishop in Glasgow, stated that he had 200 to 300 persons amongst his congregation who were chiefly small shopkeepers or publicans, but certainly 'not of the working classes'. The vast bulk of these Catholic Irish businessmen had premises in the slum districts of the old inner city which had the highest concentrations of Irish immigrants. Throughout the mid-century, they provided services required by their poorer Catholic neighbours, as doctors, undertakers, shopkeepers, publicans, pawnbrokers, food, clothes, and furniture dealers, lodging-house keepers, booksellers and teachers. As late as the 1860s, many of these businessmen chose to reside in or near the districts where their Catholic clientele lived in the heaviest concentrations.[30]

Rarely did a Highland migrant living in the central districts of Glasgow, on the basis of the census data, find it necessary to eke out an existence as a dealer or a hawker, although their involvement in shopkeeping and spirit trades indicates that they possessed their fair share of the commercially minded (Table 4). Unlike the Irish, Highland migrants were to be found engaged in significant numbers as clerical workers. The 3.0 per cent of employed Highland males who were in professional occupations demonstrate the Highlander capacity to integrate at the more exclusive levels of society. The census data did not yield any "professionals" among the Irish.

Highland and Irish Migrants in the Glasgow Police Force

A significant proportion of Highland males (10 per cent) residing in the sampled central zones were police officers. An examination of the city wide recruitment and participation of Highland and Irish migrants in the police force may reveal attitudes and practices influencing migrant entry into a form of employment to which such migrants traditionally had access. There is evidence that the Highland component of the force had been large for decades and in the first half of 1846 almost half of the 173 men recruited to the force were Irish.[31]

In January 1856 Highlanders accounted for almost one-third (32 per cent) of the force while 21.9 per cent were Irish-born. In the period 1856–1857, 23.5 per cent of those joining the force were Highlanders and a slightly greater proportion, 26.7 per cent, were Irish. These Highlanders were, in general, younger than the new recruits taken as a whole: 84 per cent were under 30 years of age and three out of five were under 26. Over two-thirds were unmarried. The Irish recruits were slightly older but still overwhelmingly young men and slightly over half were married. In this respect it was the Highlanders who were out of line with the profile of the recruits as a whole: the great majority of the Highlander recruits were young single men.

It would also appear that the great majority of the Irishmen serving on the force were from the province of Ulster which tended to reflect the general profile of Irish migrants residing in Glasgow. Eighty-three per cent of the Irishmen serving on the force in January 1856 were Ulstermen. Nearly half of these men were natives of the three counties of Antrim, Down and Londonderry. A similar pattern of geographic background can be discerned for the new Irish recruits in 1856–1857, although Londonderry men were less prominent. The Highlanders joining the force tended to come more from the north – west and northern Scotland than Highlanders in Glasgow generally. Perhaps as few as one – in – ten of the Highlanders entering the force in the mid – 1850s were from south Argyle. It is perhaps not surprising that the suitability of these Highlanders for work in a large industrial city was sometimes brought into question. Yet it is noticeable in the intermittent criticisms against the rawness and inexperience of members of the force that seldom did anyone take exception to the presence of Irishmen on the force. The previous employment recorded by recruits would indicate that the great majority of the Highlanders who sought a place on the force did not possess skills which would be in demand in an urban context. In contrast, the majority of Irish recruits claimed a trade.

Although both migrant groups were represented in most of the city's police stations there was a degree of clustering along ethnic and religious lines. There was a total absence of Irish – born in the harbour police force and Highlanders dominated in this division, with many in senior posts. The surnames, geographic origins and contemporary comment would suggest that there was a strong Orange presence in the Calton police station and a Catholic dominance in the south side division located in the Gorbals. The religious persuasion of applicants would appear to have influenced recruitment patterns and it would seem that many in promoted posts were taking the opportunity to recommend favoured applicants, making preferential appointments or exclude potential recruits on the basis of ethnicity and religion. Care must be taken, however, not to overestimate the extent of discrimination. The types of applicants themselves may have varied significantly from division to division. It should also be noted that both migrant groups were well represented in most of the city's stations. Compared to the situation in Belfast, where the town police were customarily distinguished from the Royal Irish Constabulary by being referred to as the 'Protestant' police, and where only five Catholics were employed in a force of 160 men around the same period, the Glasgow constabulary was far more accessible for the Catholic Irish even if they did encounter discrimination when attempting to join particular stations. Interestingly, the Irish presence on the force in Glasgow was at its lowest points in those years, 1861 and 1869–70, following periods of tension between the Catholic Irish and Protestants in Glasgow.[32]

At times of peak demand for labour, the city authorities may in fact have been hard – pressed to find suitable recruits let alone condone or ignore discriminatory practices. A perennial problem confronting city officials was the high rate of turnover amongst the recruits on the force. The force consisted of a core of long – serving career men and a much larger group of short-serving recruits continuously moving off in search of more attractive employment. The Irishmen joining the police force remained longer than the recruits as a whole and this perhaps indicates that Irish migrants, despite generally having more industrial or commercial experience, found greater difficulty in obtaining better employment in the city or elsewhere. For those capable of seeking a livelihood within sectors of the skilled labour market, the service had few attractions.

Conclusion

In this comparative examination of the assimilation of Highland and Irish migrants in local economies within Glasgow during the mid-nineteenth century an attempt has been made to present employment patterns of the two groups. In both the central areas and in the suburb of Anderston the census data and other evidence presented suggest that the two migrant groups were taking up quite distinct positions in the local economies. In Anderston the textile and pottery industries were exceedingly important for the Irish of both sexes but of little consequence for Highlander employment in the district. For the female Highlanders domestic service was by far the major source of employment while Irish girls were largely excluded from the jobs in this sector. In the central districts shoemaking, labouring, dealing and hawking were much more important types of economic activity for the Irish than they were for the Highlanders. The latter, however, were attracted to the central districts by the opportunities in retailing, the food industries and the heavy industries more so than was the case with the Irish.

Yet it is only when the differences within sectors and industries are examined that the full extent of the variations in migrant group occupational position becomes apparent. The Highland migrants were far more successful in gaining access to the skilled occupations in the construction, metalworking, machinery and shipbuilding industries while the Irish male workers in these industries were largely concentrated in the jobs offering low levels of pay and status. There were, however, a significant proportion of Irish migrants finding there way into the more skilled occupations in the heavy industries, a finding which challenges Handley's assertion that the Irish immigrants were almost entirely absent from such positions in this period. Compared to the Highland migrant performance, however, the Irish had been far less successful in securing jobs offering pay, conditions and status that removed them from the lower working class. Indeed, the Highland migrants were well represented in all strata of society and were to be found in the top positions in commerce, industry and the professions. Only a tiny fraction of the Irish immigrants could be classified as belonging to the middle strata of society. The more detailed examinations of migrant group recruitment to the Glasgow Police force and employment as female domestic servants confirm that there was a strong degree of ethnicity in the patterns of recruitment and points to discrimination and prejudice operating in these sectors of the labour market.

In conclusion, Highland migrants appear to have possessed the social and occupational attributes which gained them access to employment and career opportunities in the city which, in turn, enabled them to establish themselves at every level of society. Whatever other factors might have impeded their full assimilation in the new urban, industrial environment, occupational position did not exclude them from entry to every social strata. In contrast, the Irish immigrants, generally clustering in the lower occupational status positions of the new urban order, would, as a result experience a long delay in their structural assimilation into mainstream society. The barriers to occupational and social mobility which had initially consigned the great majority of Irish immigrants to those jobs offering low pay and status and little security would not be easily overcome by subsequent generations in an urban community which recruited its skilled workforce from all the regions of Scotland, including the Highlands.

Appendix

The basic source of much of the data presented in this study is the census enumerators' books of the 1851 census of Scotland. Since the main concern was to extract information on the migrant groups, but place this data within the wider socio-economic context, a stratified sampling procedure was adopted to provide an adequate number of sample cases on which to base a statistical description and analysis.[37] The household was chosen as the unit of analysis, using place of birth of the head of household as the criterion of assignation. The information on individuals within households provided the source of occupational data. The occupational categories adopted were, with slight modification to take account of historical context, those used in other studies of Irish immigrants in Britain.

After careful consideration, three census registration districts were selected for sampling. The western suburb of Anderston was chosen as were the old, central parishes of St Andrew's and Outer. These central parishes were sampled as a single composite sample which made it possible to compare the migrant group experience in two distinct types of locality: an industrial suburb (Anderston) and the old centre (St Andrew's and Outer).

As the study was primarily concerned with examining the two migrant groups, the sampling method had to yield a sufficiently large number of cases of Highland and Irish migrants but it also had to include the population as a whole. A one-in-eighteen sample was therefore drawn in each of the sample areas, allocating each case, or household, to Highland, Irish or 'Other' categories. This was then followed by a one-in-six sample of every household, excluding the eighteenth, and collecting those cases which were Irish and Highland and separating them appropriately. Yet a further sample was taken of every second household excluding the sixth and eighteenth, extracting only Highland households. This sampling procedure provided samples of every second household which was Highland, every sixth household which was Irish, and a sample of every eighteenth household which was in the districts selected for investigation.

It was not possible using the stratified sampling procedure to offer tests of statistical significance on the data presented. Great caution is therefore needed when interpreting the data yielded by such a method. As well as adopting a tentative approach to the results, an effort was made to ensure that the samples of the migrant groups were sufficiently large to partially compensate for the lack of statistical validation. This methodology has its weaknesses but it does make possible detailed analysis of two minority groups in a large urban population.

Data was also derived from the 1861 census to provide more detailed information on migrant group involvement in particular occupational areas. In some instances these searches ventured beyond the boundaries of the census districts into other areas of the city most notably the harbour area of Broomielaw adjacent to Anderston.

REFERENCES

1. See, for example, S. Thernstrom, *The Other Bostonians: Poverty and Progress in the American Metropolis, 1880–1970*, (Cambridge, Mass., 1973); M. Anderson, *Family Structure in Nineteenth Century Lancashire*, (Cambridge, 1971); L. H. Lees, *Exiles of Erin, Irish Migrants in Victorian London*, (Manchester, 1979).
2. Among the earlier histories of migrant influx into lowland towns are J. Handley, *The Irish in Scotland, 1798–1845*, (Cork, 1945); J. E. Handley, *The Irish in Modern Scotland*, (Cork, 1947); D. F. Macdonald, *Scotland's Shifting Population, 1770–1850*, (Glasgow, 1937). The case study approach has been adopted in the following works inter alia: R. D. Lobban, 'The Migration of Highlanders into Lowland Scotland, 1750–1890', PhD thesis, University of Edinburgh, 1969; B. E. A. Collins, 'Aspects of Irish Immigration into Two Scottish Towns', unpublished M. Phil. thesis, University of Edinburgh, 1978; C. W. J. Withers, *Highland Communities in Dundee and Perth, 1787–1891: A Study in Social History of*

Migrant Highlanders, (Dundee, 1986); R. D. Lobban, 'The Irish Community in Greenock in the Nineteenth Century', *Irish Geography,* 6, 1971, pp. 270–281; B. Aspinwall and J. M. McCafferty, 'A Comparative View of the Irish in Edinburgh', in R. Swift and S. Gilley (eds.), *The Irish in the Victorian City,* (London, 1985). A more general examination of the migration process can be found in T. M. Devine, 'Temporary Migration and the Scottish Highlanders in the Nineteenth Century', *Economic History Review,* 2nd series, XXXII, 1979, pp 344–358, and T. M. Devine, 'Highland Migration to Lowland Scotland, 1760–1860', *Scottish Historical Review,* LXII, (2), 1983, pp 137–149. There is of course much recent historiography on migration within the lowlands. For current historical thinking on the Irish in Scotland see T. M. Devine ed., *Irish immigrants and Scottish Society in the Nineteenth and Twentieth Centuries. Proceedings of the Scottish Historical Studies Seminar, University of Strathclyde, 1989/90* (Edinburgh, 1991).

3. A. B. Campbell, *The Lanarkshire Miners. A Social History of their Trade Unions, 1775–1874,* (Edinburgh, 1979), p 180; Handley, *Irish in Modern Scotland,* pp 134–5.

4. Handley in both his studies provided a wealth of impressionistic evidence on the position of the Irish in Glasgow and other Scottish towns but did not attempt a systematic description of the Irish presence in the occupational structure.

5. See appendix for the design of the study and research methods used to extract information from the census enumerators' books. A fuller account of the design of the study and research methods can be found in W. Sloan, 'Aspects of the Assimilation of Highland and Irish Migrants in Glasgow, 1830–1870', unpublished M. Phil. thesis, University of Strathclyde, 1987, pp 13–19

6. Printed Census of Scotland, 1851; A. Gibb, *Glasgow: Making of a City,* (London, 1983), p 124; This figure for Highland born excludes those born in the county of Perth. Extensive examination of the census enumerators' books for Glasgow at the mid-century would indicate that very few of the Perthshire-born residing in Glasgow came from the Highland part of the county.

7. *Parliamentary Papers* [hereafter P.P.], VI, Committee on Manufacturers, Commerce and Shipping, Q 5348; N. Murray, *The Scottish Handloom Weavers,* (Edinburgh, 1978), pp 21–22, 62–71; for the development of Anderston in the early nineteenth century see J. N. Cooper, *Simply Anderston,* (Glasgow, 1971); Sloan, 'Highland and Irish Migrants in Glasgow', Chapter 1.

8. Sloan, 'Highland and Irish Migrants in Glasgow', Chapter 1 for a much fuller and more detailed account of the industrial developments taking place in Anderston from the 1820s onwards.

9. The tabulated data presented in Table 2 are derived from the census enumerators' returns for the Anderston District (see Appendix). As a result of rounding-off the percentages, not all the totals at the foot of the columns add up to 100.

10. The unskilled category is almost entirely composed of those returned as 'labourers' in metal, machine and shipbuilding. However, a number of teenage employments, mainly 'foundry boys', have also been allocated to this category.

11. Handley in his study of the Irish in Scotland comments that 'Throughout the second half of the nineteenth century, the vast majority of Irish immigrants

and the first, second and third generations of those who had settled in the country in the early decades of the century, took their places in the ranks of the industrial army that laboured at unskilled and semi-skilled jobs: in the mine and iron and steel works, in the shipyards . . . in machine-shops and factories, in the numerous little foundries and workshops that existed . . .', see Handley, *Irish in Modern Scotland*, pp 134–135; Campbell's study of the Lanarkshire miners gives a more optimistic picture of Irish penetration of skilled employment. If, in the Larkhall district, none of the 50 skilled metalworkers' jobs were taken by Irishmen, in the Coatbridge area 23.8 per cent of the 706 skilled metalwork positions were taken by natives of Ireland. Apparently, the Anderston data indicate an even greater incursion into the skilled positions, see Campbell, *Lanarkshire Miners*, p 180.

12. Information on the occupations of the men married in St Patrick's R.C. chapel between 1855 and 1870 was extracted from the registers. Only for 1855 was it possible to identify the place of birth, which was given by nearly all of the newly weds. Since 82.2 per cent were Irish-born, it is perhaps reasonable to assume that the great majority in subsequent years were natives of Ireland.

13. Strathclyde Regional Archives, Register of Porters, 1834 to 1853. The applicants were expected to supply satisfactory character references.

14. The absence of dates on the Harbour register makes it impossible to establish any sequence in the granting of licenses.

15. *Report of the Glasgow Carters' Committee, 1835,* (Mitchell Library Pamphlets, Glasgow). It was the informed opinion of the President of the Carters' Committee that carters settled in large numbers in Alston Street and Stockwell Street. A search of the 1861 census enumerators' books for Alston Street indicated that there had probably been some drift away from this locality close to the Broomielaw but not so in the case of Stockwell Street.

16. For the position of Irish migrants in the west of Scotland cotton spinning industry in the first half of the nineteenth century see W. H. Fraser, 'The Glasgow Cotton Spinners, 1837', in J Butt and J. T. Ward (eds.), *Scottish Themes: Essays in Honour of Professor S.G.E. Lythe,* (Edinburgh, 1976).

17. Census of Scotland, 1861. This survey covered the working class housing areas sweeping out from the potteries.

18. Sloan, 'Highland and Irish Migrants', pp 31–32.

19. P.P. 1836, XXXIV, App. G, Royal Commission on the State of the Irish Poor, p117.

20. P.P. 1841, VI, First and Second Reports of Select Committees on Emigration, Q 1212.

21. Lees, *Irish in London,* p 95.

22. J. Strang, *Comparative View of the Money—Rate of Wages in Glasgow . . .,* (Glasgow, 1862), p 19.

23. Gibb, *The making of a City,* pp 93–99; J R Kellet, 'Property Speculators and the building of Glasgow, 1780–1830', *Scottish Journal of Political Economy,* Vol VIII, 1961, pp 211–232; W. Forsyth, 'Urban Economic Morphology in Nineteenth Century Glasgow', in A Slaven and D H Aldcroft, *Business, Banking and Urban History. Essays in Honour of S G Checkland,* (Edinburgh, 1982), pp 166–193; E Gauldie, 'The Middle Class and Working Class Housing in the Nineteenth

Century', in A. A. Maclaren, *Social Class in Scotland, Past and Present*, (Edinburgh, 1976), pp 12–35.

24. Gibb, *The making of a City*, p 92; Forsyth, 'Urban Economic Morphology', pp 175–181.

25. Forsyth, 'Urban Economic Morphology', pp 175–181.

26. T Johnston, *History of the Working Classes in Scotland*, (Glasgow, 1920), p 379.

27. Glasgow Saturday Post, 23 April 1853.

28. Scottish Guardian, 18 July 1845; *Glasgow Saturday Post*, 23 April 1853; *Sentinel*, 23 June 1866.

29. Senex, *Glasgow Past and Present*, (Glasgow, 1884), Volume II, pp 106–107; *North British Daily Mail*, 2 July, 1853; 2 July 1853: J H Treble, *Urban Poverty in Britain, 1830–1914*, (London, 1979), p 49.

30. *Glasgow Free Press*, 5 May 1860.

31. Sloan, 'Highland and Irish Migrants', Chapter 3, for a detailed description of the recruitment of migrants to the Glasgow Police Force in this period. Much of the evidence presented in that chapter derived from the Registers of Constabulary, Strathclyde Regional Archives.

32. A C Hepburn, *The Conflict of Nationality in Modern Ireland*, (Edward Arnold, 1980), pp 35–36 for information about policing in Belfast; Sloan, 'Highland and Irish Migrants', p 91.

37. For the benefits and weaknesses of stratified sampling as a means of extracting data on a minority group in a population, see R S Schofield, 'Sampling in Historical Research', in E A Wrigley (ed.), *Nineteenth Century Society: Essays in the Use of Quantitative Methods for the Study of Social Data*, (London, 1972), pp 166–169.

12

The Regional Structure of Textile Employment in Scotland in the Nineteenth Century: East of Scotland Hand Loom Weavers in the 1830s

NORMAN MURRAY

Introduction

The crucial contribution of textile manufacture to the rapid growth of the Scottish economy in the late eighteenth and early nineteenth centuries is well established. It has been convincingly argued, for example, that even as late as the 1820s Scottish textiles employed approximately 90% of the 'occupied' labour force with the respective importance of cotton, linen and woollen working being ascribed the relative ratios of 6:3:1.[1] The next important 'manufacturing' industry to textiles in the first quarter of the nineteenth century was considered to be iron. It, however, absorbed only half of the numbers employed in woollen working; it was considerably less important than linen; and iron manufacture was clearly of marginal significance when contrasted to the Scottish cotton industry.[2] But the economic importance of textiles was much wider than the industry's function as a labour outlet. Other indicators, such as capital investment, output and market expansion clearly point to it as being a — if not *the* — leading sector.[3]

The rapid growth of textiles into such a prominent position depended in the early nineteenth century, with only minor variations between fabrics, upon a number of basic processes. Of these, spinning and weaving were by far the most important. In the previous century technical advances in both of these processes had been patented.[4] The new machines were, however, adapted at different rates to the twin processes with the mechanisation of spinning almost invariably pre-dating that of weaving; and although the power loom's productive advantage over other weaving technology was widely acknowledged by 1800, considerable improvements had, nonetheless, to be achieved before it could be successfully deployed for the weaving of all textile fabrics.[5]

Such improvements encompassed some refinements to the power loom itself. But much more crucial to the successful mechanisation of the weaving process was the strength of the spun thread; for without strong yarn, warps, and particularly wefts, could only be used on power looms with extreme difficulty. It is not surprising, therefore, that the new weaving technologies were first applied to heavy cottons, since cotton fibres were the strongest raw material. Thereafter, their use widened to lighter, usually plain, cottons and then to other fabrics. It must be stressed, however, that the adoption of the power loom in Scotland was fitful and slow, this arising partly out of its initial unsuitability for fine weaving. It was claimed in 1833, for example, that the hand loom weaver 'could work a great many things which it would not be in the interests of any power loom manufacturer to make, especially all the finest goods'.[6] Thirty years earlier power loom weaving in Scotland, even in cotton, had been in its infancy, while the encroachments into other fabrics were little more than experimental.

Clearly, therefore, hand loom weaving technology was largely responsible for the increased output of woven cloth in Scotland in the early nineteenth century. Yet, with the notable exception of the flying shuttle, such technology, had, with some local adaptations, not been improved since the Middle Ages.[7] This meant that Scottish textile production remained a labour-intensive activity and that hand loom weavers were more significant than their allegedly more productive—and mechanised—counterparts in this process. This was especially true of the east of Scotland with its greater concentration on woollen and, particularly, linen weaving.[8]

Quantifying, with any claim to precision, the size of this important occupational group in the early nineteenth century is an almost impossible task. Before the parliamentary enquiries of the 1830s such an exercise is bedevilled by the paucity, and unreliability, of available data on the numbers who worked at the hand loom at any given time. Perhaps this was not surprising given the wide variations in such factors as industrial organisation, fabrics worked and geographical location.[9] Equally important was the fact that an empirical approach to the study of socio-economic matters was yet to be developed. Underlining this point, crude population enumeration was still in its infancy and, in Scotland, the statutory registration of births, deaths and marriages did not become compulsory until 1855.[10]

To obtain tolerably accurate figures regarding the size of the hand loom workforce, therefore, historians must rely heavily upon the official enquiries of the 1830s—and particularly upon data provided in 1839 by the Assistant Commissioners to the Royal Commission on Hand Loom Weavers whose final report was published in 1841.[11] The Scottish scene was examined by two Assistant Commissioners, Jellinger C. Symons and Dr.

John D. Harding, the former concentrating his enquiry on the south of Scotland while the latter scrutinised the state of the trade in the east of Scotland.[12] It is with the area investigated by Dr. Harding that this examination of the regional structure of textile employment in Scotland in the nineteenth century is principally concerned. Almost inevitably, the essay's main chronological focus will be the late 1830s.

The first objective will be to view the east of Scotland workforce in an overall Scottish context. Thereafter, detailed investigation of the trade at various centres will be attempted, concentrating initially on such economic aspects as the size of the workforce, fabrics worked, local organisation and the state of the trade. This will then lead to an investigation of some of the factors which affected living standards such as wage movements and dietary patterns. The essay will conclude with an examination of industrial organisation with particular reference to labour and capital in the hand loom weaving trade of the east of Scotland.

Dr. Harding estimated that in 1838 33,474 weavers worked in the East of Scotland.[13] This represented 39.6% of the Scottish total, as enumerated by the two Scottish Assistant Commissioners. There are, however, good reasons for believing that this proportion, approximately 40% of the Scottish total, was constant *throughout* the first half of the nineteenth century. Firstly, in the early decades of the century the predominant fabrics woven in the east were flax and wool and, with the notable exception of Perth, cotton weaving was little known in the area. Thus power loom encroachment into the area was slow and even in 1838 the amount of cloth produced by the power loom in eastern Scotland was small in comparison to the rest of the country, and even smaller in relation to overall United Kingdom production.[14] This trend continued post-1838, if for different reasons. It can be argued, for example, that the rapid diminution in the 1840s and their demise thereafter was only partly due to competition from the power loom sector. Two other related factors were of considerable significance. These were the age structure of the workforce and the availability of alternative employment.[15] It is reasonable to argue that there were fewer opportunities in the east of Scotland, which experienced a slower rate of industrialisation than the west, for ex-operative weavers who were young enough and fit enough. The conclusion must therefore be that even in the declining years of the trade four out of every ten hand loom weavers in Scotland were located in the eastern counties.

Accepting then that throughout the first half of the nineteenth century some 40% of all hand loom weavers in Scotland resided in the east, some estimates of their numbers over the period can be made by using this percentage in relation to figures generally accepted to represent the overall Scottish total.[16] This suggests that the approximate number of hand loom weavers in the area over time were as follows:

Approximate Number of Hand Loom Weavers in the East of Scotland

1790	18,000	1830	31,200
1800	23,200	1840	33,500
1810	26,400	1850	10,000
1820	31,200	1860	4,000

But the geographical term 'East of Scotland' is in itself vague and was probably arbitrarily delineated by Dr. Harding in his investigation.[17] To gain some insight into the lives of the websters of the area, however, a more detailed examination of the pattern of geographical concentration is required.

Geographical Distribution

As elsewhere, the hand-weaving trade of the east of Scotland was characterised in relation to such aspects as fabrics worked, industrial organisation and skills required by a 'bewildering variety of contrasts'.[18] These differences were determined partly by the availability of raw materials and markets and partly by the increasing encroachment of the particular form of capitalism which controlled the domestic trade. The only common factor was that all the operatives, irrespective of fabric, worked the same, or basically similar, piece of machinery to produce cloth. Since certain sectors of the trade tended to concentrate on particular locations in the east, it is illuminating to examine in some detail the experience of weavers in certain centres. Needless to say, the most comprehensive evidence relating to such specific areas is found in the Assistant Commissioner's Report.[19]

Dr Harding's report was based on evidence culled from four Scottish counties—Perthshire, Fife, Angus and Aberdeenshire—and clearly did not encompass the entire 'east' of Scotland. The investigation into the Border area was left to his colleague, J. C. Symons, and no evidence was furnished on the extent of the trade north of the city of Aberdeen. Perhaps neither of these represented serious omissions because the investigation into the state of the trade in the south of Scotland was comprehensive and searching while in the far north there were only a few, mainly 'customer' weavers, among the sparse population.[20] One possible serious gap, however, was the lack of reliable data concerning the websters of the city of Edinburgh and its environs, for neither of the Assistant Commissioners produced details about the capital or its neighbouring burghs. Yet it was well-known that, from an early date, fancy weaving had been introduced to this area by French settlers; and it was equally well-acknowledged that Leith was an important linen producing centre.[21] Given, therefore, the inadequate scope of data available it is necessary to adhere to Dr. Harding's rather restricted geographical definition of the 'east' of Scotland.

In Perthshire there were two sizeable concentrations of websters, the county town of Perth and the township of Auchterarder. The number of hand looms in Perth in 1838 was estimated at 1,355 all of which wove cotton fabrics, mostly working for Glasgow 'houses' and producing umbrella ginghams (663 looms), pullicates and checks (523 looms) and shawls (169 looms). Interestingly enough, the only healthy sector of the Perth trade in the late 1830s was thought to be the town's traditional umbrella gingham production which had been introduced in the early 1700s.[22] Like Perth, the trade in Auchterarder was entirely devoted to cotton production and came under the control of Glasgow 'manufacturers'. Here some 500 hand looms produced pullicates, ginghams and stripes. By the late 1830s they were sharing some of the experience of their counterparts in Perth; their numbers were in decline and their condition was said to be one of 'great privation and occasional distress', the contemporary panacea for their ills, emigration, being denied to them because they 'did not have the means to put this cure to the test.'[23]

Perthshire apart, cotton weaving was of little importance in the east of Scotland. The same was true of one feature normally associated with the cotton trade, its control by Glasgow houses. The exception was the town of Kinross in Fife where an estimated 350 weavers wrought pullicates and 'sometimes' *mousseline de laine*, while 50 further operatives produced woollen plaid shawls. Allegedly, the entire hand loom trade of Kinross was organised by merchants in Glasgow.[24] Apart from being controlled by capitalists in western Scotland, however, the cotton weavers of Kinross seemed to have little in common with their counterparts in the woollen sector for it was noted in 1838 that the average weekly wages of the former was 4s.6d. while the latter could earn 14s.3d. In fact, the Assistant Commissioner found the meagre rates of pay for the weaving of cotton in the town somewhat difficult to accept until 'an examination of many individual cases in the agent's books' had been 'corroborated by the evidence of the witnesses'.[25] Woollen manufacturers and agents were quick to point out, however, that they had reached a local agreement with weavers for the maintenance of wages. Kinross woollen weavers explained the capitalists' enthusiasm for this type of agreement to the latter's fear that 'a deterioration in the fabric might be the result of any reduction in wages'.[26] Clearly, their counterparts in the cotton sector in Kinross did not share such apprehension.

Elsewhere in Fife the trade was concentrated in two major urban centres, Dunfermline and Kirkcaldy, and in three smaller towns, Newburgh, Cupar (with Ceres) and Auchtermuchty. Unlike Kinross, however, cotton weaving was of only marginal importance in any of these areas and control of but a small fraction of the trade by Glasgow manufacturers can only be discerned at Auchtermuchty.[27]

The largest weaving centre in Fife in the late 1830s was Dunfermline, where Dr. Harding estimated that there were 2,947 hand looms, all weaving linen, mainly engaged in harness work producing damask table cloths, table covers and napkins. Most of the looms were owned by the weavers themselves in 1838; only 156 were the property of 'workhousemen' while 218 belonged to 'manufacturers'. There had recently been a noticeable increase in the number of hand looms in Dunfermline.[28] Yet in 1838 the trade was depressed with an estimated 617 looms lying idle 'the recent embarrassments of American commerce' being cited as the root cause of the difficulty in the linen sector.[29] The second most important weaving centre in the county of Fife was Kirkcaldy. In this town linen also dominated the trade with 2,775 hand looms producing ticks, dowlas, fine sheeting and sailcloth, the last fabric being exclusively the domain of 'stout men'. The strength and skill required for weaving sailcloth was reflected in the high rates of remuneration received. The corollary was that the weaving of ticks and dowlas, often the province of 'lads and women' was poorly rewarded. Payment for the production of fine sheeting was also poor, particularly in lines which were worked by 'old men and boys'.[30]

The first of the smaller Fife towns examined by Dr. Harding was Newburgh where an estimated 'steadily but slowly increasing' total of 600 looms operated in 1838. They all wove linen fabrics, principally dowlas and sheetings for resident entrepreneurs. As well as weaving the ancillary activity of pirn winding seems to have become a specialism of the town. Not only did women and children wind pirns for the websters of Newburgh but they also provided this service for those rural weavers within an estimated ten-mile radius of the town who worked for Newburgh houses.[31]

At Cupar, the second of the smaller towns investigated, there were 667 hand looms with an additional 'perhaps' 500 looms in the neighbouring village of Ceres. Again, they were exclusively engaged in linen production, working sheeting, dowlas and osnaburghs. Witnesses who gave evidence to Dr. Harding spoke of very low wages and subsequent privations, including the inability to purchase basic items to food. It was concluded that at Cupar and Ceres 'the weavers hardly ever eat meat; many cannot afford even meal and milk twice a day; potatoes form the principal article of food.'[32]

An estimated 1000 hand looms were in production at Auchtermuchty. A minority of these, between 50 and 100, were cotton looms working for manufacturers in Aberdeen or Glasgow. Eight other looms were singled out for attention because of the exceptionally high wages paid to their operatives; they were woollen looms who worked for capitalists at Tillicoultry near Stirling. But by far the largest proportion of Auchtermuchty weavers, probably in excess of 90% of the total in the town, produced ordinary linen fabrics. Nearly half of these linen looms were controlled by Newburgh houses.[33]

Just north of the Tay, the geographical distribution of the workforce did not differ markedly from that obtaining in Fife for here also two major centres of the trade were located in the coastal towns of Dundee and Arbroath. Inland, there were another two sizeable weaving towns, Kirriemuir and Forfar, and two smaller, but nonetheless important centres at Brechin and Montrose.[34] All were situated in the county of Angus.

Possibly because of the size of the workforce the Assistant Commissioner found some difficulty in enumerating, with any accuracy, the number of hand loom weavers in Dundee, which was certainly the largest weaving centre in the east of Scotland. Eventually Dr. Harding recorded the number of weavers in the town at between four and five thousand, all of whom were engaged in linen fabrics. The basis for this calculation, however, was a petition signed in 1834 by 4,673 weavers who favoured payments by the yard rather than by the piece.[35] Other studies suggest that this figure was a reasonable estimate as to the number who worked the hand loom in Dundee in the late 1830s confirming that Dr. Harding set safe parameters. The main fabrics produced in Dundee and its vicinity (the figure included 700 who were said to reside in Lochee) were heavy lines viz. hempen sacking and cotton bagging. It should be stressed that the latter was something of a misnomer, 'Cotton' bagging derived its name from the use to which it was applied rather than the material from which it was made.[36]

More precise figures were given for Arbroath, where 2,000 hand looms were said to be working in 1838. All were engaged in linen production and 500 were located in factories, engaged in the production of canvas. The principal market for linen cloth produced in Arbroath was England and the number of weavers in the town was 'rather increasing than diminishing'.[37] Dowlas was the main product of the domestic looms of Arbroath and it seems that adult males did not comprise the majority of those who operated them. It was claimed, for example, that 'small loom weavers' included 'many women and old men'.[38] The clear inference was that the factory-based looms of Arbroath were worked exclusively by adult males. Nor surprisingly, their rates of renumeration were considerably more attractive than those of their domestic-leased counterparts.[39]

Like Arbroath, the number of hand loom weavers in the inland centre of Kirriemuir was estimated at 2,000, employed in the production of dowlas, sheeting and osnaburghs, all linen fabrics, and destined mainly for exportation. Unlike Arbroath, in one respect, the trade in Kirriemuir was reckoned to be declining in the late 1830s.[40] Both centres, however, showed similarities as regards wage rates for sharp divisions in rates of pay were also discerned in Kirriemuir between the 'best hands' and 'old people and boys'.[41] The weaving trade of Kirriemuir was not organised locally being controlled by the manufacturers of Dundee and nearby Forfar.[42]

Almost inevitably, the capitalists of the latter town also controlled the trade of Forfar where the hand loom weaving capacity in 1838 was stated as 2,589 looms. These were all linen looms almost all of which were organised on a domestic basis, producing such 'common' fabrics as osnaburghs, tow sheeting and flag sheeting. It was alleged that as many as 10% of the hand looms of Forfar were idle in 1838.[43] No explanation for this difficulty was offered. It is likely, however, that Forfar was experiencing problems in foreign markets while the downturn in general economic activity did not help matters.[44]

This was certainly the experience of the trade in Brechin, a little to the north-east of Forfar, where 870 hand looms specialised in producing canvas, dowlas and sheetings. French demand apparently absorbed approximately one third of the output of Brechin's looms while an indeterminate amount was destined for the American market.[45] It was stated that the number of weavers in Brechin had increased by approximately one third between 1824 and 1838, this expansion having occurred despite the Brechin trade 'having been in such a depressed state for some time'.[46] Unlike their co-workers in Forfar, however, the websters of Brechin ascribed the plight of their trade to particular causes while implying one specific remedy for its ills. Among the reasons listed for the recession were 'the depressed state of America; the duties on corn, timber, articles of French produce and others, which prevent the free interchange of our goods for those produced in other countries'.[47]

The least significant weaving centre in the county of Angus was Montrose where, in 1838, the number of operatives was estimated at between five and six hundred. Atypically, less than 20% of the hand loom weavers of Montrose worked on the domestic system, five-sixths of the town's websters being based in factories.[48] All the weavers of the town, however, wove flax, producing the finer and heavier lines, dowlas, sheeting, sailcloth and bagging. Unlike their counterparts in other parts of Scotland the weavers of Montrose were considered to be on remarkably good terms with their employers 'to whose liberality they consider themselves much indebted'.[49]

Like Montrose, most of the hand looms in the most northerly weaving centre in Scotland, Aberdeen, were 'factoryised'. Of the city's 1,430 hand looms, 1000 worked linen fabrics, 300 produced woollen carpets and 130 were engaged in the cotton trade. The only hand looms in Aberdeen still organised on the domestic system were those which produced cotton and approximately 20% of linen looms; the remainder, approximately 1000, were based on factories.[50] Carpet weaving was singled out in 1838 as being the only buoyant sector of the city's weaving trade; otherwise the number of hand looms was felt to be diminishing, 'the manufacturers having turned their attention to power loom weaving and spinning'.[51] Significantly enough, Aberdeen was the only weaving centre in the east of Scotland in 1838 where power loom competition gave rise to such apprehension.

As a general principle the Assistant Commissioner did not visit, during his enquiry, places containing less than 400 weavers. Even some sizeable centres of the trade, for example, Dunblane and Balfron which had more than the requisite number, were omitted as were others which were 'comparatively remote' or 'from want of sufficient information'.[52] There were, in addition, in the east of Scotland many townships, large villages and rural hamlets where hand loom weaving comprised a very significant element of the local economy. It has been reasonably estimated that, in addition to the more sizeable centres examined in detail, there were another 8,000 hand loom weavers in the area.[53] Clearly, detailed information regarding these rural websters must be sought from sources other than the official enquiry. It is safe to assume, however, that, like most of their counterparts in the towns, rural weavers were engaged in the production of plain, linen fabrics and that, invariably, they operated the domestic system.[54]

Aspects of Industrial Organisation

In 1750 the structure of the hand loom weaving trade of Scotland was entirely domestic. Whether working on the 'putting out' system, for manufacturers or doing 'customer work' weavers worked either in their own homes or in simply-constructed loom sheds immediately adjoining them. In the east of Scotland, as elsewhere, an increasing majority of workers belonged to the former category, working in their own homes material obtained from manufacturers or their agents who paid the weavers when webs were satisfactorily completed.[55] Some contemporary organisers of the trade, however, perceived inefficiencies in this system arguing that schedules and work specifications could not be enforced and that the allegedly common practice of weft embezzlement could not be curbed. This led to the introduction of some structural adaptations in the industry,[56] for hand loom shops, or factories, had evolved in the Scottish trade, each housing a varying number of hand looms. By 1838 in the south of Scotland, for example, 3,505, out of a total of 52,164 looms, were factory-based.[57] There is clear evidence to indicate that the trade in the east had also undergone such structural change.

All the carpet weaving of Dunfermline, as well as all the town's heavy linen work, for example, was performed in factories in the 1830s. In the same year there were two hand loom factories in Leith producing sail-cloth. Over 1,000 of Aberdeen's weavers were factory-based; a quarter of Arbroath's 2,000 hand looms were similarly situated, as was five sixths of the total hand weaving capacity of Montrose.[58] Moreover, the increasing number of dandy looms being employed throughout the weaving industry in Scotland tended to be factory-based.[59] It is clear, however, that when placed in perspective, factory weavers represented only a small minority of the workforce even in the east of Scotland and that the typical webster of the area, even as late as 1840, was still the domestic out-worker.

Customer weavers were the modern counterparts of the household weavers of medieval times, 'working up the consumer's prepared material to the customer's order'. Their existence in parts of Scotland in the 1830s cannot be doubted. It was recorded, for instance, that in 1831 there was one customer weaver for every 179 persons in Inverness-shire and that, in the same year, the respective ratio for Berwickshire was one per hundred.[60] Even as late as 1858 some remnants of this form of organisation existed in the south of Scotland.[61] The number of customer weavers operating on that basis in the east of Scotland in the late 1830s is, however, less easy to ascertain. Dr. Harding referred to, but did not include in his enumerations, 'a class of weavers only to be found in the remote rural districts, who procure their own materials, and weave coarse linens and woollens, either to the order of their neighbours, or for sale by themselves, known as "customer-weavers" '.[62] The fact that the Assistant Commissioner did not include them points to their scarcity and this is reinforced by their geographical distribution. Clearly their numbers were small in relation to the whole workforce of the east of Scotland. Moreover, after 1800 it is likely that the growth of capitalist organisation reduced the vast majority of weavers to the position of mere wage earners working for employers.[63]

The existence of various forms of industrial organisation in the weaving trade was not the only aspect of it which exhibited diversity. At any time there could be found different stages of its evolution into a full-time occupation. The trend to full-time weaving in linen in the early nineteenth century is beyond reasonable doubt; there is evidence, however, to suggest that full-time status was not the norm by 1820. For example, when John Duncan entered the trade at Drumlithie in 1824 weavers not only worked on local farms at harvest time but also migrated south to do seasonal work on the larger agricultural units there.[64] This was not an isolated example. Fourteen years later, it was strongly implied that the east of Scotland trade was still, for some, a seasonal activity. Of the total number (22,000–23,000) hand looms in the east of Scotland in 1838 engaged in 'ordinary or light work', dowlas, common sheetings and osnaburghs, only 17,000 were said to be operational in summer.[65] Clearly part-time weaving still existed in the east of Scotland in the late 1830s. There are good reasons for believing, however, that it was far from typical by that date and undertaken mainly in response to seasonal, cyclical – even sectoral – depression in weavers' primary economic activity.

Firstly, increasing urbanisation — it was in towns that their numbers increased rapidly — made it difficult for websters to participate in rural-based tasks. Secondly, some contemporaries testified to the fact that weavers were not suited to such arduous outside work as reaping and stacking.[66] Thirdly, as elsewhere, many weavers had been recruited to the loom in an era of comparatively high wages and this had, allegedly, induced many of them to cut their links with other sources of employment.[67] Fourthly, the information obtained by Dr. Harding refers to the late 1830s when the trade was suffering from sectoral and cyclical depression, while slackness in summer was an established feature of the trade.[68] In short, weavers were seldom more than weavers when webs were available and this was particularly the case in sectors of the trade where expensive equipment had been acquired and where the requisite level of skill necessitated constant practice.[69]

The last category of weavers identified by contemporaries were the itinerants of the trade. Variously labelled 'migratory' or 'tramping' weavers they were described as the 'most dissolute and immoral' class of websters in Scotland. The most common malpractice associated with itinerant weavers, at least two-thirds of whom are said to have been of Irish origin, was decamping with unfinished webs which were the property of manufacturers. This seems to have been most prolific in rural Ayrshire and Lanarkshire, however, and no direct reference is made to their existence in eastern Scotland.[70] There were a number of Irish weavers in the area, especially in the larger towns, and many of them paid scant respect 'to the necessity of regular and unremitting exertion'.[71] And although the Assistant Commissioner was not reluctant to compare their social behaviour unfavourably with their Scottish co-workers, he made no mention of Irish weavers displaying migratory predilections.

The workforce, however, comprised only one aspect of industrial organisation; the capitalist side of the trade was also very important. The control of hand loom weaving by yarn merchants had been well established in the linen trade in the eighteenth century and this had been carried over into cotton.[72] Typically, those who described themselves as 'manufacturers' were really yarn merchants and were the employers of the vast majority of Scottish weavers. With capital invested in raw materials, warehouse and stock, these 'manufacturers' were the organisers of the putting-out system, the scale of their capital and organisation varying considerably with the larger ones working through agents in outlying areas.[73] The importance of certain towns in this kind of organisational structure was that they formed the nuclei of industrial activity from where work was sent out, frequently on an agency basis, to smaller towns and rural areas. The predominant rôle played by Glasgow in this cannot be disputed as regards the cotton trade, for the manufacturers of that city issued work to centres as far apart as Irvine and Maybole to the west, and Perthshire and Fife to the north-east.[74] This organisational pattern was broadly mirrored in the east of Scotland linen trade in 1838; not only did large coastal centres, Dundee, Dunfermline and Aberdeen, control the weaving trade of the area but a significant rôle in this process was also played by smaller centres such as Newburgh and Forfar.[75]

It is difficult, however, to determine the scale of the typical manufacturer's enterprise, if such a term had any meaning in an east of Scotland context.

At Dundee, for example, the capitalists of the weaving trade were generally regarded as 'a respectable class of men [and] from these God-fearing employers many of the best families in Dundee have sprung'.[76] Reinforcing this point, a number of witnesses to the 1834 and 1835 Hand Loom Weavers Select Committees testified to the respectability of the larger houses in the trade.[77] On the other hand, contemporaries also referred to the increasing proliferation of small manufacturers, or 'corks', in the trade and, almost invariably, ascribed its difficulties to the cut-throat competition between these 'men without capital'.[78] Often they included agents in this category for in much of the literature the terms 'agent' and 'cork' were used synonymously. There is little doubt that agents, or middlemen, featured prominently in the weaving trade of the east of Scotland. In rural and semi-rural settings and in larger towns they performed the vital functions of issuing webs, collecting finished cloths and arranging payments for weavers.[79] Like their 'manufacturer' colleagues, however, it is not possible to ascertain their numbers with any accuracy. Suffice to say that weavers themselves were convinced that there were too many agents and small corks in the trade in the 1830s.[80]

Typically then, the east of Scotland hand loom weaver, even as late as 1840, whether he lived in a rural community, small town or larger centre, worked for an employer who was unlikely to be locally based and who usually conducted his business through an agent. Alternatively, he might weave for a small, probably local, 'cork'. Almost invariably, he worked in his own home or in a loom shed immediately adjoining it. His profession, of necessity, involved other family members since a number of ancillary tasks such as entering and pirn winding, had to be performed. These functions, however, normally did not carry any financial return while his own reward could fluctuate widely depending in part on the fabric worked, and on the strength and skill required to produce it. The webster's wage also depended on the length of the piece which was almost always arbitrarily determined by the supplier (the measure usually employed in Scotland – the ell – had no standard length).[81] Nonetheless, he owned his own loom, dictated his own working hours and occasionally engaged in other economic pursuits. In theory, at least, he had so far not tasted the strict discipline imposed upon his counterpart in spinning who had by this date unquestionably experienced the harsher working environment which was an integral part of the factory system. On the other hand, the east of Scotland hand loom weaver had almost certainly endured a steady decline in real wages and consequent fall in living standards, which meant that he could no longer enjoy the webster's traditional independence. By the late 1830s he may well have regarded his co-worker in the 'dark satanic mills' with some envy.

REFERENCES

1. J. Sinclair, *Analysis of the Statistical Account of Scotland*, (London, 1826), p. 321.
2. *Ibid.*
3. T. C. Smout, *A History of the Scottish People, 1560–1830*, (London, 1969), p. 233; *Glasgow Herald*, 4th May 1801.
4. P. Mathias, *The First Industrial Nation. An Economic History of Britain 1700–1914* (London, 1969), p. 126.
5. S. D. Chapman, *The Cotton Industry in the Industrial Revolution* (London and Basingstoke, 1972), p. 25. 'The Rise, Progress, Present Condition and Prosperity of the Cotton Manufacture', *The Edinburgh Review*, XCI, June 1827, p. 17.
6. H. Hamilton, *The Industrial Revolution in Scotland*, (London, 1966), p. 101.
7. At Dunfermline, four weavers were commended and rewarded between 1799 and 1810 for refining hand loom weaving technology. Later in the nineteenth century several weavers, James Mills and James Morrison of Paisley and Andrew Arbuckle of Cambusland, were instrumental in effecting important improvements to the hand weaving of fancy goods. N. Murray, *The Scottish Hand Loom Weavers 1790–1850: A Social History*, (Edinburgh, 1978), p. 9.
8. J. H. Clapham, *An Economic History of Modern Britain, the Early Railway Age, 1820–1850*, (Cambridge, 1926), p. 179.
9. Murray, *Hand Loom Weavers*, pp. 13–17; 22–28.
10. S. G. E. Lythe and J. Butt, *An Economic History of Scotland 1100–1939*, (Glasgow, 1975), p. 100.
11. *Final Report of Royal Commission on Hand Loom Weavers, P. P.*, 1841, (296), X.
12. *Hand Loom Weavers, Assistant Commissioner's Report from South of Scotland, P.P.*, 1839, (195), XLII; *Assistant Commissioner's Report from East of Scotland, P.P.*, 1839, (195), XLII.
13. *Assistant Commissioner's Report from East of Scotland, P.P.*, 1839, (195), XLII, pp. 185–192; 204–208.
14. Chapman, *Cotton Industry*, p. 25. N. J. Smelser, *Social Change in the Industrial Revolution: An Application of Theory to the Lancashire Cotton Industry, 1770–1846* (London, 1967), p. 148.
15. Murray, *Hand Loom Weavers*, pp. 73–75.
16. *Ibid.*, pp. 18, 23.
17. *Assistant Commissioner's Report from East of Scotland, P.P.*, 1839, (195), XLII, pp. 198–212.
18. Chapman, *Cotton Industry*, p. 61.
19. *Assistant Commissioner's Report from East of Scotland, P.P.*, 1839, (195), XLII, pp. 198–212.
20. Chapman, *Cotton Industry*, pp. 159–160.
21. D. Bremner, *The Industries of Scotland. Their Rise, Progress and Present Condition*, (Edinburgh, 1869), pp. 152–154; *Edinburgh Evening Courant*. 9th March 1815; 13th March 1815; Lythe and Butt, *Economic History*, pp. 171; 180–181.

22. *Assistant Commissioner's Report from East of Scotland*, P.P., 1839, (195), XLII, pp. 204–205.
23. *Ibid.* p. 212.
24. *Ibid.*
25. *Ibid.*
26. *Ibid.*
27. *Ibid.*
28. *Ibid.* pp. 202–203.
29. *Ibid.*.
30. *Ibid.* pp. 207–208.
31. *Ibid.* p. 212.
32. *Ibid.*.
33. *Ibid.*.
34. *Ibid.* p. 211.
35. *Select Committee on Hand Loom Weavers' Petitions*, P.P., 1834, (556), X.
36. *Assistant Commissioner's Report from East of Scotland*, P.P., 1839, (195), XLII, pp. 205–206.
37. *Ibid.*, p. 209.
38. *Ibid.*
39. *Ibid.*
40. *Ibid.*
41. *Ibid.*
42. *Ibid.*
43. *Ibid.*, p. 210.
44. Murray, *Hand Loom Weavers*, pp. 57–58.
45. *Assistant Commissioner's Report from East of Scotland*, P.P., 1839, (195), XLII, p. 211.
46. *Ibid.*
47. *Ibid.*
48. *Ibid.*
49. *Ibid.*
50. *Ibid.*, pp. 208–209.
51. *Ibid.*
52. In his preface to his Report to Her Majesty's Royal Commissioners, Dr. Harding stated that his enquiry was generally welcomed by the weavers who 'attended in large numbers, and appeared to take a lively interest in listening to the [public] examinations', *Ibid.*, p. 184.
53. *Ibid.*
54. B. Gaskin, 'The Decline of the Hand Loom Weaving Industry in Scotland during the Years 1815–45', (unpublished Ph.D. Thesis, University of Edinburgh, 1955), pp. 15–17.
55. Murray, *Hand Loom Weavers*, p. 17.
56. Smelser, *Social Change*, pp. 130, 142.
57. *Assistant Commissioner's Report from South of Scotland*, P.P. 1839 (195), XLII, p. 211.
59. Smelser, *Social Change*. p. 142.
60. T. Craig Brown, *The History of Selkirkshire, or Chronicles of Ettrick Forest* (Edinburgh, 1866), p. 179; Clapham, *Economic History*, pp. 159–160.

61. H. Hutchison, 'Fenwick And Its Parish', *Scottish Field*, Vol. XCIX, (1972), p. 19.

62. *Assistant Commissioner's Report from East of Scotland, P.P.*, 1839, (195), XLII, p. 185.

63. Hamilton, *Economic History*, p. 100.

64. W. Jolly, *The Life of John Duncan, Scottish Weaver and Botanist with Sketches of his Friends and Notices of the Times*, (London, 1883), pp. 67–69.

65. 'This proportion [of part-time weavers] is quite different in different places, and is constantly varying in each place. Many of the weavers in the small towns and villages assist, either themselves, or through some members of their family, in getting in the harvest. Field labour, herring and whale fishing and mason's work are in most cases, the only other pursuits in which they engage. On the whole, I am of the opinion that at least three-quarters of them are engaged "exclusively" in weaving'. *Assistant Commissioner's Report from East of Scotland, P.P.*, 1839, (195), XLII, p. 184.

66. *Scottish Patriot*, 25th April 1840; *Glasgow Saturday Post and Paisley and Renfrewshire Reformer*, 9th July, 1842.

67. This certainly had been the case in weaving centres in the south and west of Scotland. M. McCarthy, *A Social Geography of Paisley*, (Glasgow, 1969), p. 67.

68. *Glasgow Herald*, 14th July 1843; *Transcript of Brown's Diary*. 19th September 1828, Library of the Scottish College of Textiles, Galashiels.

69. G. D. H. Cole and R. Postgate, *The Common People, 1746–1938* (London, 1838). p. 63.

70. *Assistant Commissioner's Report from South of Scotland, P.P.*, 1839, (195), XLII, p. 45; *The Statistical Account of Ayrshire by the Ministers of the Respective Parishes* (Edinburgh, 1845), pp. 884–885.

71. ". . . from their (Irish weavers) generally commencing without even the least capital, from their not possessing that strong anxiety for a decent outward appearance, and anxiety to conceal any visible signs of poverty, (that 'honest pride' so universal in Scotland), and from their being in the habit of living and associating exclusively with their own countrymen, the general appearance and example of the Irish is by no means beneficial to their Scotch neighbours", *Assistant Commissioner's Report from East of Scotland, P.P.*, 1839, (185), XLII, p. 195.

72. A. Slaven, *The Development of the West of Scotland, 1750–1960* (London, 1975), p. 103.

73. Hamilton, *Economic History*, p. 138.

74. *Select Committee on Hand Loom Weavers, P.P.*, 1834, X, p. 219, q. 2931.

75. *Assistant Commissioner's Report from East of Scotland, P.P.*, 1839, (195), XLII, pp. 210, 212.

76. E. Gauldie, *The Dundee Textile Industry 1790–1885 from the Papers of Peter Carmichael and Arthur Stone* (Edinburgh, 1969), p. 21.

77. *Select Committee on Hand Loom Weavers, P.P.*, 1834, (556), X p. 23, qq. 521–523; p. 45, q. 696; p. 63, q. 872.

78. *Select Committee on Petitions of Several Cotton Manufacturers and Journeymen Cotton Weavers, P.P.*, 1808, (177), 11, p. 99. *Select Committee on Hand Loom Weavers, P.P.*, 1834, (556), X p. 44, q. 692; p. 155, q. 2052.

79. *Ibid. Weavers' Journal*, 31st December 1835.

80. *Ibid.*; Gaskin, 'Decline of Handloom Weaving', pp. 65–66.

81. 'The manufacturers in these, and many other places, pay the weaver by "The piece". A "piece" is supposed to contain a certain number of "mill ells" of warp which again are supposed to contain a certain number of inches; but these "mill ells" – not being a standard measure – vary considerably in their actual length, and the quantity of cloth woven is not ascertained by actual measurement. Thus it happens that one weaver may produce a longer web than another, and yet receive no more pay; and also that whilst the wages continue nominally the same, they may be secretly depreciated by increasing the quantity of warp actually given out'. *Assistant Commissioner's Report from East of Scotland, P.P.,* 1839, (195), XLII, p. 193; "With respect to a more exact specification of the length and breadth of the pieces of goods to be manufactured, I am of the opinion that the only method which would be completely satisfactory, is payment by the measured standard yard". *Ibid.,* p. 195.

INDEX

Abbotsford, 172.
Aberdeen Comb Works, 85.
Aberdeen Granite Association, 94–95.
Aberdeen Granite Supply Company, 88.
Aberdeen, 6, 84–85, 94, 96–98, 105, 129, 135, 138, 223, 225–26, 228.
Aberdeenshire, 221.
Abernethy, 26, 28–30.
Achray, 29.
Adam, William, 27.
Addie, James, 73.
Africa Company, Royal, 25–26, 36.
Airlie (parish), 145–147, 149, 152–54, 156, 160, 161.
Airlie Estate, 144–45, 148–49, 155, 157.
Airlie, Lord, 151.
Aitcheson, Basil, 188.
Albion Company, 118.
Alexander, Colonel, 77.
Alexander, John, 67–73, 75.
Alexander, John, 96.
Alford, 84.
Alison, W.P., 184.
Allan, Colin, 85.
Alloa, 16, 48, 119.
Alyth, 145–147, 150–152, 156, 160–161.
America, United States of, 50, 95–96, 113, 117.
American Centenary Exhibition, 73.
Anderson and Boyes and Company, 119.
Anderson, Dr. James, 85.
Angus, 221.
Angus brothers, 70.

Angus, John, 69.
Angus, Robert, 66, 67, 69.
Arbroath, 6, 224, 226.
Ardnamurchan, 34.
Argyll, Archibald, Duke of, 46
Argyllshire, 32, 46, 87.
Associated Colliers of Scotland, 13.
Auchenharvie, 14.
Auchmedden, 64.
Auchterarder, 222.
Auchtermuchty, 222, 223.
Ayr, 35, 15, 129.
Ayrshire, 3–5, 13–17, 74, 228.

Bain, James (later Sir James), 65.
Baird grandsons and grand-daughters, 64.
Baird James, 60–65, 67, 71, 76–78.
Baird, Alexander Junr., 60–64, 71, 75, 76.
Baird, Alexander, 59–60.
Baird, David, 62–63.
Baird, Douglas, 61–65, 71, 75.
Baird, George, 62–65, 71, 75.
Baird, Jane, 65.
Baird, Janet, 65.
Baird, John, 60, 63.
Baird, Robert, 61–64, 71, 75.
Baird, William & Company, 58–59, 71–72, 75.
Baird, William, 59–60, 62–63, 71, 76–77.
Balfour Beatty, 113.
Balfron, 226.
Ballochney, 16.
Bank Act, 133.
Barony pit, 76.
Barre Quarries, Vermont, 96.